Introduction to Global Logistics

Second Edition

Introduction to Global Logistics

Delivering the goods

John Manners-Bell

KoganPage

Publisher's note

Every possible effort has been made to ensure that the information contained in this book is accurate at the time of going to press, and the publisher and author cannot accept responsibility for any errors or omissions, however caused. No responsibility for loss or damage occasioned to any person acting, or refraining from action, as a result of the material in this publication can be accepted by the editor, the publisher or the author.

First published in Great Britain and the United States as *Global Logistics Strategies* in 2014 by Kogan Page Limited
Second edition published in 2017

2nd Floor, 45 Gee Street
London EC1V 3RS
United Kingdom
www.koganpage.com

Martin P Hill Consulting
122 W 27th St, 10th Floor
New York NY 10001
USA

4737/23 Ansari Road
Daryaganj
New Delhi 110002
India

© John Manners-Bell, 2014, 2017

ISBN   978 0 7494 7825 4
E-ISBN   978 0 7494 7826 1

British Library Cataloguing-in-Publication Data

A CIP record for this book is available from the British Library.

Library of Congress Cataloging-in-Publication Data
Names: Manners-Bell, John, author.
Title: Introduction to global logistics : delivering the goods / John
    Manners-Bell.
Other titles: Global logistics strategies.
Description: Second edition. | New York : Kogan Page, 2016. | Revised
    edition of the author's Global logistics strategies, 2014. | Includes
    bibliographical references and index.
Identifiers: LCCN 2016033992 (print) | LCCN 2016043466 (ebook) | ISBN
    9780749478254 (paperback) | ISBN 9780749478261 (ebook)
Subjects: LCSH: Physical distribution of goods. | Business
    logistics--Management. | BISAC: BUSINESS & ECONOMICS / Production &
    Operations Management. | BUSINESS & ECONOMICS / Distribution. | BUSINESS &
    ECONOMICS / Facility Management.
Classification: LCC HF5415.6 .M317 2016 (print) | LCC HF5415.6 (ebook) | DDC
    658.7--dc23
LC record available at https://lccn.loc.gov/2016033992

Typeset by Graphicraft Limited, Hong Kong
Print production managed by Jellyfish
Printed and bound by CPI Group (UK) Ltd, Croydon, CR0 4YY

CONTENTS

PREFACE TO THE SECOND EDITION

In the two years since the first edition of this book was published, the logistics and supply chain industry has changed significantly. Many of the trends which were highlighted then have continued to transform the industry.

Not least amongst these has been the consolidation of the sector through further mergers and acquisitions activity. Many of the companies that were referenced in the first edition have been, or are in the process of being, acquired. For example, Norbert Dentressangle, which was itself a major acquisitive player, has been bought by US-based XPO Logistics and global express parcels company, TNT, looks set to fall to FedEx.

E-commerce has been one of the driving forces behind the changes that have been experienced. Retailers, manufacturers and logistics providers have struggled to adapt to the new market conditions, not least the volatility caused by marketing events such as 'Black Friday'. Home deliveries have also been particularly problematic, causing many parcel carriers to look at developing alternative delivery strategies.

New market entrants and disruptive technologies have also appeared on the scene. Amazon is now regarded as being the biggest disruptive force to impact the industry since Deutsche Post shook things up in the early 2000s. More recent start ups such as Uber could make even more of an impression.

There is also evidence that ethical supply chain strategies have increased in importance at Board level. Some global manufacturers and retailers, stung by criticism following disasters such as the Rana Plaza factory collapse in Bangladesh in 2013, have adopted a more holistic approach to supply chains, integrating a focus on profitability with sustainable environmental and ethical practices.

It is for these reasons that, as well as a complete update of existing material, three additional chapters have been added to the book. These relate to innovation and disruption, an analysis of new supply chain technologies as well as a new section on sustainable supply chains.

The logistics and supply chain sector continues to be a dynamic and exciting environment in which to operate. New technologies and business models will ensure that this pace of change will, if anything, increase over the coming few years.

ACKNOWLEDGEMENTS

As with the first edition, this book would not have been possible without significant contributions from colleagues within the industry.

I would like to thank Ken Lyon for his insight and understanding of the supply chain technology sector and his contribution to the chapter on innovation and disruption. His wisdom and foresight has proved an invaluable resource over the years I have known him.

I would also like to extend my gratitude once again to Thomas Cullen for his contribution to the chapter on vertical sector supply chain and logistics practice.

Additional thanks goes to Yola O'Hara for her efforts in creating the many charts and figures that illustrate the topics explored.

From Transport Intelligence, I would like to thank the entire Research Team and specifically highlight the work of David Buckby for his work on European road freight markets.

I would also like to thank Julia Swales, my publisher, and Kogan Page for their continued support. This has allowed me to make many years of research available to a broad and diverse audience of students, academics and industry practitioners.

Acknowledgements

Introduction

The global logistics industry is vast, both in terms of market size and the huge numbers of people employed in the sector. It is therefore surprising that its role in the development of the global economy is generally overlooked. Without the inexpensive and reliable transport of freight, manufacturers would not be able to tap into the cheap labour resources based in remote locations throughout the world. Nor would retailers be able to provide ever-increasing levels of service to their customers, ensuring shelves are always stocked whilst inventory is kept to a minimum.

In the last two decades the logistics industry has undergone a transformation, as a flurry of mergers and acquisition activity in the 1990s and 2000s led to the creation of a number of giant diversified transport-based groups. Deutsche Post DHL and TNT were at the forefront of this trend, aggressively building logistics enterprises diverse in both geographies covered and services offered. In the process many well-known, mid-sized companies disappeared but even large operators, such as Tibbett & Britten or Exel, were not immune.

The origins of the acquisition frenzy of the 1990s and 2000s can be traced back to the implementation of certain elements of supply chain theory in the 1980s. At this time there was a sea-change in the way in which retailers and manufacturers viewed inventory. Just-in-Time manufacturing became the industry mantra resulting in smaller, more frequent movements of goods. Companies started to focus on the physical centralization of stock, a goal facilitated by the growth of trade blocs such as the EU and NAFTA. Much has been written on this subject and this book does not intend to re-examine supply chain theory – only in so much that it has helped sculpt the logistics industry we know today.

As a result of these changes to manufacturing strategy, transport became critical to supply chains and the lowly freight company became a major partner in ensuring that goods reached the intended recipient on time and in good condition. It is clear that the evolution of supply chain management resulted in much higher standards across the industry, and gave the major road freight operators the opportunity to develop their value proposition. Up until this point they had struggled to compete in a market characterized by low barriers to market entry and exit.

The intensity of the M&A activity came about due to a 'perfect storm' of market conditions. These included the demand for higher value, out-sourced logistics services by manufacturers and retailers; the availability of cheap private equity-sourced cash; the globalization of the world's economy; the liberalization of the world's postal markets and the rise of e-commerce. This is discussed in more detail in Chapter 2.

Suddenly the perception of the sector was transformed from being a rather boring, commoditized, low margin jumble of transport and warehousing services, to that of a dynamic, value adding driver of the global economy.

Since the first major acquisition that kicked off the period of frenetic consolidation (that of TNT Express by the Dutch Post Office in 1996), there have been a variety of different trends that have influenced the strategies of the market leading companies. At this time (the mid-1990s), the ability to offer global 'one stop shopping' became an ambitious goal for major logistics companies in their attempt to differentiate their services from their competition. Although no one believed that any one logistics company had a complete portfolio of services in all geographies or in fact that manufacturers and retailers would be willing to put all their eggs in one basket even if they did, there was a trend for a rationalization of the number of LSPs utilized by a shipper that is ongoing today.

At the same time the management concept of 'out-sourcing' was taking root. It was believed that logistics companies could take advantage of manufacturers' and retailers' desire to focus on their core-competencies and spin off the management of their distribution activities to Logistics Service Providers (LSPs). By greater engagement with their clients, logistics companies had the opportunity to offer more value adding, higher margin services (such as postponed manufacturing, call centres, inventory ownership, etc).

However, the impact of out-sourcing on the logistics industry has not been entirely beneficial. There is no doubt that in revenue terms the trend has been massively important. However, the majority of contracts (especially in the consumer and retail sectors) are undertaken at low margins, and in truth there have not been as many opportunities to engage with clients at a more-value adding level. This is not to say that some sectors, such as high tech, have not encouraged innovations from their logistics providers – only that most have remained stubbornly unwilling to give up control of what they believe to be a competitive advantage.

Another problem faced by logistics operators is contract 'churn'. As markets became more mature, logistics companies were continually chasing contracts that came up for renewal once every three to five years. Contracts were awarded predominantly on the basis of price, and so the industry was participating in a race-to-the-bottom in terms of profitability. Margins on logistics contracts have bottomed out at around 3 per cent – hardly the high value, high margin business many companies had hoped for. A mitigating factor in these low margins is the fact that many logistics companies have become 'asset-light' – no longer major owners of trucks and warehouses – and that consequently return on capital is significantly better than the headline figures might suggest.

By the mid-1990s, the out-sourcing argument had gained traction, and investors continued to promote companies that were heavily involved in 'contract logistics' such as Exel and Tibbett & Britten, to mention two. Others such as Christian Salvesen, Hays, TDG and Wincanton were also favoured. It is no coincidence that all these companies were British, as the out-sourcing trend had started in the UK's retail industry, driven by super-market giants such as Tesco and Sainsbury's.

Many of these companies were emboldened by positive investor senti-ment to expand out of the UK and into Europe, where there was the expec-tation that the emerging out-sourcing trend would develop at a faster pace. Although there was nothing wrong with this strategy, the execution proved to be flawed. Competition in local markets was much greater than expected, and integration of acquisitions poorly handled, which ultimately left these companies exposed financially. Consequently the only one of these players still independent today is Wincanton, albeit having sold off its extensive European network of subsidiaries.

The exception to this was Exel, which was acquired due to its strength, rather than weakness. It had acquired Tibbett & Britten in 2004 and had become a powerhouse in both the contract logistics and freight forwarding sectors (more on the latter, later). It was acquired by Deutsche Post to trans-form its own 'Solutions' division and propelled it into market leadership under the DHL Exel Supply Chain brand.

At around this time, the internet or 'dotcom' boom was occurring, and this added a certain level of hysteria to the acquisition market. Logistics companies were quick to position themselves as the providers of the infra-structure enabling 'clicks and mortar' e-retailers to fulfil customer orders, both warehousing and transport. Inflated expectations arose and this trans-lated into much higher prices which companies had to pay for even very ordinary acquisitions.

Despite the fact that it would be another decade before the dotcom ex-pectations were realized, the pressure on companies' management to expand through acquisition was remorseless. Several years into this particular phase of the sector's evolution, there were now fewer good quality targets available to buy, and in many cases due diligence being undertaken was cursory.

It is at this point in the timeline that the bottom fell out of the market with the bursting of the dotcom bubble. Companies such as ABX Logistics (a division of the Belgium Post) had followed Deutsche Post's lead in building a pan-European network of road freight companies and freight forwarders. The resulting European recession of the early 2000s quickly led to a reverse in strategy as bullish volume forecasts proved to be unachievable and companies struggled to pay back the loans they had taken to make their acquisitions.

It is fair to say that all logistics companies were affected by the downturn. However, those with the deepest pockets, such as DHL and UPS, were able to ride out the storm. Others such as ABX and Thiel Logistik were not so fortunate.

Although it would be too simplistic to conclude that at this point the investment community fell totally out of love with 'contract logistics' or 'solutions' as it may be called, this reversal for the sector coincided with the rise of the international freight forwarder.

Up to this point, freight forwarding had been widely viewed as a non-value adding 'necessary evil' for moving goods across borders and booking space on ships or aircraft. Business practices had not changed for many decades, if at all since the 19th century. However, as globalization gathered pace it became obvious that the freight forwarder, with links throughout the world (and especially in up and coming markets such as China) would become a critical element in supply chains.

The race was on to build owned networks of forwarding operations. Deutsche Post had acquired Danzas (and subsequently Exel which included MSAS); UPS bought Fritz and Menlo Worldwide Forwarding; Schenker (itself now part of Deutsche Bahn) bought Bax Global to name just a few.

The pace of globalization translated into big annual increases in international air and sea freight volumes. Forwarders' counter cyclical business model (which allowed them to make better profit margins in a downturn, and better revenues in an upturn – see Chapter 5) was applauded. Their 'asset light' nature, managing rather than owning transport assets, provided high returns on capital expenditure. Suddenly forwarding was no longer the poor relation of the logistics world, playing second fiddle to more sophisticated, value adding logistics.

The rise of the forwarder has been temporarily slowed by the 'Great Recession' of 2009. The 'Black Swan' event, starting in the United States' sub-prime mortgage market, resulted in a meltdown of global freight volumes. Retailers and manufacturers, gripped by uncertainty, placed a moratorium on orders with their suppliers in the Far East. Volumes plunged by 25 per cent or more as they sought to run down inventories located in distribution centres in Western Europe or North America. This had a dire impact on the shipping and air cargo industry, with the spare capacity resulting in a catastrophic fall in rates and near bankruptcy for many carriers.

Since then there has been a recovery, but there are now fears in the investment community that the forwarding industry will never again regain its stellar growth trajectory. Wage inflation in China has made goods produced in the Far East less competitive and prompted some manufacturers to adopt near-sourcing strategies (sourcing goods from suppliers based closer to the major consumer markets of the West). Natural disasters have shown the fragility of extended supply chains, and risk is now being increasingly taken into account when looking at sourcing strategies. On top of this, the growth of Asia as a consumer market will lead to greater levels of regionalization (as opposed to globalization) with the fastest growing sector being intra-Asia movements of goods. This will lead to the dilution of forwarders' yields.

Objectives of this book

This book has been written to enable the reader to understand:

- The history and development of key logistics segments
- The demand-side trends and political, economic, social, technological, environmental and legislative forces that have driven changes in the industry
- The internal supply-side dynamics and micro-economics that have combined with these forces to facilitate change
- Technological developments that will influence and potentially disrupt the future of the supply chain and logistics industry

Introduction to Global Logistics will look at all the pressures that have led to the emergence of today's vibrant global logistics industry – from both the 'demand' (ie manufacturing and retailing) and the 'supply' (ie logistics provider) side perspective. In addition to the roles of the contract logistics and freight forwarding sectors, it will also examine the dynamics of the express parcels, container shipping, air cargo, road freight and intermodal industries. Whilst global macro trends are highly important to the long-term future of these sectors, conversely it is the structure and competitive nature of these sectors that has a 'bottom up' influence on supply chain management and hence global economies. For example, hyper-fragmentation and competition in the European road freight industry has been a key input into the formulation of manufacturers' and retailers' centralized distribution strategies.

The development of logistics clusters

A further section of the book reveals how this centralization of inventory has translated into the geographical clustering of logistics facilities. In Europe, Netherlands and Belgium dominate the regional distribution centre market, although the accession of new countries to the EU means that many companies are now looking eastwards as Europe's economic centre of gravity shifts. In the United States, gateway locations are important, and the growing role of Mexico as a near-sourcing location will inevitably impact on distribution strategies. In Asia, the emergence of region-wide distribution hubs is still at a nascent stage due to lack of economic integration and weak transport infrastructure. However, the key locations for distribution property in China, the largest market in the region, are examined in detail.

The fundamental role of technology

Technology has been fundamental to the huge advances the industry has made over the past few decades. Supply chain management and execution systems have provided the visibility that has allowed manufacturers and retailers to drive down inventory levels whilst retaining customer service levels. Warehouse processes have become more efficient, as have transport operations increasing the utilization of vehicles. In a crossborder context, systems have facilitated the international movement of goods, enabling shippers, customs authorities, freight forwarders, shipping lines and air cargo operators to work more effectively. Technology will, in the future, continue to make the logistics industry more efficient. 'Sense and respond' technologies will make supply chains more agile, thereby reducing risk by better informing management decisions. It may even drive the industry towards new business models.

Innovation and disruption

In fact, technological innovation and the disruption it brings will characterize the long-term prospects of the supply chain and logistics industry. The present incumbents need to be aware of the threat of new market entrants – such as taxi app company Uber or online retailer Amazon – which offer new and more efficient operating models. The democratization of technologies, for instance through the proliferation of affordable smart phones, provides enormous opportunities in the emerging 'sharing' economy. At the same time, companies need to be able to exploit developments such as the Internet of Things, Big Data, autonomous vehicles and even 3D Printing if they are to prosper in the new environment, rather than fall victim to it.

Ethics and sustainability

Although this book concentrates largely on the internal dynamics that have helped to shape the industry, external issues of public policy are never far away. This is certainly the case with ethics and sustainability. In terms of the environment, great strides have been made by all transport modes in reducing polluting emissions, sometimes due to government regulation, and sometimes due to the commercial sense that it makes to improve efficiencies. In terms of ethics, companies sourcing goods from around the world are starting to realize that even if they out-sourced production, they still retain moral responsibility for the conditions in which their goods are manufactured and the environmental practices of their suppliers. The most visionary companies have come to see that by combining a focus on sustainability, societal impact as well as profits, they can position themselves as industry leaders, and reap the rewards of the value that this brings.

What is clear is that after a turbulent period of transformation, there is no sign that change in the logistics industry is slowing down. A powerful mix of demand and supply side factors means that further restructuring is possible, if not probable. The shift of the economic balance of power towards Asia; increasing supply chain risk; the price of oil; further mergers and acquisitions and even near-shoring/re-shoring are just some of the 'known' issues that logistics providers will need to contend with. Twenty years ago nobody would have considered that the German Post Office would be a market leader in the international express, contract logistics, road and freight forwarding sectors or that China would be so important to the world's logistics industry. It is likely that in another 20 years the market environment will be just as unrecognizable.

What's shaping the global logistics market? 01

The global logistics industry in its present form has come about as a result of a confluence of demand-side and supply-side trends. Political, economic, social and technological factors have facilitated major changes in the way in which multinational manufacturers supply global consumer markets and how retailers source their goods. This, in turn, has allowed many of the larger logistics service providers (LSPs) to differentiate their service offering from smaller competitors by leveraging their global scale, technological capabilities as well as financial and human capital.

Figure 1.1 The confluence of demand-side and supply-side trends

Globalization Inventory reduction Out-sourcing Supply chain complexity	Industry transportation	Wider service portfolio Product differentiation Liberalization of markets Enhanced value proposition

CHAPTER LEARNING OBJECTIVES

This chapter will familiarize the reader with:

- The key macro-economic and demand-side drivers that have brought about today's logistics industry
- How the logistics industry has gone far beyond simple transport and warehousing services, becoming the glue that holds together the systems that underpin the global economy

Trade and globalization

One of the driving forces behind the trend towards the free movement of goods between countries has been the World Trade Organization (WTO), an inter-government organization born out of the reconciliation talks at the end of the Second World War. It essentially fulfils an anti-protectionist role, recognizing that the economic upheavals that gave rise to extremism in Europe and Asia in the 1930s were partly as a result of barriers to trade. These were created ostensibly to protect jobs, but in fact resulted in exacerbating the economic crisis and sowing the seeds of political discontent. As well as promoting free trade, the organization also provides a mechanism through which countries can settle trade disputes. The WTO has been very successful in preventing arguments over issues such as quotas and 'dumping' escalating into full-scale trade wars.

Negotiations since the first round of talks in 1947 have been aimed at reducing and then eliminating all tariff and non-tariff barriers. After many successes, the last Doha round of talks faltered, breaking down temporarily in 2008 over an inability to agree on the liberalization of trade in agriculture and industrial products. In essence, developing and developed countries could not agree on the appropriate level of support for farmers. Since its initiation in 2001, the Doha round has struggled to make progress. However, finally in 2015 it was able to conclude an agreement over the reduction of tariffs on high-tech goods as well as over export subsidies for agricultural goods. Despite this, for the first time the 164 members of WTO declined to reaffirm the mandate of the Doha negotiations, and many now think that in future the organization will focus its efforts on smaller packages of trade reforms (Donnan, 2015).

However, perhaps the defining success of the WTO has been the development of China as the powerhouse of global industry. By acceding to the World Trade Organization, the Chinese government committed to root and branch reform of its economy, which has subsequently allowed it to grow to a position of global importance.

One of the consequences of China's accession, along with other economies in the Asia Pacific region, has been economic integration that has in turn transformed the supply chains of sectors such as consumer electronics, clothing and furniture. This has had a profound effect on freight transport and brought about the emergence of large, integrated logistics providers, capable of supporting such complex, international supply chains. In turn, these new supply chains have transformed the pattern of sea and airfreight routes.

However, tariffs are common on many products and some governments still turn a blind eye to anti-competitive practices. The inability of the WTO to get things done through the multilateral nature of its negotiation process has meant that developed nations have turned to direct, bilateral or regional agreements in the hope that they will accelerate trade growth.

Below are a few examples of new trade groups:

- **Trans-Pacific Partnership:** Following an agreement in November 2011, the leaders of nine trading partners – Australia, Brunei Darussalam, Chile, Malaysia, New Zealand, Peru, Singapore, Vietnam and the United States – announced the creation of the Trans-Pacific Partnership (TPP). Japan has since also become part of the agreement meaning that it now covers 40 per cent of the global economy.

- **TTIP:** In March 2013, the European Commission recommended that member states give the official go-ahead for a trade agreement with the United States – the Transatlantic Trade and Investment Partnership (TTIP). It said that there could be economic gains for the European Union of 119 billion euros a year – and for the United States of 95 billion euros a year. There is a rush to conclude the deal before President Obama leaves office in 2017 as many believe that a new president would not be as keen.

- **ASEAN:** Members of the Association of Southeast Asian Nations (ASEAN) together with the group's six major trading partners began negotiations in May 2013 to form the world's largest economic bloc. This came into existence (Asian Economic Community) at the end of 2015. The ASEAN+6 trade deal will establish an integrated market of 16 countries in the Asia Pacific region, with a population of more than 3 billion.

Other smaller deals include one between the EU and South Korea and an agreement between the EU and Canada which came into existence in 2014.

These deals will inevitably result in changes for the logistics sector. It is unlikely the sector will experience the sort of supply chain revolution that was seen in the 1990s, as the economies involved already have strong trade links. However, if, for example, the barriers to merging airlines in the United States and European Union could be removed, there is a major opportunity to transform the structure of airfreight. Additionally, the market for integrated logistics companies might become more broad-based as economies become more interdependent.

Although its remit has extended far beyond its original goal, the world's largest free trade area is the European Union. The success of the Single

European Market (SEM), which was created in the early 1990s, transformed the way in which manufacturers and retailers could supply their customers in the region. The SEM had deep-seated implications for production and distribution that could consequently be centralized and rationalized to a much smaller number of locations. More latterly the geographic centre of Europe has shifted eastwards with the accession of the Central and Eastern European economies such as Poland, Hungary and most recently, Bulgaria and Romania.

The North America Free Trade Agreement (NAFTA) has had a similarly major impact on the flows of goods. An increasing number of manufacturers are choosing to supply the giant US consumer markets from production locations and distribution facilities in Mexico, where costs are substantially lower.

Looking ahead, trade deals that lead to the creation of Single Markets, whether in Asia, Middle East, South America or Africa, have the potential to revolutionize distribution strategies in the same way in which they were in the European Union.

Growth in trade

World trade is a key driver of the international logistics market. Although most elements of road freight may be dependent on domestic economies, airfreight and sea freight are dominated by the performance of trade between nations – that is 'world trade'.

Figure 1.2 World Trade Growth: Value of world merchandise exports, 2005 to 2015

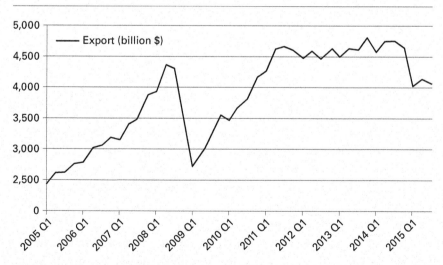

SOURCE: World Trade Organization, 2016a

World trade has been very dynamic over the past decade with underlying development being driven – until very recently – by strong growth of export and import traffic from China and related economies. To some degree the rates of growth since the end of 2009 were flattered by an element of 'bounce-back' from the severe dip seen in the recession, but the underlying trend was still evident. Volumes have also been boosted by trade between China and other emerging economies as supply chains in the region become more integrated and China's rise as a consumer market continues.

One of the most important background factors underlying the dynamics of global trade has been the recent depressed nature of consumer demand in Western markets, especially Europe. Of course up to 2008–9 such demand was the main driving force behind air and sea volumes, moving product between the new assembly locations in China and the retail markets of the West. These trades have not gone away; however, their growth has moderated.

China, the world's largest exporter, has undergone a degree of change in terms of exports. The huge leaps in volumes seen in previous years have moderated to low single digit percentages. There are indications that volumes between China and other emerging markets are filling some of the void left by lower export activity to the Eurozone in particular, but again this is a recent trend and it is unclear how prolonged this will be.

Figure 1.3 China Exports 2009–2015 US $m

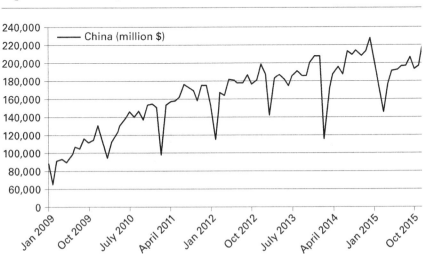

SOURCE: World Trade Organization, 2016b

The global logistics industry is already seeing a major change to the relationship that drove its development for the last three decades and before. On average, between 1990 and 2008, real GDP grew at 3.2 per cent a year, whilst world trade grew at twice this rate. This relationship was considered to be 'hard-wired', that is until the financial crisis of 2009. Since then, the 2:1 ratio has been replaced with a direct 1:1 correlation, meaning that most trade forecasts were firstly affected by the downturn and secondly by a structural change in market growth (Harding, 2014).

Why is this? There are several reasons:

1 Developed countries – including the Eurozone – have yet to fully recover and therefore there is less demand for imports of consumer goods.

2 Developing countries have been forced to focus their investment on domestic infrastructure to maintain their rate of economic growth. Of course, China is the best example of this.

3 The downturn has created more protectionist policies that have acted as a drag on international trade. Since the financial crisis, governments around the world have quietly enacted 1527 'beggar-thy-neighbour' measures to protect their domestic markets (GTA, 2013). Of these, 89 per cent remain in place today. Amongst these are Russia's e-commerce regulations which led to DHL, UPS and FedEx suspending international services into the country for a week. Likewise Argentina has made it very difficult for its citizens to buy international goods over the internet in order to prevent flights of currency.

4 Governments around the world have actively suppressed short-term consumer demand in their own economies. It may seem counter-intuitive that governments should try to dampen economic growth at this time, but perhaps inadvertently, this is exactly what has happened. They have done this through a combination of encouraging consumers to pay down debt, increase savings level (for example, through tax breaks) and most importantly by restricting pay awards (so-called 'austerity packages'). Looking at Emerging Markets we can see the same effect, albeit for different reasons. China and India have yet to really join the consumer revolution, and one of the major reasons for this is the Savings Rate (that is, household savings as a proportion of GDP) in these countries (Roberts, 2015). In China this rate is 50 per cent, compared to a global average of 20 per cent. This level is due to the level of precautionary savings by Chinese families as people put away money for their old age, housing, education and healthcare. Jitters in the Chinese economy have encouraged the rate to rise rather than decrease.

The growth of Asian trade

The past decade has seen a major shift in trade patterns, with traditional tradelanes, connecting China with the United States and Europe, losing some of their importance. Africa, for example, is amongst the fastest growing markets for China, as investors target mining and infrastructure opportunities. As a result freight forwarders, such as DHL and Damco, are developing this tradelane by expanding multi-modal products combining ocean freight and airfreight services to new destinations. China is also amongst the largest trade partners for Argentina, Chile and Colombia. In 2009, China became Brazil's largest trade partner.

The development of the 'Modern Silk Road' between Asia and the Middle East is also resulting in increased trade. In fact, from 2001 to 2010, trade increased over 700 per cent and now more than half of the Middle East's trade is with Asia (WTO, 2016b).

Asia is not only seeking to increase external trade with potential trading partners such as South America, the Middle East and Africa but it is also turning inwards as intra-regional trade increases. However, in order for intra-Asian trade to really take off, infrastructure improvements are needed across the region. China, the dominant country in the region, is taking the lead as it assists with infrastructure projects in neighbouring countries. Along with internal projects, the linking of countries to one another and more importantly to China is resulting in a complex intra-Asian supply chain. As such, logistics providers have taken note and are increasingly positioning their service offerings to this market. Shifts in manufacturing, supply chain interdependence and growing consumer spend have contributed to this trend.

It is estimated that by 2030, Asia's economy will be larger than that of the United States and the European Union combined, with the region's share of world GDP increasing from about 30 per cent to more than 40 per cent (NIC, 2012). Although Asia helped to lead the recovery of the world economy, the global crisis highlighted issues the region must address, many of which are due to its dependence on export trade. To reduce this dependence, another engine of growth, domestic demand, is needed to sustain growth within the region. Improvements in infrastructure, financial reforms and greater flexibility in exchange rates are all needed to generate this demand.

For some time it has been recognized that products are now rarely manu-factured in just one country. This means that traditional ways of measuring trade are becoming outdated. For example, using a traditional trade measure, it would seem that the United States has a large trade deficit with China as regards the import of iPhones. However, using a technique that looks at where the value is added in terms of components, this deficit is negligible (Maurer, 2011). Parts are moved from Japan, Korea and Germany, as well as many other locations, to China where they are assembled by cheap, available labour. The finished good is then exported to the United States. This shows that China is not necessarily the 'world's factory' as is usually claimed, more precisely the world's 'assembly plant'.

It could be argued that the biggest changes are yet to come. The **upstream** supply chain has already regionalized as we have seen, and the next step is the regionalization of **downstream** distribution channels. What is meant by this is the development of consumer markets in Asia, Africa and Latin America. Not only will intermediate goods manufactured in Asia stay in the region – and this is the critical point – so will finished products.

This will occur due to the development of a more affluent society. By 2020, it has been estimated that 1.8 billion people in emerging markets will enter a 'consuming class', spending US $30 trillion, up from US $12 trillion today. Emerging markets constituted just below half of world GDP in 2012 up from about one-third in 2000. In the next decade this shift will continue (albeit at a much slower speed) (E&Y, 2011).

Global to regional trade networks

The world's economy is moving from globalization to regionalization of supply chains. This involves a transformation from East–West and West–East Flows to complex networks of developed and emerging markets. What is the evidence for this?

1 Global flows of goods are becoming more disparate. In 1990 63 per cent of global flows of goods moved through the top 50 routes. By 2011 this had fallen to 54 per cent.

2 Crossborder flows of goods, services and finance from emerging markets in 2012 accounted for 38 per cent of the total, up from 14 per cent in 1990.

3 South–South trade has grown from 6 per cent of goods flows in 1990 to 24 per cent in 2012 (Manyika *et al*, 2014).

This shows that trade is rebalancing – with obvious consequences to shipping lines, air cargo carriers and freight forwarders.

Perhaps the changing face of trading networks can be best illustrated by the example of VW-Audi Group. In the 1990s, flows of materials and finished vehicles originated predominantly in Europe. However, in the past few years the company has transformed itself from being a German-based exporter to the world, to a global automotive producer with a complex production footprint.

This has clearly had a major impact on its transportation and distribution requirements. Transport volumes, for instance, have increased by 25 per cent due to the multiple production locations and hubs. The company has created an intertwined network of tradelanes, supported by a range of freight forwarders and global logistics providers. This is in addition to the national and local logistics services required to support inbound logistics.

A return to 'localized' supply chains?

For many of the global consumer goods manufacturers, sales growth in emerging markets will not necessarily result in higher global flows of goods. That is because successful penetration of emerging markets relies on developing products for specific, local markets and delivering these quickly, cheaply and efficiently.

To this end Unilever, followed by its peers, has invested heavily in local and regional facilities. For example, it has invested US $500m in production and distribution facilities in Mexico as well as US $75m in a factory in Colombia.

The issue of transport provision is an important issue in this respect. Although these companies would like to work with global logistics providers, in many cases this just isn't possible. Meeting these needs will be absolutely key for the future of the logistics industry.

Another factor in the 'localization' of supply chains in emerging markets, will be the development of 'mega-cities' – usually defined as a city of over 10 million people. The top 10 fastest growing mega-cities in the world are all in emerging markets – four in China and three on the Indian sub-continent.

At a lower level, the consultancy Boston Consulting estimates that the number of cities in emerging markets with populations of more than 50,000 will be four times the number in the developed world by 2030. This demonstrates the level of urbanization that is occurring.

Another illustration is that in 2005, retailers and consumer goods manufacturers had to develop distribution channels in 60 cities in China to reach 80 per cent of the country's population. In 2020, these companies will need to be present in 212 cities to reach the same market (BCG, 2010). Logistics will increasingly be focused around cities rather than countries.

Why should this have an impact on supply chains?

- Mega-cities will create their own economies of scale, supplied by local/regional production facilities.
- Consumer goods will be customized to local tastes.
- Each city will develop its own unique ecosystem, which takes into account the movement of people, data, finance, energy, waste, goods and services.
- Transport demands will be specific to each city's needs and capabilities: poor planning and infrastructure will result in high logistics costs.
- Fulfilment, packaging, miniaturization and reverse logistics will require increased intensity of logistics provision.

Although there may be some regional homogeneity in logistics and supply chain terms, it will be very dangerous for business to take this for granted. There will be far more customization and specialization in terms of product delivery than many might hope.

The impact of supply chain management practice on logistics

For much of the 20th century the predominant manufacturing strategy was based around creating economies of scale. This involved long production runs that created high levels of stock at low unit costs. Products were then 'pushed' out into the market, with the hope that there was sufficient demand. This was termed Just-in-Case manufacturing.

During this period the transport market was characterized by:

- full loads (inbound and outbound);
- low levels of service provision required;
- long lead times;
- regular, stochastic movements.

The problem with this approach was that demand could often be volatile, and manufacturers, retailers and other supply chain partners could tie up considerable amounts of capital in inventory. Stock itself could become redundant or be lost or stolen.

There were also other problems, not least that in fast-moving sectors such as the fashion or electronics industry, product lifecycles are measured in terms of months, not years. They also need the flexibility to release new products on short lead times.

During the 1980s and 1990s, Japanese manufacturing processes were quickly adopted throughout the world – the best known of these originated in Toyota. Smaller production runs were adopted with production lines running on an 'as and when' basis depending on demand – the 'kanban' system. This Build-to-Order (BTO) strategy did away, in theory anyway, with the need for buffer stocks.

This level of agility and flexibility is perhaps best demonstrated by technology company Dell. The lead time for any one computer is now generally about five to six working days – two to three days for production and two to three days for shipping.

Along with a change in production systems, there was also the consequent introduction of Just-in-Time (JIT) delivery schedules that complemented the on-demand nature of manufacturing. This had a very major impact on transportation requirements. Suddenly freight operators were asked by their customers for more frequent services, moving smaller consignments on a less predictable basis. Efficiency was also affected as, in terms of transport costs, it is far more economic, on a per kilo basis, to run larger trucks than smaller ones.

There were also modal consequences as the flexibility of road services placed rail operators at a considerable competitive disadvantage when competing within the new paradigm. However, despite rising transport costs overall, logistics costs (including inventory financing) fell, making the trade-off more than worthwhile for shippers.

The way in which manufacturers in North America or Europe implemented a Just-in-Time supply chain strategy was very different from in Japan where manufacturers were able to achieve high levels of supplier concentration around assembly plants. For example, all 11 of Toyota's assembly and major component plants were located in and around 'Toyota City'. In contrast, Nissan's vehicle assembly plant in the UK has suppliers located in Germany, Spain and France, up to three days' journey time away.

This has put the supply chain under extreme strain, and of course makes the transport element of logistics more critical. From a manufacturer's point of view, the transport element cannot be allowed to fail due to huge consequential loss should production be affected. This risk is examined in more detail in Chapter 14.

Figure 1.4 below illustrates the impact which lowering inventory has on various parts of the production and distribution process. As the inventory (or water in the picture metaphor) falls, the business (or boat) becomes

Figure 1.4 Supply chain hazards of inventory reduction strategies

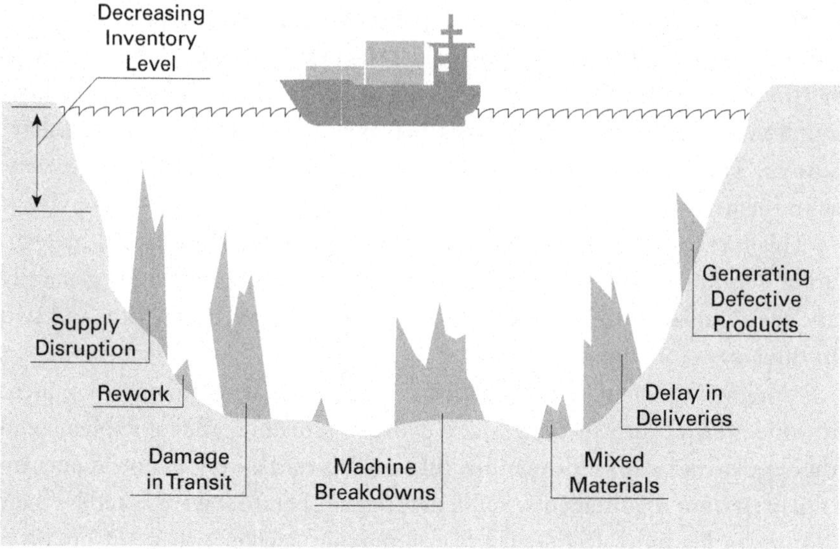

far more vulnerable to the hidden 'rocks' beneath. From a transport perspective, the hazards include mis-delivery, damage of goods in transit or late delivery.

Centralization of inventory

Distribution strategies have been largely influenced by the trade-off between the cost of moving goods to market and the cost of holding inventories. The relative cheap cost of transport has allowed manufacturers and retailers to store goods in centralized locations, and supply them over longer distances. This has many advantages:

- cost of inventory holding falls;
- less buffer stock is required in each warehouse;
- there is less 'shrinkage', that is, loss of stock through theft or damage;
- lower levels of redundancy occur;
- warehouse costs are lower.

Figure 1.5 shows that when goods are stored in close proximity to the end market (for example, in national warehouses), transport costs are low. If a regional distribution strategy is implemented, the number of national

Figure 1.5 The transport cost/inventory trade-off

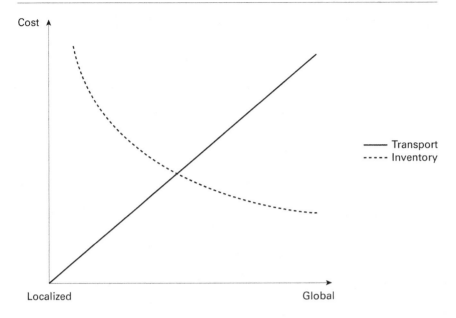

warehouses fall and so do stock levels. However, transport costs rise, due to the increasing distance to market.

The cost of transport has risen from a third of overall logistics costs in the 1980s to around two-thirds of costs in the 2010s (Transport Intelligence, 2012a). This has come about from an increase in transport-related costs (such as congestion, tolls, fuel costs and compliance) as well as a greater underlying demand caused by these changing distribution strategies. It has also derived from an increase in international transport, as more goods are supplied from centralized distribution facilities on a crossborder basis. Figure 1.6 illustrates this trend.

Taking Europe as an example, this has meant that there has been a surge in demand for European Distribution Centres in geographically central locations, such as The Netherlands. For the high-tech sector, the Holland International Distribution Council estimated at one point that about half of facilities are located in either The Netherlands, Germany or France. In contrast just under a quarter are located in large, but peripheral markets in the UK, Spain and Italy.

One challenge faced by manufacturers is that while it may be possible to treat Europe as a single market, in reality there is no such thing as a 'Euroconsumer'. Many products still need to be customized to meet national regulations or take into account cultural preferences. From a

Figure 1.6 The changing structure of supply chain costs

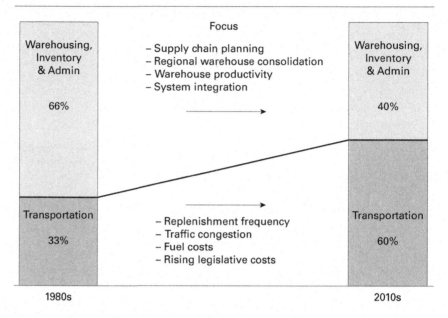

Focus
- Supply chain planning
- Regional warehouse consolidation
- Warehouse productivity
- System integration

- Replenishment frequency
- Traffic congestion
- Fuel costs
- Rising legislative costs

supply chain management perspective it is preferable for as many goods to be produced in as generic form as possible, so they can be directed to the market where there is greatest demand. Consequently the process of customization should occur late in the supply chain. The distribution centre is often the last stage when the manufacturer can undertake an intervention, and consequently a demand for 'postponed manufacturing' activities has grown up. Given that a manufacturer may have out-sourced the management of its distribution facility, it is possible for a Logistics Service Provider (LSP) to undertake these forms of value adding activities. In some cases they may be simple, such as 'kitting' (for example, adding the right sort of electric plug to an electrical device depending on the country of destination). They may also be highly sophisticated such as testing and configuring hard disk drives. In one contract UPS Supply Chain Solutions employed musicians in one of its European Distribution Centres to tune guitars imported from Asia to ensure that the customer took the instrument home in a ready-to-play state.

Out-sourcing logistics

The out-sourcing of logistics functions by manufacturers and retailers over the past 30 years has been one of the defining trends of the global logistics industry. The logistics provider's importance in terms of the overall supply chain has risen considerably with the ongoing trend towards out-sourcing of non-core-competencies.

At the outset, classical out-sourcing theory suggested that companies should identify those functions that were non-essential to its operation and then find service providers to take on those activities. This would provide a range of mostly cost-saving benefits as the service provider could, for example, make use of its economies of scale to provide a service more efficiently to an individual client. Out-sourcing peripheral roles would also have the benefit of taking staff and assets off the balance sheet.

However, more recently many logistics managers have come to believe that it is in the best interests of their company to out-source certain core activities. This means that whereas previously a manufacturer would not have considered out-sourcing its customer care, it is more likely these days to consider using a specialist contact centre provider which it believes can do the job better. It would only retain competencies in which it believed it had a competitive advantage.

As shown in Figure 1.7, the first stage of out-sourcing usually involves the transportation function. In many cases (although not all) LSPs will have

Figure 1.7 Stages in the logistics out-sourcing process

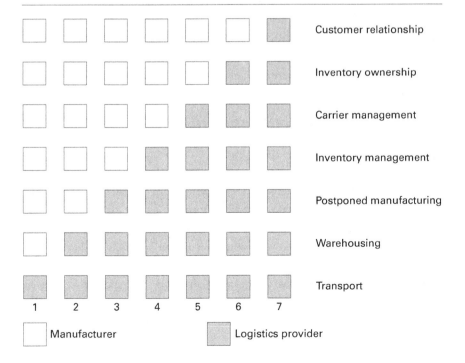

more buying power than the manufacturer or retailer they are working for, which will allow them to get better deals for trucks and materials. They may also have invested in technology, such as transportation management systems, and be better able to hire and manage driving staff. There is also the question of managing peaks and troughs of demand; working for multiple clients, a transportation provider is better able to manage spare capacity. A manufacturer whose demand is highly seasonal or cyclical, used for only part of the year, will not want to own underutilized transport assets. Finally, out-sourcing the ownership of transport assets takes them off the balance sheet, and allows the company to invest in other, more value adding, aspects of its business.

Not all types of transport are out-sourced to the same extent. For example, international transport is almost entirely out-sourced due to the specialized nature of the business. Local distribution is much more likely to be undertaken in-house, as utilization levels will be much higher and demand more predictable.

The next stage of out-sourcing is usually warehousing. This is a labour-intensive activity, and one which many companies are happy to be undertaken by a third party. The out-sourcing company can also benefit from the LSPs' economies of scale, if it combines their business in a shared, multi-user facility. As mentioned above, the distribution centre can also be used to add value in the form of postponed manufacturing and other services.

These days it has become a strategic decision to out-source logistics activities (not just the transport or warehousing, for example) and the role of logistics providers has changed as they have been allowed to penetrate further into their clients' operations and supply chains.

Reasons behind the out-sourcing trend

Companies can out-source their logistics functions for many different reasons, from the purely financial to the expectation of using a company as a catalyst for change management. It is essential that when they go into the out-sourcing process they have clearly defined the extent that they wish to engage with their logistics provider. At the most basic level, vehicle contract hire, one of the primary aims will be to take assets off balance sheet whilst retaining complete control of transport management. At the other end of the spectrum, high-end LSPs have a greater element of strategic control, often choosing suppliers, controlling inventory management and fulfilment whilst leaving the client to focus on key competencies such as product development, marketing and production.

Although the global trend is towards more logistics out-sourcing, the extent to which this has occurred differs widely from country to country. The so-called 'penetration rate' (that is, the level of contract logistics under-taken by logistics service providers as a proportion of overall spend) varies from around 40 per cent in the United Kingdom to less than 10 per cent in the Asia Pacific region. In the latter region (China in particular) there is a dearth of qualified local logistics providers and this has hindered the growth of the sector overall.

It is not only countries that have differing rates of out-sourcing; market sectors differ with grocery, non-food and clothing being the most mature and pharmaceuticals and healthcare with higher levels of in-house provision.

In 2012, market research company, Transport Intelligence, undertook a survey of 105 logistics managers in the manufacturing and retailing sectors. The vast majority of survey participants (85 per cent) were found to out-source an element of their logistics function to a third-party provider (Transport Intelligence, 2012a). The main reasons for this were the cost savings it provided (22 per cent) and the ability to gain access to specialist expertise (22 per cent). Financial benefits in terms of lower capital investment were also highlighted as a driver for out-sourcing logistics by 20 per cent of the sample. With the exception of aerospace, automotive manufacturers appear least open to out-sourcing their logistics operations.

Of those companies (15 per cent) that did not out-source any logistics activities, the main reasons cited were 'to maintain control' (48 per cent) and the fact that it was considered 'cheaper to keep logistics in-house' (30 per cent).

Of the companies surveyed, 58 per cent expected to out-source more of their logistics function in the following year.

Even though out-sourcing has now become a fact of life in most industry sectors, that is not to say that LSPs are fulfilling their customers' needs. The survey also showed that with the exception of 'range of services' and 'geographic coverage', the LSPs used by the sample fell short of shippers' expectations. Shippers appeared to be least satisfied in the areas of price, service levels and reliability.

Figure 1.8 3PL/Shipper perceived user value survey, Maximum Score = 5

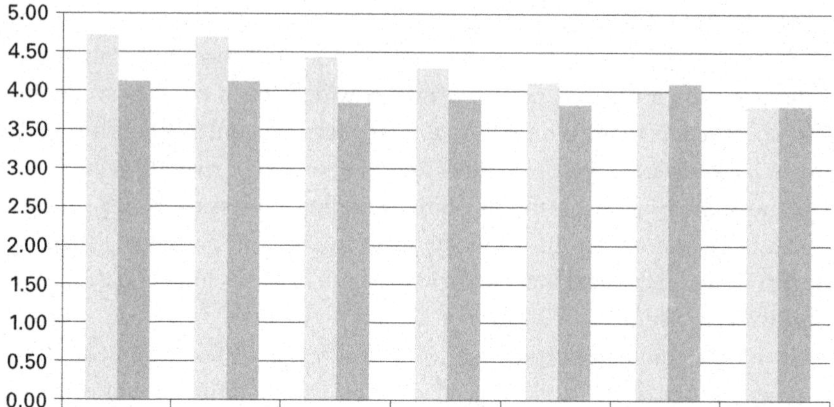

	Reliability	Service levels	Price	Customer service	Flexibility of provider	Geographic coverage	Range of services
Importance	4.73	4.69	4.44	4.30	4.10	3.97	3.79
3PL Rating	4.11	4.13	3.84	3.89	3.81	4.09	3.80

SOURCE: Transport Intelligence (2014)

Evolution towards value adding services

The need by logistics companies' customers for increasing levels of value has been mirrored by an equal desire by the logistics companies themselves to improve their profit margins. Increasing sophistication and complexity of supply chains is a considerable opportunity for LSPs to achieve this goal by moving away from the provision of commoditized activities. A survey for the European Logistics Association by AT Kearney revealed that Value Added Services (VAS) increased considerably in the 2000s, whilst expenditure on logistics as a whole fell (ELA, 2009).

Figure 1.9 outlines this trend, from the early days of logistics out-sourcing in the 1980s within fairly simple transactional relationships towards the aspiration of deeper partnerships in which solution development and management is most important. As supply chain complexity increases, so do the services that logistics providers are asked to perform. No longer is logistics seen as a tactical activity, where the gains made are purely measured in terms of transport or warehousing cost savings. Instead, customers become more engaged in the transformational impact on supply chain competitiveness that a logistics provider can achieve.

Figure 1.9 The evolution of the logistics industry

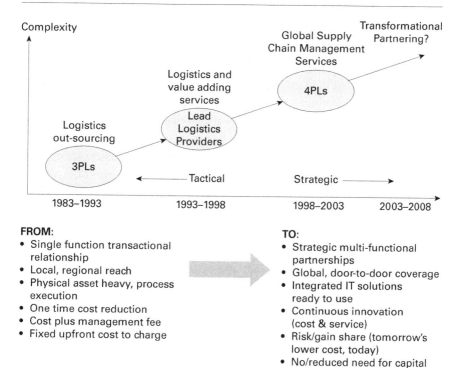

FROM:
- Single function transactional relationship
- Local, regional reach
- Physical asset heavy, process execution
- One time cost reduction
- Cost plus management fee
- Fixed upfront cost to charge

TO:
- Strategic multi-functional partnerships
- Global, door-to-door coverage
- Integrated IT solutions ready to use
- Continuous innovation (cost & service)
- Risk/gain share (tomorrow's lower cost, today)
- No/reduced need for capital

To off-shore or near-source?

As described above, supply chains have become highly globalized as manufacturers and retailers take advantage of low labour and transport costs to 'off-shore' production. However, wage inflation and rising transport costs have started to rebalance this particular equation in favour of production at locations much closer to the major consumer markets in the West.

While the BRIC countries (Brazil, Russia, India and China) have played a significant role in global growth for a number of years, other emerging markets are now showing increased promise as potential investment alternatives. There are signs that increased labour costs and skill shortages are eroding China's once-commanding edge over other markets. That said, China continues to benefit from strong domestic growth and acts as a major driver of growth in the global economy.

Separately, increasing transport costs are driving decisions about preferred production locations. 'Near-sourcing' – the effort to control costs by producing in countries adjacent or close to major destination markets – is on the rise. Markets close to the United States and Europe, such as Mexico and Turkey, are attracting increased attention.

ıg the near-sourcing trend is the growing attractiveness of emerging
as consumer markets. Weakened demand in Europe, the United
ther developed economies means emerging markets have been less
end on these countries as export markets. This has powered increased
trade between emerging markets and led to development of vibrant retail
sectors, increasing opportunities for domestic-based logistics operations.

Generally, if a product has a high manufacturing cost and is not heavy, it
is better to produce it in a region where labour is cheap. If it has a low
manufacturing cost and the goods are heavy, it is better to produce it closer
to consumer markets. In 2005, for example, it made economic sense to
produce mid-range copiers and assembled TVs in Mexico. Following an
increase in labour costs and oil price, however, a shift in the trade-off curve
meant that it became more cost-effective to build these types of product in
the United States. Likewise, the production of mid-range servers could now
be undertaken in Mexico, rather than in Asia.

In the survey of manufacturers and retailers undertaken by Transport
Intelligence, 70 per cent of the sample stated that they intend to adopt a
hybrid-model of sourcing goods from a mix of low-cost markets, such as
China, as well as countries closer to key consumer markets. The proportion
of companies continuing to source goods solely from remote markets is
relatively low (21 per cent), whilst 9 per cent of the survey are now actively
seeking to source all of their goods from markets closer to their consumers.
This switch from dependence on the more remote markets may, in part, be
countered by continued decreases in fuel prices.

The process of un-bundling and fragmentation of manufacturing, which
has resulted in the globalization of supply chains, is described in detail by
Richard Baldwin (Baldwin, 2011).

The author describes how over the last two decades 'un-bundling' of production processes has occurred across markets. This initially occurred in Europe
with the accession of Spain and Portugal to the European Union and continued
with its expansion into Central and Eastern Europe. In North America, the
establishment of maquiladoras just across the US/Mexico border had the same
effect. The facilitation of longer distance supply chains was helped by the
development of information and communications technology that occurred at
the same time as falling transport costs. In Asia un-bundling has been encouraged
by the huge disparity in wage costs compared to physical distances. For example,
wage costs in China are far lower than those in neighbouring Japan.

In many instances it makes sense to out-source high labour-intensive
processes to lower wage cost markets, although if the goods are capital
intensive and transport costs high, then out-sourcing may not take place.
Fluctuating shipping costs can mitigate or enhance the benefits of co-locating

various production stages within an end market, influencing management decisions and demonstrating the fluidity of the environment in which these decisions are taken. Timeliness, reliability, information sharing, quality and design, along with wider benefits resulting from shared labour skills and knowledge all mitigate against out-sourcing to remote markets.

An interesting part of the analysis shows that in some cases out-sourcing to remote locations will only work if a sufficiently large number of production stages are relocated. Otherwise remote companies have the penalty of being distanced from upstream supply partners and the end market. In addition to this, many companies are unwilling to relocate production if other companies are unwilling to follow. This will slow development of manufacturing clusters in developing markets as the necessary production ecosystems do not exist. Japanese manufacturers have been able to overcome this problem in one such developing market, Vietnam, by creating their own supplier parks. This is no doubt facilitated by the strength of the relationships that often exist between suppliers and manufacturers in Japanese supply chains.

This perhaps demonstrates that decisions on relocating production are highly sophisticated. With a shrinking differential in wage costs between the developed and developing world, other factors therefore come into play and very rapidly sourcing strategies can be changed. At the same time as this, Asia is transforming from a production market to consumer. This will add an extra layer of complexity into sourcing and off-shoring decisions for Western manufacturers.

Summary

This chapter has examined the main demand-side (that is, manufacturer and retailer) and supply-side (that is, logistics service provider) driven trends that have created the modern global logistics industry. It addressed the growth in trade and globalization of supply chains; the transformation of supply chains management practice from inefficient and costly 'Just-in-Case' manufacturing to 'Just-in-Time' and the impact this had on logistics companies. It also addressed how centralization of inventory has led to the development of local, regional and global distribution hubs, which itself has created the need for more transportation. Finally, the chapter dealt with out-sourcing by manufacturers and retailers to third-party logistics providers and the evolution of the sector towards the supply of increasingly high end, value adding services.

Key points to consider:

- Logistics service providers need to be increasingly agile to operate successfully in a fast-moving and complex environment.

- 'Intellectual capital' is now as important as transport assets or IT to winning major contracts from customers looking for innovative supply chain cost-cutting solutions.

- Logistics companies need geographic scope to be able to provide end-to-end services in certain globalized sectors. However, this should not be overstated, as most retail, consumer and automotive customers still have mostly national or regional requirements taking into account local consumer tastes or regulations.

- Asia is the fastest developing logistics market and, with increasing supply chain integration in the region, this will continue to be the key market for logistics investment for many years to come.

An industry in transformation: towards consolidation

02

CHAPTER LEARNING OBJECTIVES

This chapter will familiarize the reader with:

- How the logistics industry has undergone a transformation in terms of the major logistics service providers which have come to dominate the market
- The different dynamics in each logistics segment that have caused these changes
- The major deals that have been transacted
- The range of corporate development strategies that logistics companies have employed to meet the changing needs of their customers

Although mergers and acquisitions have always been a constant factor in the global transport and logistics industries, the last two decades have seen unprecedented levels of activity.

The catalyst for change was the entrance of the European post offices into the global logistics industry in the mid-1990s, in particular the Dutch and German mail operators. They brought with them considerable resources that enabled them to sustain lengthy – and costly – acquisition and integration programmes.

The present market leaders have emerged from a range of backgrounds. Post offices, railways, freight forwarders, integrators, road hauliers/truckers and former in-house distribution businesses have all built integrated service offerings in order to capture the enhanced value that can be attained through building scale operations and extensive portfolios. This has resulted in one of the most marked impacts of consolidation: the merging of traditionally discrete logistics segments.

Consolidation has also occurred within sectors, perhaps most noticeably within the shipping industry. Maersk, for example, built a market leading position through acquisition (P&O Nedlloyd, Sea-Land), although not without problems along the way. Recently the acquisition of NOL by CMA CGM was announced.

Even air transport was not immune to the seemingly inevitable process of merger. In the United States, nine major airlines have shrunk to just four – American, Delta, United and Southwest. Elsewhere in the world KLM was bought by Air France and BA and Iberia have merged.

The market dynamics of today's logistics industry have resulted from a number of trends that have created opportunity for logistics service providers. This chapter reviews these trends before examining the strategies employed by companies to exploit this opportunity.

Consolidation and fragmentation in the logistics industry

External pressures for industry consolidation

The fundamental changes in the logistics industry have been driven by a number of imperatives, both demand- and supply-side led. The speed at which change has taken place over the last decade is as a result of the mutual benefit and opportunities to both logistics service providers and users, which these trends have created.

The three charts in Figure 2.1 show how the transport and logistics industry has evolved in the last three decades:

- **Stage 1:** Right up until the 1970s and 80s each of the functions highlighted were largely discrete, with little overlap. The reason for this was partly due to a lack of sophistication in the demands of customers; partly due to national regulations that favoured, for example, in-house operations against out-sourced; and partly due to the high levels of fragmentation which meant that few companies had the management expertise, resources or backing to expand aggressively through acquisition.

Figure 2.1 Merger and fragmentation of logistics functions

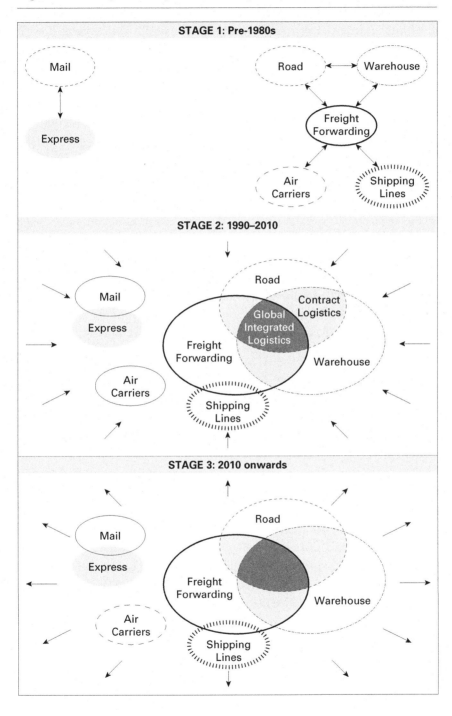

- **Stage 2:** The largest companies, already dominating their national markets, expand into neighbouring sectors. The Dutch Post Office, for example, acquired Australian transport group TNT, providing it with Express and Logistics capabilities; Deutsche Post bought international express operator DHL and a range of domestic express parcels companies before subsequently expanding into the logistics sector; Deutsche Bahn acquired road, forwarding and contract logistics specialist Schenker and subsequently Bax Global. Management justify these decisions on the level of synergy that can be achieved. Acquisition strategies are fuelled by cheap money and pressure from shareholders.

- **Stage 3:** This shows the reverse pressures that have existed since the recession of 2008 (and in some cases before). In several instances, due to the absence of expected synergies or poor integration, companies have sold off their loss-making acquisitions. TNT, for example, sold first its underperforming logistics operations and then split its express operations from its mail. DHL was forced to withdraw from the US domestic express market (as well as domestic markets in the UK, France and elsewhere) losing billions of dollars in the process. The harsher economic environment could be said to have shown up weaknesses in either business models or management.

However, large diversified groups, such as DHL, UPS, Deutsche Bahn and SNCF continue to operate despite the fact that there is little integration between many of the functions they provide. These lack of synergies make disposals more likely if and when management comes under pressure from shareholders.

Putting to one side the claims of synergy, acquisitions have delivered benefits in the form of diversification. UPS, for example, has created a much more defensive business model by developing an international express offering, largely by inorganic growth. Its profits have been helped by the development of Asia as an economic powerhouse, even when the US domestic parcels sector was stagnating. Likewise at various times in the past decade its forwarding and logistics capabilities have proved to be a useful source of revenue and profits, despite initial painful integration.

Ambitions to build diversified transport groups still exist. French-based group Norbert Dentressangle, for example, added contract logistics capabilities to its road freight operations, and more recently freight forwarding before itself being bought by US group XPO Logistics. However, others, despite access to capital, strong management and plenty of opportunity, have eschewed this approach. Expeditors, a pure-play freight forwarder based in the US, has successfully concentrated on organic growth within its sector and has been one of the best performing companies in the industry.

The push for globalization

Many logistics companies with the necessary resources have chosen to globalize their operations in line with the changing requirements of their clients. Manufacturers and retailers have increased both the level of global sourcing and the scope of the markets that they supply. This has been enabled by the reduction of barriers to world trade facilitated by such organizations as the EU, NAFTA and the WTO, as detailed in Chapter 1. The rising levels of international trade, and the increasingly integrated nature of supply chains, has created a need for logistics companies that can offer sophisticated services on a worldwide basis, including IT systems, which can provide global visibility.

Out-sourcing manufacturing to regions of low-cost production has been gathering pace for many years although the decision of where to source goods from or where to locate production facilities takes into account a wide variety of different factors, labour costs being just one.

For instance, if time to market is of prime importance then the decision may be made to 'near-source', that is, locate production in Central and Eastern Europe or in the Mediterranean region. Nowhere is this more apparent than in the clothing sector where a whole market of 'fast fashion' has developed. Retailers buying clothing may choose to near-source some product lines in order to meet short-term market trends. Product can be manufactured and delivered in weeks, rather than the three months that is usual for goods to be brought in from China. Of this lead time, a transit could comprise a month at sea rather than a few days by road from a comparable supplier in Eastern Europe.

Consequently, the response of logistics providers has reflected this. To continue the fashion logistics theme, logistics service providers have needed to develop operations that can move goods to Western markets in a fast and effective manner. This has meant establishing operations in Eastern Europe, North Africa, Latin America or the Asia Pacific region to undertake value adding activities such as quality control and packing as well as having the infrastructure in place to move the goods in an appropriate manner.

Logistics companies will in the future be expected to go even further afield by their clients. At the lower value end of the product spectrum, China is starting to lose out to even lower cost countries in Asia Pacific such as

Vietnam. For low value production it could be said that a 'ripple' is moving out throughout the region with China as its centre although it will be many years before this trend starts to have any real impact. Crudely it could be surmised that China may end up being squeezed at the bottom of the market by lower cost rivals and in the middle of the market by its Western customers' supply chain requirements (time to market/inventory cost). This will eventually result in a focus on higher quality, higher value products where more expensive but quicker air cargo (or indeed a mix of sea and air cargo), are options. For logistics companies it will reinforce the trend to develop operations in remote and difficult countries, requiring a particular set of skills.

Liberalization of markets

The liberalization of the European postal markets has been one of the driving forces behind the high level of M&A activity in the late 1990s and early 2000s. The market has been progressively opened up to private sector competition although it is more obvious in some markets – such as the UK and Netherlands – than others. However, the threat of competitors entering what previously had been monopolistic markets was the key reason for mail operators to diversify their revenues. This led the Dutch, German and subsequently the British, French, Austrian and Scandinavian post offices to embark on extensive buying campaigns, which added express parcels networks and, in the case of Deutsche Post, extensive logistics operations to their portfolio.

There has also been deregulation in Europe's rail industry, which prompted some state owned railways to prepare for a more competitive environment. ABX, a subsidiary of Belgium's SNCB, embarked on a hugely ambitious (and ultimately flawed) programme, building an extensive European logistics group. Deutsche Bahn, Germany's railways, acquired one of the world's biggest logistics companies, Schenker, and also US-based global forwarder Bax Global. This was in addition to complementary rail operators throughout Europe, such as EWS Railways in the UK. SNCF, France's national rail operator, meanwhile, has acquired logistics giant, Geodis, also French-based.

Europe has not been the only market to see major changes through liberalization. Although deregulation of the US postal market is highly unlikely, the trucking market has already seen a major transformation. The Motor Carrier Act of 1935 stipulated that companies that wanted to haul freight across state lines on a for-hire basis had to obtain authority from the Interstate Commerce Commission. Prices were determined through a collective ratemaking process made legal by federal antitrust exemption. Following deregulation starting in 1980 interstate trucking became much easier as did the setting of competitive rates. This had the effect of a huge shake-up and it is estimated that more than three-quarters of the United States' largest carriers in 1980 have since gone out of business.

Efforts to liberalize the US–Mexico crossborder trucking market started in 2000 – in the teeth of strong opposition from Teamster Unions. A pilot project permitted US trucks to cross the Mexican border and, in return, a certain number of Mexican trucks were allowed to deliver freight to destinations beyond the former 20-mile limit inside the US border. In 2015, after the programme was considered a success by the government, the market was deregulated fully, although Mexican truckers are still required to comply with safety provisions.

Even the trend towards out-sourcing of logistics, one of the prime catalysts for the change in the industry in the past three decades, can be attributed to deregulation. In many markets, in-house transport operations were favoured by regulators (and to some degree this is still the case). However, since reducing the protection of in-house operations the third-party logistics (3PL) sector has emerged, allowing manufacturers and retailers to focus on their core-competencies whilst providing new impetus to the transport and distribution industry.

In order to take advantage of this trend, logistics companies have sought to build skills, capabilities and geographic scope. The fact that in some markets (such as in the United States) it is estimated that only around 20 per cent of logistics activities are out-sourced, shows that a huge potential still exists.

Product differentiation, sector focus and supplier rationalization

Many segments within the logistics industry, such as road haulage and warehousing, are commoditized or with low barriers to entry and exit, such as freight forwarding. This has led to the market being typified at the grass roots level by low margins and high competition.

The largest companies have sought to address this challenge by making targeted acquisitions which increases their exposure to vertical sectors or supply chain segments in which there is less competition, whilst at the same time building on their own competitive advantages, such as access to finance, intellectual capital, IT capabilities and global scale.

For example, the pharmaceutical sector has attracted considerable interest from LSPs in recent years. The sector is very sophisticated in its logistics needs, requiring high security distribution, a high degree of regulatory compliance, consignment tracking capabilities as well as, in some cases, temperature control and monitoring.

Rather than attempt to build these capabilities in-house, many LSPs decided to buy niche specialists who already had the expertise and licences. Below are some examples of such acquisitions:

- UPS acquires Pieffe Group in Italy
- Kerry Logistics acquires Trustspeed Medicine Logistics
- Forward Air Corporation acquires Total Quality in the United States
- Geodis acquires Pharmalog in Europe.

One of the earliest companies to enter this sector was Exel, the forerunner to DHL Supply Chain, which acquired a number of pharma logistics specialists in 2004 and in the process built a market leading position.

In addition to vertical sectors, some LSPs have sought to add functionality at additional stages of the supply chain. Perhaps the most relevant and recent examples of this involve the e-commerce sector. For example, UPS acquired European e-commerce specialist Kiala to give it B2C downstream supply chain delivery capabilities in Belgium, France, Luxembourg, the Netherlands and Spain. Kiala had developed a platform that enabled e-commerce retailers to offer their shoppers the option of having goods delivered to a convenient retail location. Other examples include La Poste's acquisition of e-fulfilment specialist ORIUM and TNT Post's acquisition of e-retail company Kowin.

Additionally, logistics companies are increasingly being asked to provide a range of value added services, rather than just one element of transportation or warehousing. Using a smaller number of logistics suppliers benefits the manufacturer or retailer by reducing the amount of supplier administration required. It also allows them to leverage their buying power to drive down costs. Acquisition is one way in which a logistics supplier can expand its range of capabilities to meet these ever-increasing demands and improve margins.

Supplier rationalization will benefit the larger logistics companies as scale players are more likely to remain on short lists for tendering, reducing the level of competition and allowing them to access logistics spend, which was previously spread over a greater number of suppliers. This helps to increase revenues as well as the bargaining power that an LSP has with its carriers. This in turn can improve transportation management margins.

Options for growth

At present, acquisition is the most favoured route towards building global portfolios of integrated services. However, there are other alternatives available to logistics providers looking to offer a wider range of services to clients.

Organic growth

Although organic growth is viewed as being the safest way in which to develop presence in new markets, in the race to build European and global platforms it has become increasingly unfashionable. Acquisitions can deliver immediate revenue streams and an operational presence, which organic growth cannot. However, organic/acquisitive strategy options tend to be cyclical, related to the number of appropriate target companies, the availability of 'cheap money' in the financial markets and the maturity of companies' acquisition programmes.

Alliances

Alliances are a quick and easy way to offer clients enhanced services in different geographies or to add functionality. They are very common in the freight forwarding sector as they allow national or regionally based operators to compete effectively on a global basis with owned-network providers such as DHL Global Forwarding or Kuehne + Nagel.

Examples of where an alliance adds functionality include a tie-up between express carrier TNT and US trucking company Con-way. TNT's US operations mainly consist of international express delivery services to and from the United States and Canada. For delivery within the United States and Canada, the company utilizes a combination of regional partners, own operations and a relationship with Con-way, established in 2009, that provide Less-than-Truckload (LTL) services from TNT's main gateways: New York, Los Angeles, Chicago and Miami. This arrangement will probably change given that TNT has now been acquired by rival FedEx, which will have its own distribution capabilities.

Alliances work best in stable, conservative markets where the threat of competitors acquiring alliance members is low. This obviously has not been the case in the global logistics market in the last few years. In 2012 a forwarding network, World Air Cargo Organisation, had to restructure its membership in Africa/Middle East when one of its independent members, Swift, was taken over by global player, DSV.

Another weakness of the alliance model is the potential for a lack of strategic direction. Individual members may have different opinions on the future for the alliance as well as having their own distinct corporate priorities and identity. This often inhibits investment in the network infrastructure, both physical and IT. If this is the case, the alliance will have little chance of competing against fully owned and integrated players and can leave the partners vulnerable to acquisition.

Joint ventures

A joint venture is a formal relationship in which two or more parties create an entity with a shared stock ownership. JVs are typically used by companies that have complementary services or attributes to exploit a particular market.

Joint ventures were essential in the Chinese market, where legislation forced foreign-invested companies to partner with local companies. Since deregulation of the market this is no longer an obligation and many have chosen to establish wholly owned foreign enterprises (WOFE) or buy out their JV partners (such as UPS buying its JV with Sinotrans and FedEx, DTW). However, many still see advantages from JVs as they provide local market knowledge, contacts with local officials and a knowledge of regulations. Most notably this includes DHL's long-term relationship with Chinese logistics and express giant, Sinotrans.

'Piggybacking'

Expansion by 'piggybacking' involves developing services geographically on the back of the needs of a key client. This has become a frequently used mode of expansion due to the internationalization of manufacturing and retailing. Using existing logistics suppliers has various advantages:

- There is already a relationship in place that provides a level of trust that otherwise would need to be developed if an unknown supplier was contracted.

- There is often a shared business culture between senior management of both companies.

- When locating production to an undeveloped, remote market, sophisticated logistics practices may not exist.

- The global expansion of UPS Supply Chain Solutions, Schneider and Penske from the United States; Geodis from France and DHL from Germany has involved piggybacking on existing domestic clients. One of the obvious benefits of piggybacking is the immediate revenue stream that it brings, along with the potential to leverage the investment costs in the operation across a range of other clients.

Is acquisition worthwhile?

For many years the global logistics market has been consolidating owing to the reasons outlined above. However, the risk element of the trend has never really been examined in the race for scale and global scope. The number of logistics companies that have been able to grow 'successfully' through acquisition is limited.

On the whole, large companies seem to be better at acquisitions than smaller ones, although there are exceptions to this statement. Larger companies are often already experienced at undertaking acquisitions, as well as the job of integration. They are also able to employ appropriate levels of labour to oversee the integration, thereby releasing the value of the acquisition. Being global already, they are also often better able to understand and overcome cultural barriers.

Smaller logistics companies do not have this luxury. Into this bracket must fall many of the UK companies that expanded into Europe in the late 1990s. At that time the prevailing belief was that better opportunities were to be had in the mainland European market as the domestic logistics market was becoming increasingly competitive and mature. However, providers such as Wincanton, Christian Salvesen, TDG (both bought by Norbert Dentressangle, now XPO Logistics), Hays (now Kuehne + Nagel), and even Exel (now DHL) all at one point or another ran into problems. All these companies, with the exception of Wincanton, have now been taken over by larger European rivals.

However, being very big is no guarantee of success. DHL, for example, failed to turn around its domestic express operation in the United States and this cost the company several billion dollars. Rival logistics operator ABX

Logistics (owned by Belgian Railways) also faced difficulties following its acquisition programme, and it was forced to sell off poorly performing companies, and then was sold itself. Similarly, German logistics company Thiel also expanded too quickly and as a result lost its management and then sold off many of its constituent parts.

Acquisition strategies

'Blockbuster' deals

Since the 1990s, a number of global logistics companies have undertaken one or more 'blockbuster' deals to acquire immediate scale. The acquisition of GeoLogistics by Agility; TNT by the Dutch Post Office or Deutsche Post's acquisition of Danzas, AEI, Airborne and Exel are examples of these types of deals. They have then proceeded to 'in-fill' gaps in capabilities or geographies with a sequence of smaller acquisitions.

The advantage of this approach is that it gives the company immediate scale and market presence, therefore providing competitive advantage over smaller players. It also reduces the level of M&A activity required in identifying a series of potential targets, as well as approaching, negotiating with them and eventually integrating them into the parent company. It may also reduce cultural barriers if the acquisition target is from a similar business background.

However, there are many disadvantages too. Even the largest scale player does not have consistent depth of services across all geographies and segments. Therefore, whereas small, focused acquisitions can identify high-quality players that can be easily integrated into a larger company, scale acquisitions can leave buyers with ongoing management problems due to weak or badly performing business units.

Evolution strategies

An alternative to the 'blockbuster' scenario is the evolution model. The early stages of an expansion strategy usually focus around increasing presence in the home market, and consolidating market position in a core-competence. When this has been achieved, the company develops into associated competences and markets in close proximity or with similar attributes, through a range of alliances, joint ventures or focused acquisitions. In this way, a portfolio of capabilities and markets can be built without the risks involved in a

Table 2.1 Major acquisitions in the global logistics industry 1996 to date

Year	Acquirer	Target	Geography	Approx cost
2016	FedEx	TNT	Global	€4.4bn
2015	CMA CGM	NOL	Global	$1.9bn
2015	XPO	Con-way	Global/USA	$3.0bn
2015	XPO	Norbert Dentressangle	Europe/USA	$3.5bn
2015	Geodis	Ozburn Hessey	USA	$800m
2014	Norbert Dentressangle	Jacobson	USA	$750m
2012	Russian Railways	GEFCO	Europe	€800m
2010	Norbert Dentressangle	TDG	Europe	€232.8m
2008	SNCF Geodis	IBM Logistics	Global	Not disclosed
2007	Toll	Baltrans	Asia Pacific	€300m
2007	Norbert Dentressangle	Christian Salvesen	Europe	€365.1m
2007	CEVA	EGL	Global	$2bn
2005	Agility	Geologistics	Global	$454m
2005	Deutsche Bahn	Bax Global	Global	$1.1bn
2005	Kuehne + Nagel	ACR Logistics	Europe	€440m
2005	DP-DHL	Exel	Global	€5.6bn
2005	Maersk	P&O Nedlloyd	Global	€2.3bn
2004	UPS	Menlo Worldwide	Global	$150m
2004	Exel	Tibbett & Britten	Global	€480m
2003	DP-DHL	Airborne Express	USA	$1.05bn
2002	Deutsche Bahn	Stinnes (Schenker)	Europe/Global	€2.5bn
2002	Deutsche Post	DHL	Global	€2.44bn
1999	Ocean	NFC (Exel)	Global	€2.2bn
1999	Maersk	Sea-Land	Global	$800m
1999	Deutsche Post	AEI	USA/Global	€1.2bn
1998	Deutsche Post	Danzas	Europe/Global	€1.3bn
1996	TNT Post Group	TNT	Global	€1.2bn

SOURCE: Transport Intelligence (2016)

scale acquisition in areas where the company has no prior experience or skills. This approach is usually termed 'bolt-on' acquisition.

In this respect post offices have a natural advantage over competitors in other logistics fields. They already have market dominance in their own sectors owing to the fact that in most cases they have monopoly or near-monopoly positions. They therefore have no need to focus on building or protecting their own core businesses and can diversify, using the profits gained in their home market to fund the acquisitions.

Some companies have found that building a major global presence without solid foundations carries high levels of risk. ABX Logistics and German logistics companies Thiel and D.Logistics experienced severe financial difficulties due to the underperformance of acquired companies. In addition they did not have the resources required to integrate the group into a coherent entity, therefore unlocking the value of a global or European network. One of the major risks involved in acquisition is the migration of key employees and clients – this is especially the case with freight forwarding companies where client loyalty often revolves around personal contacts rather than corporate relationships.

The emergence of the 'mega-carrier'

The consolidation of the global logistics industry was forecast as long ago as 1991 by Cooper, Browne & Peters (*European Logistics*). They believed that companies from a range of different logistics backgrounds would converge in terms of services offered and geographic scope. This has been shown to be the case as the largest freight forwarders, distribution companies, express operators, shipping lines, in-house operators and of course post offices have engaged on a strategy of developing into one-stop shop providers of multiple functions.

Figure 2.2 shows the original positioning of the major logistics segments. From their relative starting points there has been convergence towards the 'mega-carrier quadrant'. Distribution companies in particular have tended to offer clients the most sophisticated logistics activities. However, this has largely been on a regional or national basis and contrasts with freight forwarders and express operators that have large global networks, but offer limited products or services.

As detailed above, the trend towards the development of a multi-service portfolio has been driven by a number of demand- and supply-side factors.

Figure 2.2 The 'mega-carrier' quadrant

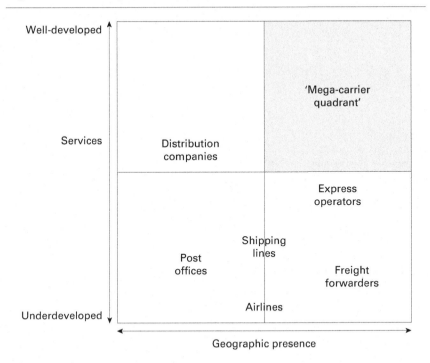

SOURCE: Cooper, Browne & Peters in *European Logistics* (1994)

The result of this has been a frenetic period of acquisition as companies have extended their capabilities horizontally into adjoining logistics segments as well as geographically. For many companies, with a few notable exceptions, the next step has been to integrate these capabilities in order to provide customers with cohesive solutions. Deutsche Post DHL acquired international express capabilities through DHL, land transport and freight forwarding through Danzas, airfreight operations by buying AEI and distribution operations through Exel, which was itself a merger of Exel and Tibbett & Britten.

It should be noted that total integration of all their acquired distribution, forwarding, express parcels, etc activities is not the goal of these companies. Rather they seek to have the processes and networks in place that can be used where necessary for a limited number of 'blue chip' clients with sophisticated, regional or global logistics needs.

Although to begin with many companies were aiming to position themselves in the top right 'mega-carrier' quadrant, the last two economic recessions have led to a counter trend. Falling volumes exposed poor

Figure 2.3 Reversal of the mega-carrier trend?

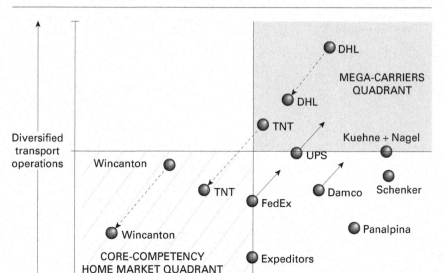

acquisitions or weak integration and management. Figure 2.3 shows that whilst some companies are still acquisitively building global presence, others including even DHL, TNT and Wincanton, have retreated towards the core-competency/home market quadrant.

The key logistics segments

Post offices

The European postal operators have been responsible for a significant proportion of the acquisition activity in the logistics market. The first post office to recognize that there was a major opportunity to develop a worldwide logistics presence was Royal Dutch Post, acquiring the express parcels and logistics company TNT in 1996.

The reasons behind the expansion of the post offices can be summarized as follows:

- Their domestic markets were in the process of liberalization and therefore the monopolistic advantage they enjoyed was passing. Diversifying into other parts of the logistics industry was a way of maximizing their brand, presence and resources, as well as utilizing the strong cash flows that they generate.

- The extension of domestic parcels operations on a European and global basis was a natural progression for postal operators to take advantage of the increased internationalization of goods flows.

- They recognized that they were in a good position to exploit the trend towards integrated, global supply chains by coordinating flows of goods, information and funds.

- E-commerce has become the major growth sector in the express and logistics industry. Post offices are very well placed to offer fulfilment services and 'last mile' delivery.

Although the Dutch Post Office was first to acquire internationally, Deutsche Post implemented the most ambitious expansion plan. By buying Danzas, AEI, DHL, Exel, Airborne Express (since sold), and subsequently a multitude of infill companies, it constructed a global mail, express and logistics company. Other post offices have tried to follow suit on a more modest basis. Royal Mail acquired a European network, General Parcel, for in the region of 750 million euros, and La Poste (through subsidiary GeoPost) took a controlling interest in DPD.

Railways

The European railways sector has also become a factor in the logistics acquisition market. This is partly as a result of liberalization of rail markets, which has seen competition increase on a domestic and international level.

The management of Deutsche Bahn (German Railways) also had the ambition of arresting the long-term decline of rail as a modal choice by acquiring freight forwarders and logistics providers (which control a large proportion of cargo volumes). In this way, they believed, railways could leverage their sizeable resources to ensure that rail was not further marginalized. By doing this railway companies would be able to acquire customers directly, thereby also increasing their level of value add (and hence improve margins). The risk of such a strategy was the alienation of existing client forwarders which following such a move become de facto competitors.

In the execution of this strategy, Deutsche Bahn has been the most aggressive of the European rail operators. It made significant acquisitions both to expand the geographic scope of its operations throughout Europe through its DB Logistics division (including Brunner Railway Services in Switzerland;

EWS in the UK; Transfesa in Spain; joint ventures in Sweden and Poland) as well as expanding its Schenker road/freight forwarding operation. The latter was transformed through the acquisition of global forwarder Bax Global.

However, Deutsche Bahn's ultimate plan of a listing of its shares on a stock exchange in a similar way to that of Deutsche Post ran into political problems. There was a fear amongst politicians and unions that by turning Deutsche Bahn into a fully commercial entity through an IPO, key interest groups would suffer. This highlighted the tensions between those who wanted full privatization and the welcome influx of foreign capital, and those who saw such a move as leading to the destruction of an important public service. Ultimately, the latter forces won and the Chief Executive and architect of these plans, Hartmut Mehdorn, eventually left the company.

Not to be outdone, French railway operator SNCF has also carried out aggressive inorganic expansion in the logistics and express sectors. Already a major shareholder in French logistics company Geodis, in 2008 it acquired the remaining stake. The deal was a major part of its plan to create an international multi-modal operator in the field of logistics and transportation. Following this, it also acquired IBM's internal global logistics operations, managing approximately 1 billion euros per year of IBM's logistics costs worldwide. These were then integrated into Geodis' existing operations to make it a global player. Geodis has certainly not scaled back its expansion plans and in November 2015 it acquired Ozburn Hessey Logistics (OHL), a US based 1.2 billion euros logistics provider.

Freight forwarders

Freight forwarders have a number of natural advantages in the present logistics environment. They have global operations and can manage complex goods flows through the information systems they have built. This has meant that they have been amongst the largest beneficiaries from the globalization trend.

Freight forwarders achieve considerable competitive advantage through scale, as the more volumes they control, the greater is their bargaining power with carriers. Therefore, many acquisitions by freight forwarders have been made to build presence on certain traffic lanes. An example of this is CH Robinson's acquisition of Phoenix International, which gave it an enhanced presence on the Asia–North America routes.

There are a number of other reasons why freight forwarders have been prominent in the acquisition market. For many years they have been under pressure from international parcels carriers that have succeeded in acquiring most of their high-margin small-consignment business. Without being able to offer the client value adding services, freight forwarders risk being marginalized. Therefore, the more innovative companies have increased the number of services that they supply, and increased the depth of relationship that they have with their clients, from ad hoc to long term. This has been achieved not least through the acquisition of capabilities.

The very fact that forwarders already have in place global networks has also made them highly attractive to logistics players that have developed from a domestic or regional focus. There are numerous examples of this, but CEVA's takeover of EGL and Geodis's acquisition of TNT Freight Management (Wilson) and German forwarder Rohde & Liesenfeld are amongst the most prominent.

Parcels networks

The main global and European parcels operators have all been highly acquisitive over the last 20 years. The primary reason why many parcels operators have chosen acquisition over alliance is that it gives them a greater level of strategic control. In the parcels industry it is essential that there is consistency of products, pricing, service and quality on a regional and global basis. Hence Royal Mail and GeoPost both chose to buy existing franchise operations, General Parcel and DPD, rather than work in partnership with them. UPS, TNT and Deutsche Post DHL have also been highly acquisitive, and for Royal Mail and GeoPost the threat of network partners being bought by competitors was also a driving force.

UPS has been one of the most acquisitive of the parcels companies investing billions of dollars in building an owned distribution network. It has also developed a substantial logistics presence in and outside of the United States. Its prime reason for this was that it wanted to take advantage of its relationships with many large shippers, as well as benefiting from the fast growth of the logistics industry. This was especially the case in sectors such as service parts logistics or high-tech logistics where it could integrate its own express operations with value adding activities. The company also acquired freight forwarding capacity through the purchase of Fritz Companies and Menlo Worldwide Forwarding.

The major integrators have focused their acquisition strategies both on Europe and developing markets. Although varying geographically, the main targets have been domestic express carriers.

In Europe two of the biggest acquisitions occurred in the UK:

1 In 2006 FedEx bought the UK Express Company ANC for £120 million. The deal marked the US integrator's return to the domestic Express markets in Europe after an absence of more than 10 years.

2 In 2005 UPS acquired UK package delivery company Lynx Express Ltd for £55.5 million.

The UK has seen consolidation of its own domestic express sector, which has historically been highly fragmented. This trend is likely to be ongoing, not only in the UK but also in other European countries.

UPS has also bought in Eastern Europe – Polish Messenger Service Stolica S.A. TNT meanwhile acquired in Spain TG+, a leading Spanish domestic distribution company. In 2012, UPS attempted to take over TNT, but this was thwarted by the European competition authorities.

Outside of Europe, the main acquisitions have occurred in China and India.

In China:

- In 2005 UPS acquired its express operations from Sinotrans, its joint venture partner. The deal was valued around 100 million euros.
- In 2006 FedEx Corporation acquired DTW Group's 50 per cent share of the FedEx-DTW International Priority express joint venture and its domestic express network in China for US $400 million.
- In 2007 TNT completed the acquisition of Hoau, a leading freight and parcels delivery company in China. This was subsequently sold in 2013.
- DHL prefers to work through its joint venture partner, Sinotrans.

In India:

- In 2006 FedEx acquired Indian airfreight company Prakash Air Freight Pvt. Ltd (PAFEX) for US $30 million.
- DHL has progressively acquired stakes in Indian air express company Blue Dart since 2004.
- UPS has a joint venture with Indian operator Jetair.

In-house logistics companies

Many of the largest contract logistics players have grown out of former in-house operations. This includes Wincanton (Unigate) and Easydis (from French retailer Casino). The German market in particular has a number of huge in-house operations some of which have been 'corporatized', either remaining in the ownership of the parent company or becoming independent. The latter provides the greatest opportunity as it allows the company to tender for business amongst competitors of its former parent company without any clash of interest. Arvato (subsidiary of Bertelsmann) is one of the best known.

Air cargo carriers

Air cargo has been one of the few industry segments to be excluded from the trend of buying value adding capabilities. One of the main reasons for this is their position in the supply chain relative to their main clients, the freight forwarders. It is estimated that forwarders control about 85 per cent of airlines' cargo revenues and attempts to develop value added services or extend the level of functionality have been resisted. The reason for this is simple enough: an airline that starts to offer a door-to-door service to shippers comes into direct competition with the forwarding community. Whereas 'disintermediation' has worked in other parts of the industry (for example, low-cost airlines sell direct to consumers via the web), no air cargo operator has yet decided that it is in their interests to alienate their existing client base.

A further problem that exists for many air cargo operations of flag carrying airlines is that freight has a low priority within their company's overall strategies. Routes and frequencies are driven by passenger volumes, rather than belly-hold freight, even though the two markets need not be in complete synchronization. Freight capacity has in the past been often sold on a marginal cost basis, as a by-product of the passenger services.

Finally, regulation of the industry has not allowed the larger airlines to develop comprehensive owned global networks that would be able to service all the needs of shippers. In the past airlines have been forced into developing marketing alliances with other airlines as an alternative to organic growth or acquisition. This may be about to change, as the negotiation of a US/European 'open skies' agreement could be a catalyst to mergers such as that between KLM and Air France or BA and Iberia. One of the results of this could be coherent cargo strategies with the development of products that reach beyond the freight forwarding community.

Shipping lines

The shipping industry is highly cyclical. Despite the sustained growth of volumes from China to Europe and the United States, the industry has been plagued with over-supply and intermittent plunges in rates and consequent problems of unprofitability.

The business of shipping is also highly capital intensive, and consequently many lines have sought to create economies of scale both in the form of larger ships but also with larger fleets. Although some lines, such as MSC, have successfully grown organically, others have bought market share through acquisition. This has been with the intent to rationalize activities, reduce costs and minimize financial risks through the scale this would, in theory, deliver.

The largest example of this in the past decade has been the purchase of Safmarine, Sea-Land and, in 2005, P&O Nedlloyd by Maersk. Despite this, the latter acquisition was largely regarded as a failure. The second and third largest companies continued to gain market share (MSC and CMA CGM respectively), whilst Maersk lost customers at the same time as failing to exploit any potential economies of scale.

One of the most recent examples of consolidation in the sector involves French shipping line CMA CGM, which in December 2015 announced it had made an offer for rival Neptune Orient Lines (NOL). The deal will secure its position as the world's third largest operator behind Maersk and MSC.

Many shipping lines were originally reticent in developing logistics services that would potentially bring them into conflict with forwarders. However, freight forwarders have less leverage over shipping lines than they do over air cargo carriers, as a much larger proportion of shippers (the manufacturers and retailers) book direct. This has allowed companies such as Maersk, NYK and APL to build logistics divisions that provide services such as consolidation at origin and distribution on a global basis.

The major shipping lines have a considerable interest in developing logistics organizations. They provide a key source of extra revenue with the potential for higher margins through value added activities.

Road freight

Europe

One of the most obvious industry segments to develop both functionally and geographically has been road haulage. As providers of capacity, road haulage companies offer a largely commoditized product with little opportunity to add value without expanding its associated services.

The major problem for companies involved in road haulage, whether domestic or international, is that the market is highly fragmented with few barriers to entry or exit. The economies of scale are limited which allows small, low overhead owner-drivers to compete effectively with large fleeted companies. Information and communications technology, which for a brief period had become a differentiator, is, at a basic level, now widely available. On an international basis, low-cost hauliers from Central and Eastern Europe, which enjoy lower fuel and labour costs, are more competitive than indigenous providers that are increasingly burdened with a range of social costs and regulations.

This market environment has prompted many of the larger logistics companies to migrate to a business model where there are higher barriers to market entry. UK companies have been at the fore in evolving into contract logistics providers where there is a requirement for:

- higher levels of capital to operate;
- more sophisticated IT capabilities;
- a higher degree of intellectual capital;
- wider geographic scope;
- higher brand equity.

Perhaps the best example of a company with its roots in the road haulage industry in Europe was Exel, which developed from the nationalized UK company, NFC. It transformed itself into a contract logistics player, with operations in Europe and the United States. Following its merger with Ocean Group, Exel became a full service logistics provider with a global network and the capability to integrate its forwarding and logistics activities for multinational clients, before eventually being bought by DHL.

Another way in which road hauliers have been able to differentiate themselves has been by developing Less-than-Truckload (LTL – otherwise known as groupage) networks. This relies on a large capital investment to build presence on a European-wide basis, as well as the IT to support the flows of goods.

With a complex of depots, companies can construct a hub-and-spoke model ensuring frequent services, but at a lower cost. This model is hardly new, but it is now emerging as a key strategy employed by the large logistics companies to increase their grip on the road freight/trucking market.

European logistics company Kuehne + Nagel has indicated its plans to expand its already large road freight network by acquiring medium-sized road freight companies. Alongside companies such as DHL, France's GEFCO and Geodis, and Denmark's DSV, the big European logistics service providers seem to regard LTL as both an essential part of their wider service offering and as a growth opportunity in itself.

North America

North American (mainly US) trucking companies have focused largely on creating scale and increasing functionality has been of secondary importance. There have been some spectacularly big acquisitions in recent years, driven in part by the entrance of UPS and FedEx into the market.

The truckload sector is highly fragmented with more than 500,000 carriers operating in North America. The majority of these carriers are smaller operators, working with less than 20 trucks. Consolidation in the truckload sector will mean carriers are able to increase capacity and volume across their networks, as well as broadening their geographical presence. This is particularly attractive for regional LTL players looking to increase scale and move into national LTL markets.

The less-than-truckload sector is much more consolidated than the truckload sector, with fewer than 10 companies in North America accounting for more than two-thirds of the industry revenue. National carriers are driving consolidation by moving into the retail markets in search of additional growth and more opportunities for profitable growth. However, the lines between the long-haul market and the regional market are being blurred as regional carriers push into the national market.

More recently the freight brokerage sector has seen high levels of consolidation. This asset-light industry has become popular owing to challenges that LTL and TL players have faced, such as rising costs and driver shortages. The fragmented nature of the sector has seen existing companies and new entrants (such as XPO Logistics) attempt to build scale through acquisitions.

The most notable acquisitions in recent years across the whole US trucking industry include:

- XPO buys Con-way Inc for US $3 billion in 2015;
- DHL buys Standard Forwarding in 2011;
- Con-way Inc's 2007 acquisition of Contract Freighters, Inc (CFI), a privately held North American truckload carrier in a transaction valued at US $750 million;
- FedEx's 2006 acquisition of the LTL operations of Watkins Motor Lines for US $780 million;
- UPS's acquisition in 2005 of Overnite Corporation for approximately US $1.25 billion;
- also in 2005, Yellow Roadway Corporation (itself a merger of two giant trucking companies) acquired USF Corporation in a transaction valued at US $1.37 billion.

DEUTSCHE POST DHL
The emergence of a global powerhouse

Deutsche Post DHL (DP DHL) has its origins in the former German state mail, telecoms and post saving bank. In 1989, the German government decided to split these business functions and give them separate management structures. In 1995 legislation was passed which turned Deutsche Post from a government department into a private company. This enabled the management to work towards full privatization although around 25 per cent of shares are still held by the German government's state holding bank, KfW. With revenues of 56 billion euros, the company is now one of the world's largest transportation and logistics groups.

The company's primary aim, originally driven by former CEO Klaus Zumwinkel, was to develop diverse revenue streams that would reduce its reliance on declining German mail volumes. As a result it became the main protagonist in the consolidation of the express and logistics industry throughout the 1990s and 2000s.

Deutsche Post's first step was to enter the air express parcels market by taking a strategic stake in DHL in the late 1990s. By 2002 it had obtained control and it began to develop DHL as its flagship brand. At the same time it acquired many other well-known names in the industry including Danzas, AEI, ASG and Nedlloyd, building a global presence.

In 2005, Deutsche Post made a transformative bid for global contract logistics and freight forwarding group Exel, itself a merger of the Ocean Group and Tibbett & Britten. It paid 5.6 billion euros for the company, a move that led to market leadership in both of these additional sectors.

However, progress has not been without major challenges along the way. In 2003, DP DHL acquired the US domestic express service provider Airborne Inc (at an acquisition cost of 983 million euros) which gave it a ground and air transport network in the United States, the world's largest express market. However, following integration, customer service and profitability deteriorated to such an extent that DHL was forced to pull out of the market in 2008, preferring instead to focus on its profitable international services. This also forced it to reappraise its domestic operations throughout the world, including UK and France.

DP DHL is still heavily focused on the European market, with almost two-thirds of its revenues generated in this region. However, through its mix of freight forwarding, express, contract logistics and road freight operations it can claim to have a greater depth of service provision than any of its competitors. Its strategic ambitions are much more conservative than they were at the height of its aggressive acquisition programme – profitability has become critical to the group's goals. This is partly as a result of its disastrous foray into the US domestic parcels market and partly due to the global economic situation. However, it is very well placed to take advantage of the dynamic growth opportunities presented by the emerging markets in Asia, Africa and Latin America.

The future of the global logistics industry

The global logistics industry is at a crucial point in its development. Not only is there a host of economic, security, legal, political and societal pressures on the industry but bubbling up from underneath is a plethora of disruptive forces, many of which are as a result of the development of new technologies. The full implications of this collision of top-down and bottom-up developments are yet to be fully realized, and the timescale in which this will play out is still unknown. However, it is clear that the industry is facing a revolution.

As a whole, the industry is driven by economic growth and as such has seen a recovery in the past five years. However, there are also a number of other macro-economic drivers that have created good market conditions for corporate development. At the same time as this there is an unprecedented level of what can be termed 'endogenous bottom-up' developments. In this category can be included the technology disruptors of which so much is being made such as 'Uberization', drones and the use of virtual reality within the warehouse environment.

Ten reasons for more M&A in the logistics industry

1 The global economy (particularly Europe) is forecast to improve, providing companies with more confidence to invest in new markets and sectors.

2 Supply chains are reaching into untapped markets in the developing world, increasing the need for global logistics companies to support their multinational clients.

3 The reverse is also happening. Asian logistics companies are looking to expand their networks into Europe and North America to support the expansion of their customers.

4 The express parcels sector is being propelled by e-commerce activity and this has made providers of last mile delivery, e-fulfilment and specialized IT solutions in demand.

5 The emergence of a powerful middle class in Asia and Latin America (Africa to a lesser degree) has created more demand for higher value consumer goods, which in turn require a higher level of sophistication of supply chain management.

6 Manufacturers and retailers are increasingly demanding more sophisticated supply chain IT capabilities which logistics service providers can obtain from purchasing niche technology providers (in the way that Amazon acquired robotics expert Kiva).

7 Retailing structures are changing in Europe with the advance of discounters such as Lidl and Aldi. Major logistics companies must diversify in order to protect their revenues and margins.

8 Increased near-sourcing will mean that logistics companies will have to develop their capabilities in low-cost manufacturing locations such as Turkey and North Africa for Europe and Central America for the United States and Canada.

9 Logistics companies are increasingly looking to expand into niche sectors such as healthcare/pharmaceutical where they can leverage their value adding capabilities and networks.

10 Major corporations and investment institutions such as private equity companies are sitting on large cash piles – M&A activity is one way in which they can achieve better returns for investors.

Global M&A database analysis

In terms of deal volumes, deal numbers ramped up during the early 2000s to reach a peak in 2006. This was the height of the M&A boom in the industry. Many large players, such as DHL, pursued aggressive M&A strategies and their competitors sought to follow them. After what can only be called a 'binge' of acquisition activity (some value adding, many not), deal volumes dropped as companies sought to integrate the operations they had taken over. In some cases (as seen with DHL), they sold off loss-making acquisitions to focus back on core-competencies.

Figure 2.4 M&A activity 1999–2013

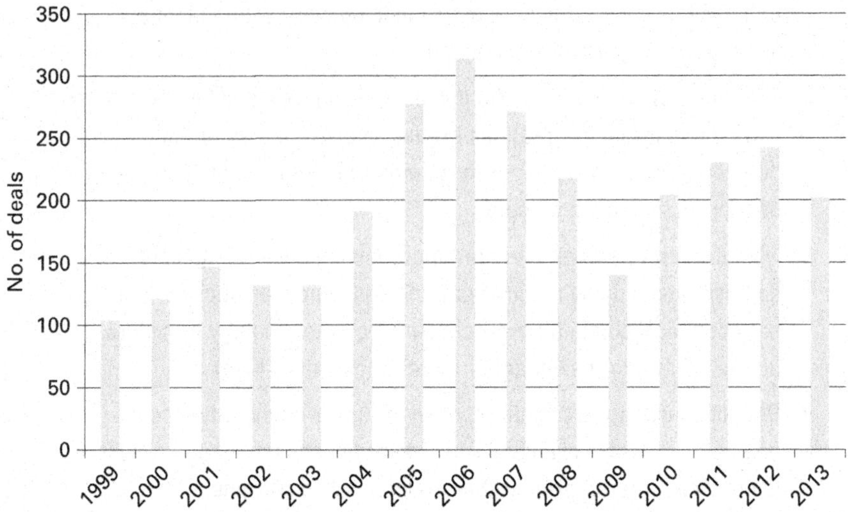

SOURCE: Transport Intelligence (2015)

The impact of the economic downturn in 2008–9 can be clearly seen in Figure 2.4. Companies had to concentrate on ensuring the profitability of their main businesses. Also, access to credit and 'cheap' money dried up. Since then, deal numbers have picked up, but are still influenced by the economic stagnation in Europe and elsewhere.

Most acquisitive logistics companies

The top 10 most acquisitive companies in the world (by number of deals carried out) account for about a quarter of all the transactions undertaken in the sector in the 15-year period between 1999 and 2013.

Deutsche Post DHL has been by far the most acquisitive in the market (see Figure 2.5). It is followed by Australian logistics company Toll Group, whose acquisition strategy related mostly to the Asia region.

European-based express company TNT is in third position and Swiss-based logistics and freight forwarder Kuehne + Nagel is in fourth. A large proportion of the deals undertaken by the latter were in the road freight sector, especially in Germany.

Figure 2.5 Top logistics companies by global acquisition volume (1999–2014)

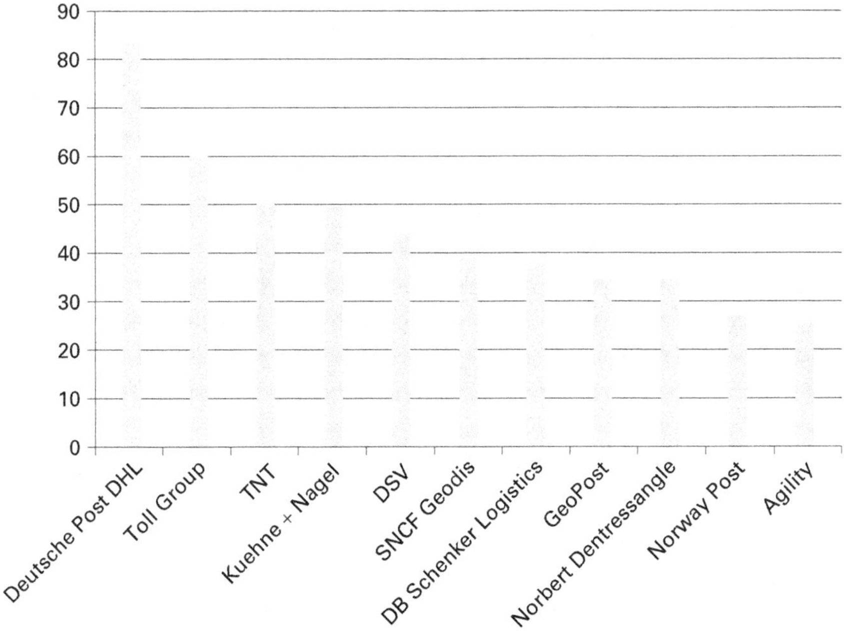

SOURCE: Transport Intelligence (2015)

Economic upturn

There is a close correlation between economic activity and M&A activity as might be expected. It is noticeable that whereas deal activity in emerging markets closely follows economic growth, in developed markets this relationship has existed only since 2007.

Why is this? One likely reason is that during the early 2000s, M&A activity in Europe in particular was driven by internal dynamics such as consolidation within the industry. Globalization, out-sourcing and the quest to add value all combined to drive up deal volumes, although GDP growth during this time was less than exciting (see Figure 2.7).

In contrast, M&A activity in emerging markets has largely grown as a result of European and North American companies wanting to tap into this economic growth story. The faster GDP growth has occurred in regions such as Asia, Latin America and even Africa, the more companies want to buy into these markets. This has resulted in deal volumes mirroring economic development (see Figure 2.6).

Figure 2.6 Emerging markets – deal activity and GDP correlation

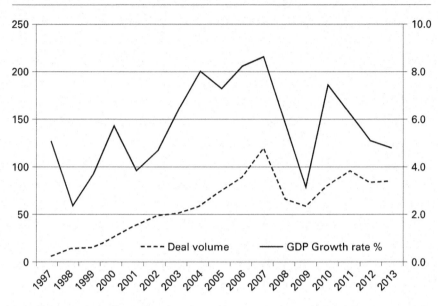

SOURCE: Transport Intelligence (2015)

Figure 2.7 Developed markets – deal activity and GDP correlation

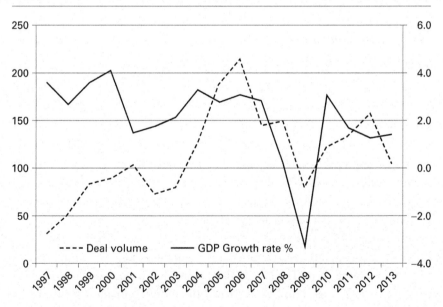

SOURCE: Transport Intelligence (2015)

Emerging v developed markets

In terms of what might be called 'mega-trends' in the global logistics industry, the development of emerging markets has been amongst the most significant. Figure 2.8 shows that from a very small base, the number of deals in emerging markets is now on a similar level to those in the developed world. This has come about due to the expansion of logistics companies based in Europe and North America into regions such as Asia, Africa and Latin America, as these economies have offered greater growth prospects.

Figure 2.8 Number of deals in emerging and developed markets 1997–2013

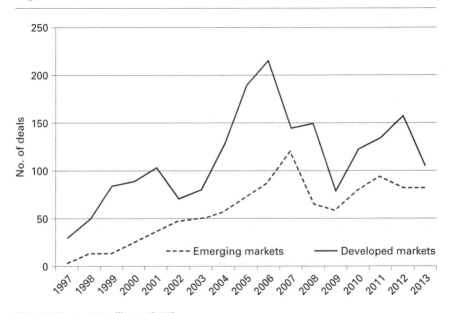

SOURCE: Transport Intelligence (2015)

There has also been a degree of consolidation in these emerging markets, as domestic-based logistics companies attempt to grow quickly in order to take advantage of strong economic activity.

Logistics companies will, in the future, be expected to go even further afield by their clients. At the lower value end of the product spectrum, China is starting to lose out to even lower cost countries in Asia Pacific such as Vietnam.

Asian logistics expansion

In 2015, two large deals were undertaken by Japanese companies: Japan Post buying Australian logistics group Toll and Kintetsu World Express buying APL Logistics from Singaporean NOL. This is something that has been expected for some time and is as a result of specific factors in the Japanese market – namely, stagnation in the economy, the expansion of Japanese manufacturing throughout Asia and a more open business culture to out-sourcing. It is perhaps surprising that it has taken so long to occur and is testament to the inertia that has characterized the Japanese culture and economy.

Japanese companies will not be alone. Chinese brands have been encouraged to expand globally by the government – Lenovo, Huawei, for example. So why not in the logistics sector? Many companies are actively looking to expand abroad (Sinotrans, for example) and it is inevitable that some big deals will be undertaken.

The impact of e-commerce

e-retail, of course, has brought about a dramatic change in the nature of goods flows. Many logistics companies were traditionally set up for the delivery of B2B goods. However, most of the growth has been in the B2C sector. Instead of full or part loads, many shipments are now single parcels as well as being low value. This has called for a completely different set of capabilities, especially as recipients, and hence their customers, are looking for a range of delivery options. This has also led to the development of new technologies to support these needs.

Disruptive technology capabilities

The transport and logistics industry faces a huge threat from innovators who are transferring replicable technological solutions from other sectors. For example, the 'Internet of Things' will provide enormous levels of data and give shippers – the cargo owners – greater levels of power. Logistics providers must develop capabilities to deal with the data flows and this will mean that they either have to build their own solutions or buy the capabilities.

Of course, there are companies such as Uber who are developing freight transport capabilities that will connect cargo owners with a vast new market of carriers – individuals using their own vehicles perhaps. Logistics companies may face the prospect of changing their business models to adapt to the evolving competition.

Other competition will come from companies such as Amazon or eBay, which are proving highly successful in consolidating small e-retailers and then using their buying power in the parcels market to drive down costs. Amazon is now starting to make deliveries itself using its own vehicles. 3D printing should also be of concern to logistics companies – starting in the service parts sector. (See Chapter 16.)

The big question is how transport and logistics companies react to these developments. Do they ignore them or try to harness them within their own business models? If it is the latter there will be many acquisitions of new start-up tech companies, which can provide the incumbents with a lifeline in this new market environment.

Industry sector speciality

Acquisitions are seen as one of the main ways in which to rapidly build up expertise in a particular sector. The intellectual capital that can be attained and the niche markets in which target companies operate, can often mean higher margins.

Drawing on Transport Intelligence's M&A database data, it can be seen in Figure 2.9 that where an industry sector speciality was indicated in the transaction details, the consumer/retail sector was by far the most popular, accounting for almost half of deals. Many of these would have been quite general in nature.

Automotive was the second most popular sector, followed by high tech and healthcare/pharmaceutical, all of which have more specific needs. The healthcare/pharmaceutical sector is a case in point. Barriers to market entry are much higher as there is a large degree of regulatory control, security needs to be high and there is a need for consignment tracking as well as, in some cases, temperature control and monitoring. Rather than build up expertise organically, many companies (such as DHL, UPS and FedEx) have undertaken acquisitions in this sector, not least because of its strong underlying growth prospects.

Private equity

Private equity (PE) companies are generally better known for investment in transport infrastructure rather than in logistics service providers. However,

Figure 2.9 M&A activity by vertical sector

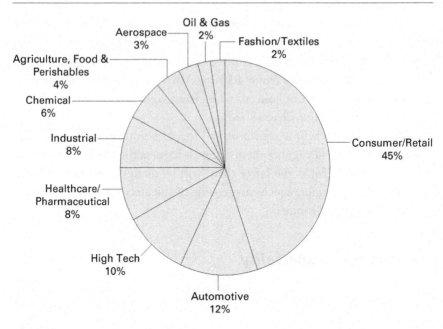

SOURCE: Transport Intelligence (2015)

although the present structure of the global logistics industry has been more influenced by the ambitious development plans of many of the companies already present in the sector, PE companies have played an important role in the sector.

Perhaps the best-known intervention by a PE company has been the acquisition of TNT Logistics and EGL, by Apollo, to create CEVA. This followed the model of combining contract logistics and freight forwarding operations, except rather than being undertaken by a trade player, the deal was initiated by private equity. Unfortunately, the deal has not worked out too well for the owners. CEVA has a huge debt burden that it has struggled to fund. Whilst its growth and operating profits have been respectable, they were swallowed up by the cost of interest, which led to a restructuring of the debt.

Other major PE companies in the European market include:

- Platinum Equity – owns 65 per cent of Neovia (formerly Caterpillar Logistics);

- Phoenix Equity Partners – own UK companies Palletways and NFT;

- Arcapita – owns UK rail group Freightliner.

What conventional private equity companies really like is to take a business with sub-optimized potential and groom it for a sale. A good example of this is Platinum Equity's purchase of Hays Logistics in 2004 and its sale, in 2006, to Kuehne + Nagel (then ACR Logistics). The company was rationalized and put on a sufficiently stable footing for Kuehne + Nagel to pay an attractive premium. This would suggest that there is plenty of potential for PE companies to be involved in the future of the industry.

Conclusion

Despite the weak state of parts of the global economy, conditions are right for continued growth in global mergers and acquisition activity. Manufacturing and retailing sectors are undergoing systemic change in a market environment influenced not least by the development of e-commerce. This transformation will force logistics companies to seek out new markets, sectors and niches.

In the next five years, deals will be driven by a number of drivers:

- Technology is becoming the most important competitive differentiator as consumer behaviour and expectations change. Companies with specialist capabilities will be targeted by larger players.

- Traditional retailing patterns are changing, due not least to the advance of low-cost retailers such as Aldi and Lidl. This will mean logistics companies will need to diversify into other sectors where there is a greater demand for value adding logistics services.

- The development of e-commerce will also be a major disruptive force. Logistics companies will need to add niche services both in fulfilment and last mile delivery.

- Near-sourcing will increase the need for logistics capabilities in emerging markets at the periphery of Europe, such as Turkey and North Africa. Geographic expansion through acquisition will be widespread.

- Fast-growing sectors, such as healthcare/pharmaceutical, offer higher margin opportunities, especially in the temperature-controlled market. Logistics companies will continue to target these niche markets for inorganic expansion, buying operations and capabilities.

- European logistics companies will also be targeted as stronger, profitable Asian companies expand their networks into Europe.

There are other big question marks hanging over the future of some of the world's largest providers. For example, CEVA, owned by PE company Apollo, has struggled to deal with the huge debt burden that was loaded on the company at inception. However, although operationally robust, surely the company must be vulnerable to an approach from a competitor and its owners open to an exit-strategy opportunity.

Summary

The global logistics market has evolved rapidly over the past two decades from one characterized by multiple, fragmented and independent transport functions, to one in which diversified conglomerates dominate. This has been mainly achieved through acquisitions, with post offices, rail operators as well as freight forwarders and road hauliers extending their functional and geographic capabilities through M&A activity. Today's market has been brought about by a range of internal and external competitive pressures; the need to match clients' globalized needs and the desire for logistics companies of all backgrounds to improve profitability. This chapter examined the most important drivers of the trend towards consolidation; each logistics sector's individual dynamics and discussed in detail how one of the market leaders, Deutsche Post DHL, achieved its position.

Key points to consider:

- Logistics companies need regional/global scale and multiple logistics capabilities if they are to compete effectively for the largest supply chain contracts.

- Although the industry has been transformed through acquisition, there is little sign that there have been any benefits in terms of profitability.

- The last 10 years have been littered with disastrous acquisitions destroying billions of dollars in enterprise value. Despite this logistics companies have continued to make acquisitions.

- Whether large or small, a successful acquisition requires extensive due diligence, strong management and good integration.

Logistics market development by geography

03

CHAPTER LEARNING OBJECTIVES

This chapter will familiarize the reader with:

- The factors that influence the characteristics of local and regional logistics markets
- How individual markets have developed exploring the specific logistics market conditions in some of the largest countries
- The impact that government regulation has had upon the development of the logistics industry
- How markets in even neighbouring countries can differ dramatically due to the local political, economic, social or geographic variables that exist

Influences on market characteristics

Despite growing globalization, logistics markets are still largely defined by national characteristics. A combination of government regulation and economics has been behind the development of transport provision. Some of the key industry drivers are discussed below.

Regulation

Up until relatively recently, most European countries operated a system of permits that acted as quantitative controls on the entry of new operators into the transport market.

In Europe, these were swept away during the 1980s and 90s by liberalization, but controls still exist in terms of quality, if not quantity. In fact, there is growing evidence that the European Commission would like to use quality tests, such as the 'Financial Evidence' regulations (that is, those that insist that operators have a certain amount of money in the bank to cover maintenance and upkeep of vehicles) to reduce the continuing fragmentation of the industry. This acts as a de facto intervention in the market by raising barriers to entry by the back door, so to speak.

In the United States, there were similarly high levels of regulation, most of which have been done away with, at least on a domestic basis. However, restrictions apply to the transport of goods from Mexico to the United States, although these are being lifted despite opposition from vested interests and labour organizations.

In many countries in the developing world, restrictions exist on foreign investment in the transport sector. For instance, the only way for a company to enter the Indian logistics market is through a joint venture with a local operator. Protectionism creates a sclerotic market in which new developments and practices are not able to develop. In these markets, logistics costs will remain high and efficiencies low.

Openness and trade

The openness of a country's economy is also important to the transport market. Belgium and the Netherlands, for example, have highly developed international road freight markets due in part to their geographical location on key transit routes, but also due to centuries' old tradition as important trading hubs.

Retail development

Consolidation of a country's retail sector is very important. In the UK, a relatively small number of very large contract logistics players have developed by doing business with a handful of giant supermarket chains. This contrasts with Italy or Spain where a fragmented retail sector in which local stores predominate has meant that logistics companies have not developed to the same sort of scale.

Import/export balance

In some developed markets, such as Europe, the balance of logistics provision will be on secondary distribution (from warehouse to retailer or consumer) as relatively few consumer goods are manufactured in the region. However, in China the transport market is still largely focused on moving goods from factory to port – a largely commoditized activity. As consumer markets in China develop, so will the secondary distribution market with greater opportunities for logistics providers to add value.

Urbanization and population distribution

The level of urbanization in a country is also a major influence over the development of the logistics sector. Countries with dense urban communities can be better served by a range of more sophisticated contract logistics and express parcels providers than those with dispersed populations.

For example, in the UK the contract logistics industry developed around retailers' regionally centralized distribution requirements. One distribution centre could effectively serve the whole of a region with transport assets being fully utilized on a daily basis. In other countries, where geographical distances are much greater between population centres, alternative strategies have to be employed, and there is a much greater emphasis on inter-regional trucking (such as in the United States). Logistics costs can consequently be considerably higher.

Geographic market profiles

The Western European logistics market

Logistics markets in Western Europe are highly competitive. Not only is there a wealth of global LSPs but there is also no shortage of medium to large national players with good logistics capabilities.

Germany

Despite a slow start due to the regulation of the market up until the mid-1990s, German logistics companies have become amongst the most highly developed and expansionist in the world. Consequently, German manufacturers and retailers have access to a sophisticated supply side that facilitates their supply chain strategies. Up until the early to mid-1990s a comprehensive permit system was still in place, which regulated not only the quality (which is normal in all markets throughout Europe) but also the quantity of road haulage capacity.

The existence of controls on the quantity and type of service that logistics companies could provide did not apply to the in-house operations of manufacturers and retailers. This meant that there were fewer compelling reasons for companies to out-source their logistics needs to the third-party market and consequently it is only over the last 10 years that service providers have been able to increase their penetration of the in-house market.

The complexity of regulations and the tariff system that existed (fixing the rates that transport companies could charge for certain products, routes and mode of transport) led to the development of 'Spedition' companies. These were essentially domestic freight forwarding operators who could manage freight movements throughout the complex German transport regime.

Despite the liberalization of the markets, the pace of change has still been slow. This is perhaps due to the conservatism of German logistics companies, which tend to be owned by families or by banks rather than shareholders. Also retailers have not been as enthusiastic to utilize logistics providers in the same way as their UK counterparts. However, automotive manufacturers have been at the forefront of adopting leading-edge supply chain techniques and working with companies such as Schenker, BLG and Rudolph Logistik to fulfil their requirements.

Out-sourcing will become more important for industries still unfamiliar with this trend, for example healthcare, public authorities and the construction industry to name just a few.

Two of the leading companies in the market are Deutsche Post DHL and Deutsche Bahn Schenker. These companies have grown out of their original functions of mail and rail and, building on the monopolies which they enjoyed for many years in their home market, expanded geographically and vertically.

One characteristic of the German market is the number of partnerships that exist between the many mid-sized logistics companies. These alliances offer customers national delivery through a franchise system and a way in which they can compete with the two market leaders in road freight, Schenker and DHL. In recent years, European operators such as Kuehne +

Nagel, DSV and Geodis have bought their way into the German road haulage market by acquiring membership of many of these alliances.

Germany has a distinct logistics market. In an economy with a very large automotive sector and large chemical industry, logistics is more skewed towards industrial logistics than other major European economies. Germany has a strong supply of specialist logistics providers, particularly in areas such as chemicals. However, with strong grocery retailers such as Metro and Lidl, German LSPs are certainly exposed to large-scale grocery retailing.

Production in sectors such as automotive and chemicals is also dominated by large corporations and their approach towards purchasing logistics services has a big impact on the sector. For example, VW, which is one of the largest purchasers of logistics in Germany, likes to do business with medium-sized German providers as well as larger LSPs. This has been beneficial for a mid-sized company such as Schnellecke Logistics which not only has a substantial business across Germany but is expanding outside Europe. Similarly, companies such as Rudolf, BLG Logistics or Rhenus have expanded into value adding logistics on the back of business from the likes of BMW and Daimler. This is all the more remarkable as two of the world's largest contract logistics providers, DP DHL and DB Schenker, are headquartered in Germany.

As a result of this the German contract logistics market remains more fragmented than elsewhere in Europe, with medium-sized providers plentiful and often looking to grow.

France

Deregulation of the French transport market commenced in the late 1980s with the scrapping of a fixed-price tariff system known as the Tarification Routiere Obligatoire. This system placed controls on the price that transport providers could charge their clients, although in practice many large shippers were able to circumvent the regulations. A permit system was also in place, which limited the number of transport companies that could operate in the market, although this had become largely redundant by the early 1990s.

The legacy of these regulations was a strong in-house logistics sector and this resulted in a slower conversion to the out-sourcing concepts that, at about the same time, were being adopted in the UK. However, in recent years out-sourcing has become a major trend in industry creating a vibrant French third-party logistics sector.

The French market was characterized by the number of strong regional players that were in existence. This was symptomatic of France's large geography, which forced a number of alliances between medium-sized companies in order to provide manufacturers and retailers with national distribution. However, a number of major national players (for example, Geodis, Norbert Dentressangle) have evolved to meet these needs through purely owned operations. Norbert Dentressangle was acquired by US group XPO Logistics in 2015.

Another reason for the slower take-up of out-sourcing in France has been the dynamics of the French retailing sector. In France the hypermarket model is widespread, where emphasis is placed on bulk purchases of goods at a discount from manufacturers, rather than the JIT delivery of product directly to the shelves. Consequently, it is perceived by retailers that there is less to gain from taking over the distribution of goods from their suppliers. As a consequence of this, the shared user model is far more popular in France than dedicated distribution operations. However, there are signs that the major French retailers (such as Carrefour) are increasingly taking ownership of their supply chains.

Although the market is far more deregulated than it was, one piece of legislation to have a major impact on the transport market has been the Working Time Directive (WTD). The French government established this at 35 hours, far lower than the EC mandatory 48-hour working week. One of the effects that this has had on the industry has been the creation of more strategically located hubs throughout the country to reduce the duration of driver trips. The impact of the WTD has been an increase in social costs. Consequently, the industry has become less competitive than its European neighbours, and far less competitive than Eastern European companies.

Another challenge for French hauliers is the rising cost of tolls, which they complain they have not been able to recover from clients in the present economic climate. The cost of using France's motorways has risen by about 25 per cent in three years.

There is the belief that the French market is being squeezed by lower cost Spanish hauliers to the west and the operators moving into the market from Eastern Europe. As well as this, German and Dutch international operators are well placed to offer both international and cabotage services. The development of manufacturing in Central and Eastern Europe is possibly one of the greatest challenges to the industry. This has led to the development of a network of suppliers throughout Europe, which are increasingly served by low-cost, lower regulated operators based in Poland, the Czech Republic, etc. French hauliers have been the victims of this trend.

Several strategies for the French road transport market have been suggested:

- They should adopt the network models prevalent in the German market, which has given small operators the necessary scale and access to resources (such as marketing and IT).
- Further consolidation in the market, especially as part of wider air/sea/intermodal/3PL groups.
- Specialization on market niches.
- Expansion into Southern Europe/Mediterranean.

UK

The UK has the most mature logistics market in Europe, mainly due to the length of time that it has been deregulated. Since the early 1970s there have been no quantitative controls on the number of logistics companies operating in the market, which has led to a high degree of competition.

The early adoption by UK manufacturers and retailers of out-sourcing their non-core activities has also helped to fuel the country's logistics sector and allowed a much faster rate of expansion than in other EU countries. At the same time, the grocery retailers have been at the forefront of introducing best practice in supply chain management, and they have encouraged logistics players to meet their sophisticated and ongoing needs.

As a consequence of this, the market has seen a high degree of development with contract logistics companies, such as Exel (now DHL Supply Chain) and Wincanton, at the forefront, differentiating their products from the smaller market entrants.

The market in the UK has matured over the past 5–10 years as large grocery chains have diversified into consumer durables, becoming the leading players in areas such as clothing or electronics. This was ideal for the big national players as they could expand volumes with existing customers, as those customers took market share from smaller retailers with less efficient logistics. Another feature of this growth is the role of globalized supply chains. A substantial proportion of cheaper consumer durables are sourced from China and consequently logistics provision has increasingly become orientated around goods moving through container ports. An example of the latter has been the growth of consolidation centres in large port-based distribution parks. Intermodal 'inland ports' have also benefited from the trend.

One of the most marked changes that has occurred in the UK retail sector has been the explosive development of e-retail. This has affected the growth of the major supermarket chains, which have been forced to adapt from 'big box' retailing to 'omni-channel' strategies. What is meant by this is that consumers have many more alternatives in the ways in which they not only do their shopping, but how the goods are delivered to their homes. The challenge for retailers is how to fulfil customer expectations of quick, cheap delivery – either on- or offline – without seeing their own logistics costs surge. The new retailing environment has seen competitors such as Amazon, ASOS and even sports equipment e-retailer Wiggle steal market share from slower moving brick-and-mortar incumbents.

Although logistics sectors such as the automotive industry are quite healthy, a high proportion of production is of luxury vehicles rather than volume models. Sectors such as chemical production may also undergo a similar change with production of bulk-petrochemicals increasingly based in the Middle East whilst higher added value production grows in the UK. Similar trends are seen in other areas of engineering. Consequently, the market for contract logistics may be as much about coordinating global production, of which the UK is an element in the supply chain, as simple export activities.

The UK has seen significant change in the structure of its logistics market. Two significant larger players, Christian Salvesen and TDG, have been bought by the French family business of Norbert Dentressangle (which has since, itself, been acquired by US company, XPO Logistics). There are also signs that Kuehne + Nagel is continuing to reinforce its already strong presence in Britain through the recent acquisition of R H Freight, although this was largely targeted at the road transport sector. What is notable about the British market is the comparative power of large LSPs such as DHL, CEVA, XPO and Kuehne + Nagel. For example, there is nothing comparable to Germany's Mittelstand, which is such a feature of its logistics industry.

Italy

The Italian road transport industry is characterized by extreme fragmentation with high levels of owner-drivers (the so-called *padroncini*) dominating the sector. Around 40 per cent of those employed in the industry are self-employed. This compares with the UK and France where the comparable figure is less than 10 per cent (Eurostat, 2009).

Whereas the German and French logistics markets could be said to have been held back by over-regulation in the 1980s and early 1990s, the opposite could be said to be true for the Italian market. Low levels of regulation as well as ease of entry and exit from the market have made it more difficult for larger transport concerns to build scale and profitability in a market typified by wafer-thin margins. The owner-drivers can compete effectively with their larger counterparts, often with far lower overheads.

The own-account sector in Italy is still strong. However, it has been found that this has been a drag on the efficiency of goods' movement throughout the country. Empty running by own-account operators is far greater than the corresponding level in the third-party market and this has been identified as a major policy issue for the government.

Cabotage is also a concern for the industry. It has been estimated that the penetration of the domestic market by foreign hauliers – mainly from Eastern European origins – has risen from 1 per cent in 2004 to 6 per cent in 2014 (Eurostat, 2014). To counter this growth, the industry believes that there should be more regulation to prevent the influx of foreign operators as well as initiatives to restore business competitiveness and generate a long-term profitability. One of the government's primary concerns is over the loss of taxation revenue caused by the loss of market share of Italian corporations.

Within the contract logistics sector, CEVA Logistics (formerly TNT Logistics) dominates the market. Partly the reason for this is the position of FIAT, CEVA's biggest single client worldwide, within Italian industry.

The lack of large Italian contract logistics players has made it difficult for other foreign-owned companies to develop scale in this sector through acquisition.

The largest single transport organization (taking into account express parcels) is DHL, which has acquired a number of large players in the express industry (such as Ascoli) and in addition has significant air, sea and road business.

Foreign investment in logistics operations has come despite the fact the Italian economy is not particularly vibrant. As the requirements of shippers become more sophisticated, the larger logistics companies will increasingly gain a competitive advantage over their smaller rivals, driving higher levels of market growth.

Spain

The Spanish logistics market was highly regulated right up to the mid-1980s. The responsibility rested on new haulage companies to prove a requirement for their services to the local authorities prior to the award of an operating permit. From the 1990s onwards, the market has been liberalized and regulation is currently in line with other developed European economies.

Spain has a highly fragmented road haulage sector, with a large number of small players offering non-specialist haulage and warehousing services. Owing to the lack of resources of these smaller companies, the development of a more sophisticated contract logistics industry has been hindered. This has led to the influx of foreign companies supporting the logistics operations of multinational retailers and manufacturers, which have recently entered the Spanish market. In many cases this has been by acquisition.

Madrid is the most important region for international goods flows whereas Catalonia (focused around Barcelona) is perhaps the most important for logistics activities accounting for a significant proportion of all logistics properties. The road network in the region has produced two major transit routes for goods. The north–south route links France with the Mediterranean, while the east–west route connects Barcelona with the rest of Iberia.

The market is highly competitive, with foreign-owned companies struggling to make any headway. UK-based company Wincanton has withdrawn its operations, although others, such as Schenker and DHL, continue to push into what is a highly strategic market. Schenker has acquired TIR and Transfesa, two of Spain's largest operators.

The Spanish retail sector has been one of the driving forces behind the growth of the logistics industry. The retail sector has undergone a transformation with the emergence of a number of major French groups such as Carrefour. The entrance of international retailers has changed a market that was previously dominated by family-owned micro-stores to one in which hyper- and supermarkets play a much more important role. Foreign logistics companies are leading the way in introducing best practice from more developed markets, such as the UK, to support these multinational retailers. The growth will also be reinforced by the trend towards out-sourcing that is being increasingly adopted by many major manufacturers and retailers.

The intermodal sector will play an important role in the development of the industry over the coming years. Ports, such as Barcelona, are investing heavily in intermodal operations as they seek to develop their European 'gateway' status. This will link them to other key Southern European countries as well as improving distribution around Spain. However, road freight will stay dominant in sectors outside of containerized freight.

The situation in Spain is similar to other European markets, if more extreme. Spain has also experienced strong consumer-led growth over the past decade. This provided the logistics market in Spain with a good opportunity to diversify from the automotive sector, which had dominated its business from the 1980s. To complement this, Spain also experienced a construction boom, which affected the logistics sector. This trend has now not only halted, but the sector has experienced considerable reversal.

The consumer industry is likely to continue to shrink and the construction sector is still deeply depressed. The automotive sector in Spain is experiencing competition from Central Europe, with no plants opening over the past decade. Spain badly needs investment-led growth of the type seen in the 1980s with one source being a 'spill-over' from German production, although this is a slow process. Consequently, the logistics market in Spain is in far from healthy shape.

Central and Eastern Europe contract logistics market

Central Europe has been a dynamic market for larger logistics companies. Although the region suffered from poor infrastructure and patchy services in the decade after the fall of the Berlin Wall, since 2000 the sector has grown enormously.

Key to the development of logistics in Central Europe has been the nature of economic growth in the region. This has been driven largely by external investment by manufacturing companies looking to exploit the region's competitive strengths. The automotive sector has been the leader in this trend, with German vehicle manufacturers the largest investors. The vehicle assembly plants that have been built are generally 'greenfield' sites with large capacity and a high level of productivity. Consequently, the vehicle manufacturers generally look to larger LSPs to provide the level of logistics services demanded by such plants. Equally, this applies to the component suppliers who have located in the region to support the assembly plants.

The impact on the region of this wave of investment was quite sudden. Previous to 2005, disposable income was too low to drive the retail sector. However, over recent years this has changed and increasingly the consumer sector has been building a substantial logistics infrastructure in most of the countries of the region. The economies of the region do vary considerably, however. Poland accounts for around half of the economy of the region, whilst certain countries, such as Slovenia, have a GDP per head approaching that of Western Europe. Other countries have much smaller economies, such as Romania and Bulgaria.

The position of different LSPs in the region is heavily influenced by the nature of local and national economies. DB Schenker, for example, has a strong presence in the Czech Republic due to the size of VW Group operations in the country, although DHL SC has penetrated into much of this business in recent years. GEFCO is strong in Slovakia due to the presence of the Toyota Peugeot-Citroen joint venture in Kolin. Glovis has established a presence in Slovakia to serve its parent Hyundai-Kia's new plant in the country.

A feature of the Central European logistics market is that there are very few indigenous contract logistics providers but a large number of local road freight operators.

Poland

One of the more mature economies of Central Europe, Poland is also the largest. Although the automotive sector is not quite as large a proportion of its economy as in the Czech Republic and Slovakia, it still has significant plants, notably run by GM and Ford. Unsurprisingly, German companies are major investors in the country and are disproportionately represented in Poland's logistics market. Poland's successful economy is now triggering growth in areas such as retail. Transport infrastructure, however, remains a problem.

Czech Republic and Slovakia

The level of automotive logistics investment in both the Czech Republic and Slovakia has been substantial. Volkswagen is the largest investor, bringing with it extensive logistics operations. The German car manufacturer not only operates the two large Skoda facilities but also has engine and body-work facilities. Consequently, many of the logistics providers who support VW Group's supply chain have a very strong presence in both countries. Schenker and Schnellecke are prominent amongst these.

Hungary

Hungary's economy may be less dominated by automotive production than some of its neighbours, yet the production at the VW/AUDI Gyor plant and the new Mercedes Benz Passenger Cars plant at Kecskemét will nevertheless dominate the logistics sector in the country. This is all the more the case as the economic crisis will depress consumer-driven sectors. Hungary is notable for having one of the few major Central European contract logistics providers in the form of Waberer's Optimum Solution.

North American logistics market

The North America logistics market is a fragmented one. Besides transportation services and warehousing and distribution services, numerous niche players offer specialized services such as reverse logistics, IT services and consulting. As the economy continues to show improvement, consolidation within the logistics market, particularly in the United States, is expected over the next two to three years. The US market, albeit a mature one, remains a focal point for North American logistics.

Trade continues to improve steadily as the North America region recovers from the 2009 recession. However, a driver shortage, tight capacity, infrastructure and government regulations are affecting the industry.

Infrastructure is a key issue for the region. Canada is seeking funding to improve roads and rail along the US–Canada border. The Mexican government has invested billions of dollars into improving its ports in anticipation of increasing Asian trade. Investments have also been made in the road and rail networks to connect the country with the United States. Owing to the high debt the US government currently has, funding for many infrastructure projects are on hold.

The need to improve the highway systems is great as many have seen little improvement since the 1950s. The eastern ports are in need of additional dredging in order to remain competitive. The US $5.2 billion Panama Canal expansion, which started in 2007, is expected to be completed in 2016 and will allow much larger vessels to pass.

Trends in distribution centres are changing as many shippers are consolidating their requirements. The number of distribution centres is declining for the average shipper and now are being located in more strategic locations throughout the region. Multi-customer distribution centres are also being utilized to provide customers and providers additional cost savings.

United States

The transportation and logistics market in the United States is highly fragmented and consists of a variety of services including third-party logistics, intermodal, brokerage and pure-play truckers and railroads. The truckload sector is highly fragmented with more than 500,000 carriers. The majority of these carriers are smaller operators, working with fewer than 20 trucks. The less-than-truckload sector is much more consolidated than the truckload sector, with fewer than 10 companies in North America accounting for more than two-thirds of the industry revenue. National carriers are driving consolidation by moving into the retail markets in search of additional growth and more opportunities for profitable growth.

Like its European counterparts, the US market was highly regulated until 30 years ago. The Motor Carrier Act of 1935 stipulated that companies that wanted to haul freight across state lines on a for-hire basis had to obtain authority from the Interstate Commerce Commission (ICC). Prices were determined through a collective ratemaking process made legal by federal antitrust exemption. Carriers were able to file their own rates, although subject to challenge from regional bureaus. Therefore, most chose to go along with the conference pricing.

The principally deregulating Motor Carrier Act of 1980 did not eliminate all of the previous rules and most states imposed some economic regulation on trucking. The Act of 1980, however, made some changes. Interstate trucking companies should still obtain ICC operating authority but the application and review process was simpler. Ratemaking was still carried out through regional bureaus but independent rates could not be challenged with the result that more carriers selected their own prices. Contract carriers were no longer restricted in how many customers they could serve.

Following deregulation, many carriers accelerated long-term expansion plans through adding terminals and equipment. Annual growth rates of 30–40 per cent were not uncommon and overcapacity forced rates down. Since deregulation, many thousands of carriers, including 74 of 1980's top 100, have gone out of business.

The sector has undergone major consolidation in the past five years with both UPS and FedEx entering the market to round out their freight portfolio. FedEx is now market leader, following a disastrous period of acquisitions by the former leader Yellow Roadway. Other big players include Con-way (acquired in 2015 by XPO Logistics) and Schneider.

A major issue within the logistics sector as a whole is unionization versus non-unionization of transportation and logistics companies and its effects on operating costs. The principal union representing transportation workers is the International Brotherhood of Teamsters. After the deregulation of the motor carrier industry, those companies without union representation saw labour costs decline far more dramatically than those with union representation. The single largest employer of Teamsters' members is UPS, employing more than 200,000.

Out-sourcing in the US market is not as far advanced as in parts of Europe, with a large proportion of business remaining in-house. The largest contract logistics player in the market is DHL Supply Chain, which was built on the back of Exel (in fact, it is still branded as 'Exel') and Tibbett & Britten. UPS Supply Chain Solutions, Ryder, XPO and CEVA are also well developed.

Shifts in domestic transport networks are starting to alter the locations of warehousing and distribution facilities. Long known as the world's leading importer, the US economy has found itself no longer able to sustain the amount of imports it had once been able to. Like the rest of the world, its trade patterns appear to have changed in this new global economy – a result of the 2009 economic decline. This situation is still the case today, despite the strength of the US economy relative to the rest of the world. Exports from the US in contrast rose, although they have now slowed, not least because of weak demand in developing nations due to the strengthening dollar. In addition, as the Panama Canal widening moves to completion, east coast ports are expanding in anticipation of gaining market share from the possible shifts in trade that is expected.

As this shift continues the rise of intermodal transportation is on the upswing. This increase is due to a number of reasons such as: the lower costs of intermodal transportation; a shift from exclusive use of trucking because of tight capacity; and the more 'environmentally friendly' use of rail versus truck.

As confidence continues to rise in the US economy, consolidation within the logistics industry is increasing: 2015 was a 'stellar' year for deals, especially in the trucking and freight brokerage sector. Many industry analysts believe the industry will experience an active consolidation period over the next two to three years with an emphasis on transportation services and non-asset based providers.

Other trends affecting the US contract logistics industry include the rise in e-commerce activity. Retailers are adapting to the rise in e-commerce by dedicating more of their distribution centres to the service. Amazon is investing heavily in distribution centres right across the country.

Another growth opportunity for contract logistics providers is the healthcare sector. The growth of healthcare has resulted in many logistics providers offering specialized services devoted to this sector.

Canada

Canada has developed economically and technologically along with the United States, its neighbour to the south. In fact, the country enjoys a substantial trade surplus with the United States, which absorbs more than 70 per cent of Canadian exports. Canada, in turn, imports more than 50 per cent of US exports annually.

The importance of Canada–US trade needs to be emphasized. With 90 per cent of Canadians living within 100 miles of the US border and 85 per cent of Canada's 20 largest cities located within 110 miles of the border, Canada–US trade is robust. Most of these imports include cars and automotive parts and energy products including oil, gas, uranium and electric power. A significant proportion of trade is crossborder intra-company transfers. Automotive parts, for example, frequently cross the border several times before entering the final assembly stage.

Growth in international trade has spurred the demand for logistics services. Owing to the growth in international demand as well as consumer demand, investments in distribution facilities in Canada have increased greatly over the past five years. The main areas of distribution facility investment were in Ontario followed by Alberta, Quebec and British Columbia.

In the oil and gas extraction sector, storage and transportation of equipment represents a significant portion of investment. Heavy equipment is kept in fewer yards located in more active areas, whilst tools and spare parts for oil and gas extraction and production are stored in distribution centres near major exploration sites.

Mexico

Mexico's logistics industry is one of great potential that has yet to be fully realized. The prospect of near-shoring is promising for Mexico as manufacturers move facilities from China to Mexico to be closer to the US market. Since 1994, the country has been a participant in the NAFTA trade between the United States and Canada. In 10 years, trade between the three countries has increased almost 50 per cent.

Fairly sophisticated crossborder logistics exists. The large-scale manufacturers on the Mexican side of the US border utilize state-of-the-art logistics processes and technology to connect their factories with global suppliers and US customers.

Though much improved over the last 10 years, the country remains reliant on old and inefficient infrastructure. Fewer Mexican companies are using contract logistics providers than those in the United States and Europe; this difference is even more exaggerated amongst small and medium-sized companies. Those companies that are using logistics providers are focusing on more routine activities such as customs clearance and freight bill auditing and payment. Mexican companies are also focused less on cost reduction than they are on improved flexibility and customer service.

Warehousing is still a less-mature market with major differences in service quality between providers. In most cases, third parties are used only temporarily. Many shippers still prefer to keep warehousing in-house, rather than to out-source, for reasons of trust and security.

Asia Pacific logistics market

Increasing intra-Asian trade, along with a growing increase in imports not only for manufacturing inputs but also consumer products, helped lead the world out of the 2009 recession. The growth of this region continues to increase as the world recovers from the economic upheaval.

Instead of specializing in producing certain types of final goods, Asian exporters increasingly have specialized in certain stages of production and have become vertically integrated with each other. For example, the iPad final assembly is in China; however, most of the components are actually manufactured in other Asian economies, including Korea, Japan and Taiwan. Growth of crossborder supply chains is growing and will continue to do so; however, China will continue to be the focal point of the Asian supply network. China now accounts, directly or indirectly, for about half of all imports of intermediate inputs within Asia. For many of its Asian partners, China has become the single most important destination of intermediate goods exports.

Adequate infrastructure is needed to support this integration amongst Asian countries. To do so, individual Asian governments have launched initiatives to improve the road, rail, port and airport networks. Although government-sponsored infrastructure improvements are underway, logistics providers such as DB Schenker are investing in the rail network to link Europe with Asia whereas TNT, and others, have invested in the road network to link Southeast Asia with China.

As integration amongst the Asian countries continues to evolve, China is experiencing a shift in manufacturing locations. Historically, manufacturing was located in the eastern parts of the country. However, owing to rising wages, production is shifting to the west of China in search of lower costs. Other manufacturers are opting to relocate to other Asian countries such as India, Vietnam or Thailand whilst some are choosing to move closer to the markets they are serving in the United States or Europe (re-shoring).

To sustain its growth, China recognizes the need for a strong domestic economy and as such it is now seeking to stimulate domestic consumption to spur this on. Higher levels of disposable income have led to increased demand for a variety of consumables. This has, in turn, placed higher performance demands on the overall supply chain, from manufacturers who have ramped up supply, to the LSPs who provide the service link to the retail outlets. The larger retailers, in particular those with multiple outlets, are now expecting higher levels of service from their manufacturers such as daily deliveries and orders, which may include a high percentage of case or split-case picking.

Japan

Japan is considered to be Asia's logistics leader in terms of sophistication and transportation connectivity. However, Japan's logistics sector has been largely ignored by foreign investors in the past, their focus clearly on neighbouring China's huge and fast-growing market. In any case, economic stagnation, cultural barriers and the dominance of the Japanese conglomerates ('*keiretsu*') have created a market that has proved largely impenetrable until recently.

To complicate matters, Japan's industry is refocusing on services rather than manufacturing although out-sourcing has still not caught on to the same extent as in most other developed markets – the major manufacturers traditionally operated their own logistics subsidiaries. Japanese companies have also preferred to own rather than lease their warehouses or distribution facilities. However, this trend is changing, led by companies such as Nippon Express.

There are several reasons why prospects are good for global contract logistics players in Japan. Firstly, there are signs that the long, systemic downturn in the market is finally acting as a spur for Japanese companies to sell off their logistics subsidiaries and open up to third parties. This will not only support balance sheets, but also introduce new thinking and efficiencies.

Secondly, Japanese companies, as with many global manufacturers, are shifting their production abroad – mainly to China. The increased internationalization of the product flows naturally suits global logistics companies, which have significant capabilities in these key markets. This is an area in which domestic Japanese logistics companies are not as strong.

In this regard, DHL Supply Chain stands out. It was an early entrant into the market through Exel's earlier acquisition of Fujitsu Logistics in 2004. The company is organized along regional lines, with strong cooperation between the Japanese and Chinese businesses.

China

Owing to its huge growth, China occupies a special position amongst national logistics markets. Yet as many companies have found out, this is far from an unalloyed benefit, for the Chinese market may well be described as 'large but difficult'.

The Chinese economy is far from being a straightforward free market. It can be divided into three parts: the state; the 'State Owned Enterprises' (SOE); and the private economy. This structure has a huge impact on the nature of logistics provision with much of the SOE sector resistant to the concept of out-sourcing, especially to non-Chinese companies.

The ironic aspect of this is that private sector growth in China has been hugely dependent on Western logistics operations. Around 60 per cent of the Chinese economy is based around the Pearl River Delta, which owes its origins to its proximity to Hong Kong Port. The profile of the private sector and its appetite for contract logistics is quite different from that of the SOE sector. A great deal of the Chinese-owned business is export orientated producing consumer goods such as furniture, clothing and consumer electronics, often as part of a wider supply chain.

This results in complex interfaces with contract logistics providers. Chinese suppliers will frequently feed into the supply chains of large global OEMs or retailers, run by global LSPs. Yet providers still do not form a substantial market for contract logistics. This is, in part, due to the position that Chinese suppliers play in the global supply chain. However, it must be seen as a major opportunity for growth in the global contract logistics market. At present, the services that are bought are a mixture of road freight, port services and sea freight, frequently coordinated through a forwarder. However, it would be a logical evolution of these supply chains for them to be coordinated and developed with contract logistics input.

The situation of global companies operating in China is also complex. Their need to support operations is becoming more complex as the nature of investment changes. Up until very recently, the bulk of non-Chinese investors were located in the Pearl River Delta – especially Shenzhen – and their supply chain very much resembled that of Chinese suppliers. However, this is changing. Investors such as retailers are increasing as well as producers of consumer durables selling into Chinese markets.

This requires new types of logistics provision, but these investors often struggle to find what they need. Non-Chinese contract logistics companies have struggled to establish operations in much of China, with local regulatory authorities discouraging competition to local companies. Consequently, major investors increasingly rely on internal management structures to purchase and plan individual logistics functions. In short, they have in-sourced much of what is out-sourced in other markets.

This enables them to buy individual services such as transport or warehousing from local companies. There are examples of more extensive relationships that might be called contract logistics; however, it is difficult to tell what the exact nature of the relationship is. One example is the German retailer Metro, which has agreed to use Shuanghui Logistics to support its frozen food operations. Shuanghui Logistics is owned by the food processing company Henan Luohe Shuanghui Industry Group, which is owned by the local government in Henan province. It is presumed that Shuanghui will be using its existing frozen food infrastructure to support its own food distribution activities.

At present, even the pioneering fast-moving consumer goods (FMCG) companies are focused on the big eastern urban conurbations. As the cities in the western interior of China become more prosperous these companies are facing the need to support sales in these locations. The problem they will have is that the logistics provision is even weaker here than in the eastern cities, which at least had the platform of port activities on which to build. With the reluctance of local authorities to let non-local logistics service providers gain large market shares, it appears likely that China will emerge into a patchwork of smaller and medium-sized contract logistics providers based on locality and relationships with local political authorities and business interests.

That said, Toll Group (a subsidiary now of Japan Post) is in the process of constructing a physical network throughout China, supporting both Western FMCG companies such as Colgate-Palmolive as well as Chinese competitors. The future of truly private contract logistics LSPs with a pan-Chinese presence, either Chinese or non-Chinese owned, is hard to ascertain. There are certainly important contract logistics providers who are capable of providing the most sophisticated services, but their ability to reach across China may well be constrained.

The situation in the automotive sector is not so different. Almost all global vehicle manufacturers' operations in China are joint ventures. These operations have traditionally had complex supply chains with substantial quantities of components being imported. This has made substantial demands on logistics provision, with freight forwarders being used to coordinate the flow of components. Companies such as Schenker or DHL, who have large forwarding businesses, are able to interface these with contract logistics operations in vehicle manufacturers.

These contract logistics operations are different from those found in the West as assembly plants schedule environments tend to be less 'JIT' with components consolidated at forwarders' consolidation centres near major ports. This situation is changing as more components are produced in China, although it is reasonable to say that large Western LSPs have a 'foot in the door' for supporting these plants. However, the situation is hugely complicated by the relationship with the Chinese joint venture partners. These companies – who usually have their own car production assembly operations as well – are junior partners in terms of engineering and production management, but are often responsible for logistics provision. They will seek to impose their own in-house or related logistics companies on the joint venture. This is not always as bad as it sounds. A few such logistics service providers are sophisticated companies capable of supporting large-scale car production activities. A good example is Anji-CEVA (formerly known as Anji-TNT), which is a joint venture between the SOE Shanghai Automotive Industry Corporation and CEVA. Yet even here such a company is largely concerned with providing services to SAIC companies, not other Chinese VMs.

India

As Asia's third largest economy, India is witnessing a boom in economic and trade activity. Unfortunately, the growth rate has outpaced the country's infrastructure. Owing to the lack of modern infrastructure, World Bank estimates that India's logistics costs are approximately two to three times higher than best practice in developed countries.

The growth in external trade and the growth across major industry segments such as automotive, pharmaceutical, fast-moving consumer goods (FMCG) and the emergence of organized retail have favourably impacted the growth of the warehousing industry. At present, a large proportion of the warehousing industry is controlled by small, unorganized companies and as such, these facilities serve mainly as storage facilities. Those warehouse operators that do provide value added services charge a premium for such services as reverse logistics, kitting, labelling, etc. Another complication for the warehousing industry is the fact that India's tax system is complex. To avoid multiple taxation, companies typically have warehousing operations in every state. The result is a large number of small warehouses across the country, which lack the latest warehousing processes and technologies and do not offer economies of scale.

Until a few years ago, Indian firms out-sourced only transportation and basic warehousing. That has changed in the last few years, particularly after the economic slowdown. Customers from retail, apparel, IT and telecom sectors are out-sourcing quality checks, packing, labelling, store-ready delivery, parts of inventory management and billing function.

However, providers of warehousing services are in need of capital and know-how from investors and operators. As a result, several government plans are in place to expand and modernize the industry in India. For example, as part of rail infrastructure improvements, India Railways has proposed the development of freight logistics parks at six locations between Delhi and Mumbai. The parks will be operated as joint ventures with India Railways and the respective state governments.

Local logistics providers are expanding operations as well as international rivals. Safexpress has more than 5 million square feet of warehousing space across the country and is planning to set up 32 logistics parks and add another 5 million square feet in the next two years. This will be helped by the phasing out of the central sales tax which has created high levels of inefficiency.

South America

Until recently, South America had enjoyed an unprecedented increase in international trade due to demand for commodities such as minerals, oil, steel and agricultural goods. Demand for these goods was driven primarily by Asia, particularly China, whose need for these manufacturing inputs prompted many Chinese companies to invest in not only South American companies but also the region's infrastructure in order to gain access to the commodities more easily.

This situation changed when the Chinese economy started to weaken, meaning that demand for raw materials plummeted on international markets. This exposed weakness and corruption in South America's economies, especially Brazil, on which many of its neighbours relied.

Infrastructure remains a major issue for the region. Congestion at ports and airports, lack of paved roads and outdated rail systems have caused delays in the transport of goods and commodities to global markets. However, the last few years have seen major investments in the transportation infrastructure of most South American countries, particularly in Argentina, Brazil, Chile and Peru, although this has still left the region lagging behind.

Diversification into other industries is greatly needed in this region as commodity prices for raw materials tend to fluctuate wildly on the global market. To maintain a more stable economy, South American countries such as Brazil, Argentina and Chile are successfully expanding their economies into such industries as pharmaceuticals, winemaking, automobile and aerospace and apparel manufacturing.

Intra-South American volumes are increasing as road and rail networks connecting east to west South America are created. Brazil is the largest country, economically and geographically within the region, and 26 per cent of its total trade is with other South American countries. For landlocked countries such as Bolivia and Paraguay, more than half of their trade is intra-South America.

As the economies of Argentina, Brazil and other countries in the region expand, increases in trade have provided many new opportunities for global and regional 3PLs, ocean carriers and other transport operators. Intermodal connections between the key southern Brazilian cities of Sao Paulo, Rio de Janeiro and Belo Horizonte have improved significantly in the last three to four years. Major logistics providers such as Schenker, Expeditors, Panalpina and Kuehne + Nagel have increased their investments in warehousing and related logistics services in Brazil and they expect further heavy investment in the country's logistical infrastructure over the next few years.

Brazil

Brazil is the most important market in South America by a considerable margin. The country is a significant trade partner not only globally but also regionally and is a global producer of aircraft, consumer goods, steel, vehicles, rubber and paper. Along with local providers, global logistics providers such as DHL, Kuehne + Nagel, Panalpina, Expeditors, CEVA and UPS have all established operations to support Brazil's growing manufacturing and agricultural activities.

As with the rest of South America, Brazil's infrastructure has not kept up with the growth the country has experienced in the past few years. The government has introduced plans for infrastructure improvements, private companies have invested in Brazil's infrastructure and logistics providers are investing in the country's infrastructure. Still, the World Economic Forum recently described Brazil's infrastructure as 'appalling'.

Brazil is facing mounting pressure to improve and expand the country's infrastructure. Based on the World Economic Forum's report, Brazil's road infrastructure is lacking and maritime shipping suffers from insufficient capacity. Brazil's road network carries more than 61 per cent of domestic freight whereas 70 per cent of the country's exports are transported via ocean vessels.

Brazil is a global top 10 producer of vehicles and parts. In terms of logistics suppliers, CEVA is the leader with a presence in all areas of the market across the continent. It even has a strong presence in the finished vehicle logistics market. However, just as strong in terms of inbound logistics is DHL Supply Chain. GEFCO has also developed its presence in the region, in part to support the operations of its parent PSA. Medium-sized US LSPs also have a useful presence in South America. Typical of this is a company such as Crowley Logistics, a Florida-based maritime and land transport LSP that provides support to vehicle manufacturers with supply chains in the United States but production facilities in South America (for example, Ford).

With an annual production of 650 million pairs of shoes, Brazil is the third largest producer of footwear in the world after China and India, according to the Brazilian Footwear Industries Association. Brazilian shoe production is concentrated in the area of Vale dos Sinos, which accounts for the majority of shoe production. Benefiting from this specialization, DHL Supply Chain manages a distribution centre on behalf of Nike in Louveira, Sao Paulo. The company provides receiving, storage, order picking, distribution and reverse logistics for three Nike units: footwear, apparel and equipment. Other logistics providers that provide services to the footwear and retail industry include Damco, CEVA and GEFCO.

Middle East

Although it might be perceived as an emerging market, the Middle East in terms of logistics is quite different from most others. The Middle Eastern economies vary substantially, from Egypt with its large population and growing economy based on tourism and manufacturing, to the oil and gas driven economies of the Gulf. In terms of contract logistics, however, it is the latter that have made the running.

The dominant industry in the region is obviously oil and gas. Logistics provision in the oil and gas sector is not usually described as contract logistics as the oil companies involved generally own much of their own logistics infrastructure, such as oil storage and terminals. To a lesser extent this also applies to areas of oil and gas storage. However, an important market for out-sourced logistics companies is that of oil field maintenance. This mix of air transport and inventory management is largely dominated by the leading global LSPs who are often linked in to global oil and oil field services companies worldwide. That said, there is substantial activity in this area by local contract logistics players as well, particularly serving state-owned oil companies.

Another aspect of the Middle Eastern economies over the past decade is their programmes of diversification. Typified by the Emirate of Dubai, Gulf States in particular have invested in areas such as airlines, tourism and ports. The latter, in particular, has had a direct impact on the logistics sector. By building a large complex of container ports as well as substantial airfreight facilities, Dubai has sought to position itself as the logistics provider for a huge area of the Middle East, Central and Southern Asia. It has been partially successful with the Port of Dubai acting as an important trans-shipment point for India. This has also meant that contract logistics providers, both global and Middle Eastern based, have established Dubai as an important centre of operations.

The sectors served by Dubai-based logistics operations tend to be in the area of consumer durables. Electronic products in particular are suitable for strategic inventory holding in Dubai, but increasingly pharmaceutical logistics is attracted to the mix of good-quality temperature-controlled warehousing and intensive airfreight services. Tourism and hotel support logistics is also important.

Africa

The African logistics sector is more a collection of national markets than other, more integrated regions. Despite continuing severe infrastructure issues, Africa's growth has continued to be helped by the strength of its biggest trading partner, China, although logistics costs in Africa remain high, constraining the development of the sector. Corruption is rife in many parts of the continent, and this not only creates delays but adds to the cost of moving goods. Other problems include labour unrest and a major skills shortage.

However, the opportunities are clear. Africa is a resource-rich continent, and the growth of developing countries, such as the BRIC group, has led to huge demand for these resources. Despite this, the logistics sector will only take off when African industry moves up the value chain and manufacturing becomes more important. This may be a little way off, as although labour costs in Asia are reducing manufacturing's competitiveness in China and elsewhere, there is little sign that Africa is able to fill the void.

South Africa is increasingly being viewed as an important emerging market with large investment opportunities. South Africa's automotive industry has been growing quickly with vehicle manufacturers such as BMW, Ford, Volkswagen, DaimlerChrysler and Toyota basing production plants in the country. Manufacturers have established plants in South Africa to take advantage of low production costs, coupled with access to new markets as a result of trade agreements with the European Union and the Southern African Development Community free trade area. Opportunities also lie in the production of materials (automotive steel and components).

South Africa is also becoming increasingly important as a location for clinical trials, although there are longer regulatory timelines involved in setting up a trial in this country than in the developed world. However, compared with other 'emerging' markets, such as Eastern Europe and India, timelines are similar and costs are increasingly competitive.

There are significant opportunities for growth in the South African temperature-controlled logistics sector, but the market is not free of challenges. As the South African middle class expands, there has been increased demand for frozen foods. There has also been a growing trend towards using third-party logistics providers. However, most retailers operate their own distribution centres. In addition, land to build is scarce causing the cost of land to almost double since 2007. Building costs are also escalating rapidly.

Nigeria is the second largest market in Africa. The principal interest that Nigeria holds for foreign logistics companies stems from its major oil production operations. The country is a top 10 player as far as production and reserves are concerned, and most of the major oil multinationals are active within the market, the largest being Shell.

By making the country more investor and importer friendly, the authorities hope to make Nigeria a hub for the West Coast of Africa. Establishing a Free Zone makes relations with customs easier and more formal, although corruption in this market, and in fact throughout the whole region, is endemic.

Summary

At a local and national level, the logistics industry is significantly influenced by characteristics such as: regulation and liberalization; the development of the retail sector; international trade and commerce as well as levels of urbanization and population distribution. This chapter looked at the world's largest logistics markets in Europe, North and South America, Middle East, Africa and Asia; their origins, attributes and prospects.

Key points to consider:

- Whilst globalization has impacted upon the strategies of the largest logistics companies, particularly air cargo, shipping and freight forwarding, national logistics markets are still dominated by road and distribution.

- Governments still exert considerable influence over the logistics sectors through a range of quantitative and qualitative measures, seeking to control the industry through barriers to market entry.

- Despite this, levels of fragmentation are generally very high and this impacts on rates and the long-term sustainability of the industry in all countries.

- As developing countries adopt more Westernized retail practices and the sector becomes more consolidated, the logistics market will become more sophisticated, benefiting larger players.

- Likewise, as developing countries become less export-orientated, there will be a need for more value adding domestic distribution services.

The emergence of logistics clusters

04

CHAPTER LEARNING OBJECTIVES

This chapter will familiarize the reader with:

- The reasons behind distribution centre location
- How transport infrastructure plays an important role in this decision
- The functions that different types of distribution centres fulfil in the supply chain
- Why non-transport-related issues, such as rental costs and availability of labour, also play an important role
- The key locations of distribution centres in Europe, North America and China

Where to locate distribution centres?

'Primary' supply chain attributes

Manufacturers and retailers spend many millions on restructuring their logistics systems to ensure that customer expectations are met whilst inventory and transportation costs are minimized. This is a fine balance but getting it wrong has obvious implications in terms of efficiency and sales. Every company's distribution strategy is different but in the process of deciding where to locate distribution hub or hubs, a number of primary supply chain attributes first need to be assessed.

Location in supply chain

The relative position of a distribution node in the supply chain has a very important influence on its geographic location. If its function is to carry out primary logistics activities (for example, feeding vendor managed inventory into a large manufacturing site) the overarching need will be to locate the hub near to its customer. If, however, the hub is designed for secondary logistics purposes (for example, to distribute finished goods to a mass consumer market) then its location will be more governed by the need for geographic centrality.

Customer distribution profile

Leading on from this latter point, the customer distribution profile is obviously of prime importance to the location of a hub. This may mean geographic centrality, although this is not always the case. If the customer distribution profile is global (for example, a medical technology spare parts operation) then the 'connectedness' of an airport may be the overwhelming requirement, more than its physical location.

Type of product that is being shipped

This is important both from the perspective of a product's physical attributes as well as intrinsic value. If small packages are being shipped, location next to a parcels hub or airport will be important. For higher volume/lower value goods, location at a road interchange or proximity to a seaport may be more important.

Customer service levels required

In sectors where suppliers have to offer their customers a very high level of service (such as in the after sales market), achieving deliveries in small time windows will have a major effect on the structure of a distribution network. This may require a network of close-to-customer Forward/Field Stock Locations (FSLs), replenished from national or regional distribution centres.

'Secondary' supply chain attributes

Once these 'primary' supply chain attributes have been identified, a system of subsidiary factors can then be prioritized and 'weighted' in importance.

Air links

Where volumes include air cargo, proximity to an airport is obviously important. However, not any airport will do, as the level of 'connectedness' is essential. According to research undertaken by Chicago's Northwestern University, Paris, London, Frankfurt and Amsterdam are the four most connected cities in the world, with the highest ranked US city being Chicago followed by New York, Atlanta, Dallas and Houston. In Asia, Tokyo, Beijing, Bangkok and Hong Kong are the best connected. As well as the number of distinct routes, frequency of flights has to be taken into account, as well as other potential environmental factors such as night flying bans.

For high value-density shipments, the need for proximity to an international air express hub has led spare parts operations, retailers, high-tech companies, etc to cluster around airports such as Memphis (FedEx), Louisville (UPS) and Wilmington, Ohio (DHL) in the United States, and in Europe at Paris (FedEx), Cologne (UPS) and Brussels (DHL). In Asia Pacific, DHL has a major hub in Hong Kong; Shanghai is growing in importance through UPS's investment, and FedEx has its main hub in Guangzhou, southern China.

Shipping links

Similar issues of 'connectedness' exist for sea freight. As well as the number of routes available from a seaport, fleet deployment (number of ships), container carrying capacity (number of TEUs) and number of shipping lines are important factors. At a country level, China, Hong Kong and Singapore have the highest level of connectivity, according to the UN Conference on Trade and Development (UNCTAD). These countries are followed by the United States, United Kingdom and the Netherlands.

At a port level, Shanghai, Hong Kong, Singapore, Los Angeles, Rotterdam, Antwerp and Hamburg offer the most choices for shippers and have consequently attracted substantial investment in distribution centres.

Good port-to-port links are just part of the equation. Efficiency in loading/off loading and congestion in and around the ports have become major factors in recent years, given the increase in global shipping volumes. This has had a major impact on routing decisions with some shippers by-passing West Coast US ports and opting to distribute from hubs based near to ports such as New York or Charleston.

Competition for space in and around ports has led to the development of 'inland ports'. This has resulted in the growth on the 'Inland Empire' in California and intermodal ports such as Duisport in Germany.

Road links

For most manufacturers or retailers, road links are the most important modal factor in the location of a distribution hub, influencing access and time to market. In Europe, this has led to the development of hubs around towns such as Venlo, Eindhoven or Roermond in the Netherlands, all of which are on key arterial routes between the manufacturing and consumer centres of Germany, France, the Netherlands and Belgium, the main ports of Rotterdam and Antwerp, and the airports of Amsterdam, Brussels and Cologne, to name but a few.

In Western Europe, the quality of road infrastructure is generally very good which makes the decision on location reasonably easy, with plenty of options available. Regions competing for distribution hubs generally have to stress other advantages. Companies could base their logistics hubs as easily across the border in Germany as in Venlo – in this case it is a range of other non-modal factors that are more important such as labour laws and costs. However, elsewhere in the world this is not the case. Few companies choose to site their distribution hubs outside of the main metropolitan areas in China, for example, as road networks are still relatively undeveloped.

Non-modal factors

Generally, where there is little to choose between locations on the basis of transportation, decisions will be made through a combination of the following factors:

Cost of rental, land and build costs

The costs of renting, buying and building distribution warehousing varies considerably even over relatively short distances. For instance, in Europe rental at Heathrow Airport in London is highest, many times that of regions such as Limburg, Netherlands or even of Frankfurt Airport, Germany. Building costs are highest at Vienna, Austria and cheapest in Marseilles, France. Land costs, meanwhile, are most expensive in Heathrow and cheapest in Antwerp, Belgium (Savills, 2012).

Labour

Labour is an increasingly important factor in the location of a distribution centre. Legislation in some countries has made the workforce significantly less flexible than in others. As several hundred staff may be employed in any one centre it is essential to ensure the ability to take on and lay off staff during seasonal and cyclical peaks and troughs.

Labour availability is also important. Where there is full employment, the costs required to staff an operation rise considerably – and in some cases it is impossible to recruit good quality staff. Warehousing and hub employment remains unattractive to many people and therefore companies often have to resort to either higher wages or other benefits such as training and qualifications. This is the route that UPS took with the local government authorities in Louisville to overcome staffing shortages at its Worldport hub. Workers are paid to take a degree level course and are rewarded for academic success and loyalty to the company. This has been very successful in ensuring the retention of staff, as well as motivation.

Other factors

Other factors involved in the location of distribution centres include the flexibility and efficiency of customs regimes (an important competitive advantage for the Netherlands) as well as the availability and quality of a large number and range of logistics service providers.

Centralization of distribution in Europe

The characteristics of European distribution structures and how they operate depend largely on: the industry sector; the geographic markets that those industries serve; the product type; and the location of manufacturing facilities. Generally, over the last decade or so there has been a move towards centralized distribution of products in Europe, due to the removal of customs barriers and the improvement of transport infrastructure across Europe.

Most distribution structures around the world follow similar patterns and normally fall into one or more of the following distribution centre functions:

- Global distribution centre: often located close to the worldwide manufacturing site and serves to distribute goods to the different worldwide geographic regions.

- European distribution centre (EDC): serving as a central storage of goods for the European, Middle East and Africa (EMEA) regions and takes care of replenishment of the different regional distribution centres.

- Regional distribution centre, serving as a main distribution centre for a specific region within EMEA, for example the UK/Ireland region or the Nordic region.

- Country/local distribution centre, serving final distribution to customers.

These functions are generic and every company and industry sector will adapt these structures to fit their business. The amount of adaptation depends on the product type, historical development, availability of investment and strategic intent. In the fresh food industry, for example, global or European distribution centres are unusual owing to the perishable nature of their products. The product type therefore dictates a local distribution structure. This contrasts with the high-tech spare parts industry, where one can see all of the above distribution structures, owing to the fact that spare parts need to be delivered within a few hours and are expensive, requiring a centralized distribution structure combined with local delivery points.

The industry trend towards European distribution centres has been driven by large-scale changes in the European transport, supply chain and logistics sector. Over the last decade or so, many barriers to crossborder transactions between countries within the European Union have been removed. Companies therefore have been able to centralize European supply chain structures leading to large cost savings.

Companies such as Deutsche Post and Schenker have built, through acquisition, European and Global structures allowing them to service the pan-European and global supply chain requirements of their largest customers. However, this is only a relatively recent development, and many retailers and manufacturers are still operating 'national' supply chain structures (that is, within country borders) as part of an overall global strategy. This is evidenced by the fact that logistics companies are still winning national, rather than multinational, logistics contracts. In spite of this, many larger multinationals have moved to a pan-European structure and have benefited from large supply chain cost savings as a result.

The implication of these trends has meant fundamental changes in the use of warehousing and distribution property. Clearly, a move to a centralized European structure means less demand for smaller, national distribution centres and an increased demand for larger, central pan-European and regional distribution centres (see Figure 4.1).

Several European countries possess many of the key attributes that make them good locations for distribution facilities. The most popular are Belgium, Germany and the Netherlands:

- Belgium benefits from its proximity to seaports (such as Antwerp) and airports (Brussels), its transport infrastructure and the incentives it offers to investing companies.

- Germany benefits from being the largest economy in Europe, its proximity to rail hubs and its infrastructure.

Figure 4.1 Preferred/future European distribution centre locations

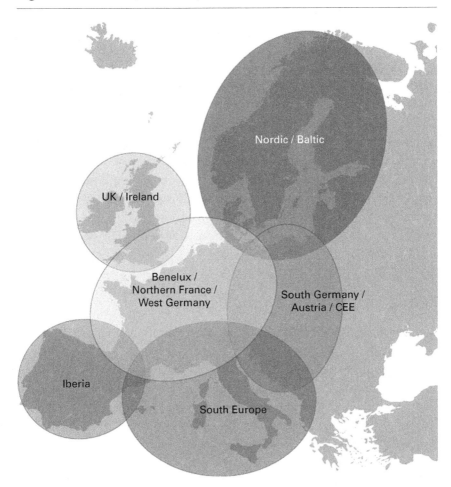

- The Netherlands benefits from its proximity to seaports (Rotterdam) and airports (Amsterdam Schiphol), its transport infrastructure, the incentives offered to investing companies, the multilingualism of its nationals and the positive business environment (including flexible customs regime).

Slightly less attractive are Denmark, France, Ireland and the United Kingdom.

For many manufacturers and retailers, the expansion of the European Union has required a new pan-European distribution strategy. With 10 of the EU's most recent members located in Central Europe, many European companies are looking to extend the reach of their supply chains in an eastward direction. The focus of these companies' efforts has been concentrated in Poland, the Czech Republic, Slovakia and Hungary. Retailers such as

Carrefour, Auchan and Tesco have partnered with logistics providers to extend relationships into Eastern Europe and European manufacturers such as Volkswagen, Volvo, Fiat and Unilever have relocated part or all of their production facilities to the region.

Clearly, the accession of Central and Eastern European countries into the European Union has had an impact on European distribution. These countries are attracting many Western companies for location of production and/or distribution facilities owing to their relatively less expensive land and labour costs. This, in turn, is changing distribution structures. The infrastructure does not currently exist to serve all these new markets from a central distribution location in Benelux, where most European distribution centres are based. Therefore, as distribution throughout the region becomes centralized, locations in the more developed Eastern European countries such as Poland or Hungary have been favoured as well as in eastern Germany (see Figure 4.2).

Future locations for strong demand

For pan-European distribution, the strongest locations for European distribution centres will continue to be the Netherlands, Germany, France and Belgium, for the short term at least. Germany is likely to experience significant growth in EDCs, due to the accession of Central and Eastern European countries. Existing structures with European distribution centres located in Benelux or France can be enhanced in the short to medium term with additional 'satellite' regional distribution centres strategically located in Northern Europe (Nordics), the United Kingdom and Ireland, Southern Europe, Eastern Europe and Italy/Greece.

On a national level, a general trend can be observed in many European countries, where new-build warehousing and distribution property is being sited outside of main capital cities, in locations with good transport links, availability of labour and less expensive land, rental and lease costs. Examples of these include:

- south and east of Paris and Lyon;
- east of Madrid in San Fernando de Henares, south of Madrid and Tarragona;
- Rhine-Neckar area or North Hessen in Germany;
- Wroclaw, Silesia, Poznan and Lodz in Poland;
- Brno, Plzen and Ostrava in the Czech Republic;
- Gyal and Gyor in Hungary;

- Transilvania, Ploiesti and Banat in Romania;
- Daventry, Kettering, Stoke, M1 corridor above Northampton in the UK (Nottinghamshire, Leicestershire and Derbyshire);
- Kempen, Limburg, Liège and Hainaut in Belgium;
- for the Netherlands, the following areas will be active: Coenhaven, Vlothaven in Amsterdam, Spaanse Polder in Rotterdam, De Hurk/ Ekkersrijt and De Kade in Eindhoven, Lage Weide in Utrecht and Trade Port in Venlo;
- Piacenza, Novara and Chieti in Italy.

Of course, ports are key strategic locations for warehousing and distribution property: Rotterdam, Le Havre, Barcelona, Hamburg, Marseille and Antwerp will see further expansion of warehousing space. Airports too will continue to be popular locations.

Figure 4.2 European strategic distribution locations

Centralization of distribution in the United States

Geographically, distribution space in the United States is divided between coastal areas and 'inland ports' (see Figure 4.3). Traditionally, ports in California, Seattle, Florida and the East Coast around New York and New Jersey have been a magnet for warehousing and distribution space. However, a lack of space around the Ports of Los Angeles and Long Beach has seen the growth and development of the Inland Empire, situated slightly further in from the coast.

The saturation of coastal space has also seen the development of 'inland ports' in locations such as Chicago, Atlanta and Dallas. Other locations include Kansas City, Memphis, Columbus, Harrisburg and Front Royal, Virginia. Goods arriving at ports such as Jacksonville, Savannah and Charleston on the East Coast are transported to distribution centres in Atlanta. Here goods are stored, ready for dispersal throughout the east of America.

These 'inland ports' have also seen an increase in activity due to the increasing level of goods that are arriving from Asia Pacific and in particular China. The volume of goods arriving on the West Coast has increased dramatically in the last 10 years. These goods are transported from West Coast ports via rail to Chicago and Atlanta for distribution to the east of the United Sates. Dallas likewise acts as a distribution hub, located between the West and East Coast of the country.

Dallas, and Texas as a whole, has also increased in significance as a distribution hub owing to its location on the border with Mexico. US manufacturers are increasingly using warehousing space in Northern Mexico where costs are cheaper. As a result, warehouses are also needed on the US side of the border from where goods can then be distributed to the rest of the country.

As ports become more congested, companies are delaying breaking containers until trains can carry them much further inland to locations such as Texas. Companies are also starting to use deepwater ports in Mexico as an alternative to the ports of Los Angeles and Long Beach, which has increased the importance of movement between Mexico and Texas.

Business-related taxes play an important role in determining where to locate a logistics hub. Sales and use tax, the cost for unemployment insurance for employees, corporate income tax, personal property, inventory and fuel tax rates are all important factors.

There have been major changes in distribution patterns in the retailing sector. The past decade has seen Walmart consolidate its national presence across the United States. Walmart now has a well-established infrastructure of distribution centres across the United States. This is characterized by centralized distribution centres around the centres of gravity of major markets.

The continuing change in this market sub-segment – which also applies to major home products company Home Depot – is the reorientation of its supply chain to sourcing from China. This has had the effect of major retailers relocating their warehousing to adapt to the new supply chain geography. Until recently, product was generally delivered to regional distribution centres, usually multi-modally. However, such is the volume of product entering the United States that specific facilities have been created to consolidate and store inventory before it is fed out to the distribution system across the country. Obviously, these have tended to be located on the US West Coast, particularly around Los Angeles. However, there are important new locations. For example, the port of Tacoma, which has grown on trans-Pacific volumes, has seen the furniture retailer IKEA open a development of 800,000 square feet.

More extreme is the growth of facilities on the East Coast. Notable is the development of a facility of 900,000 square feet by Walmart at Jacksonville port on the Atlantic coast of Florida. The logic behind such development is the ability to by-pass congested ports and rail capacity coming out of the West Coast.

Figure 4.3 United States – main distribution centre hubs

In terms of developments further down the supply chain, there have been several contradictory developments. On the one hand the continued move to big-box retailing had led to a consolidation of logistics infrastructure. However, there is a marked shift towards less commoditized retailing emerging over the past two years both in non-food and food retailing in smaller shops.

Another clear trend in US retailing is the move towards internet-retailing activities. Probably the highest profile brand in this area is the e-retailer Amazon, which has diversified in other product areas. Its market penetration is strong across the United States and it has constructed an established network of large facilities.

Key hub locations in the United States

Atlanta

Owing to Atlanta's geographic location, the area is a popular hub for warehousing and distribution facilities, particularly for logistics and transportation providers as well as retailers. The growing automotive industry in not only Georgia, but also surrounding states, South Carolina, Tennessee and Alabama, is also spurring growth.

The region serves as a major transportation hub. Close proximity to major interstates allows truck companies to reach 80 per cent of the United States within two days.

Atlanta also benefits from Atlanta Hartsfield-Jackson International Airport, which is the eleventh largest air cargo hub in the United States, as well as the Port of Savannah which, located a few hours to the south, is the second busiest US port for containerized export tonnage.

Chicago

Chicago is a major transportation hub, in which all modes of travel and freight movement intersect. Five federal highways and six major railroads pass through the city. The region also has a port and offers airfreight services via the Chicago O'Hare International airport and Midway International airport.

The state of Illinois has the second largest rail system in the United States, with almost 10,000 route miles of track and 39 freight rail companies. As a result, Chicago is not only a major hub for the nation's rail system, but also one of the largest intermodal systems in the country. Congestion is a major problem for the road network within the Chicago area.

Louisville, Kentucky

Louisville is the home to UPS's Worldport, the global headquarters for UPS Airlines, located at the Louisville International Airport. One of the area's largest employers, UPS also has numerous warehousing and distribution facilities in the area including two temperature-controlled centres. In total, UPS has approximately 70 customers that utilize its facilities, mostly in the high-tech and healthcare industries.

Canadian Pacific, Norfolk Southern and CSX operate in Louisville. CSX recently built an intermodal hub which connects the city with its Northeast Ohio intermodal network. Besides its rail connections, Louisville also is accessible via three major interstate highways – I-65, I-64 and I-71 as well as two inland ports on the Ohio River, which connects with the US inland waterway system.

Memphis, Tennessee

Memphis is called a 'quad-modal' hub – that is, goods may be transported by river, road, rail or air from this city. Memphis sits on two major national interstates – I-40 which links it to California to the west and North Carolina to the east, and I-55 which links the city to New Orleans to the south and Chicago to the north.

The Memphis International Airport is the largest cargo airport in the United States. FedEx, headquartered in Memphis, utilizes the airport as its primary hub. UPS also considers the airport as an important air hub for its operations.

Los Angeles, California

Los Angeles is a major location for warehousing and distribution centres owing to its position as a major West Coast port. Located to the south of Los Angeles, the Riverside-San Bernardino-Ontario area is one which is collectively known as the 'Inland Empire'. Owing to a large supply of vacant land and a transport network where many highways and railroads intersect, the Inland Empire has become a major shipping hub.

The LA/Ontario International Airport is a major West Coast air and truck hub for UPS whilst Los Angeles International Airport serves as a major West Coast hub for FedEx.

The Ports of Los Angeles and Long Beach handle about 40 per cent of the nation's Asian imports. Both Union Pacific and BNSF railroad companies provide direct rail access for the ports.

Centralization of distribution in China

As a region that is responsible for more than 35 per cent of total global exports, Asia's airports and seaports are consistently ranked as some of the largest in the world for tonnage carried. In fact, the top eight largest global ports are located in this region. Many Asian countries are expanding these ports as well as building new ones to accommodate growing trade. In addition, four Asian airports are ranked in the top 10 largest global cargo airports – Hong Kong, Shanghai, Incheon and Tokyo.

As trade continues to increase throughout the region, Asian countries are investing in much needed infrastructure projects within their borders. As individual countries improve their networks, the need to link these countries is also increasing. Intra-regional trade and the need to transport goods efficiently to outside markets are the primary reasons for the need of a combined network. As such, international organizations, China, the ASEAN economic community and logistics providers are pushing to improve links throughout the region.

For years, the United Nations Economic and Social Commission for Asia and the Pacific (UNESCAP) has worked with Asian countries to develop the Asian Highway. Conceived in 1959, it did not receive much traction until about 10 years ago. Since then, 23 Asian countries have signed the Asian Highway agreement and are working towards completing a 141,204-kilometre network that will integrate the region.

Logistics providers are also connecting countries via road and rail service offerings. Perhaps one of the best-known offerings is TNT's Asia Road Network. Established in 2005, the network is modelled after TNT's European Road Network and is wholly managed by TNT. The network stretches across 127 cities in seven countries across South East Asia and China for a distance of more than 7,650 kilometres.

Agility's integrated trucking network provides shippers with an option to truck directly to several major cities in South East Asia and China as well as direct connections to major airports and ports in the regions. According to the company, the service provides shippers with a cost-effective alternative to airfreight with savings of 30 per cent to 40 per cent.

Countries within the Asia Pacific region have varying levels of intermodal infrastructure, and face different geophysical and institutional challenges in upgrading existing infrastructure, or in the creation of new intermodal terminals. The Asia Pacific countries are at differing stages in devising solutions for removing inefficiencies and competition between companies operating different modes. The respective governments and industry groups, however, recognize the benefits attained by establishing intermodal freight systems to deliver improved economic performance.

However, compared with the integration of markets in the EU, progress towards market integration is at a very early stage and, consequently, the vast majority of secondary distribution throughout the region occurs on a national, rather than intra-regional basis. Rationalization of tariffs, customs clearance and duty procedures have yet to allow the development of region-wide distribution centres to anywhere near the same extent as in Europe.

Key distribution hub locations in China

Since the mid-2000s, the significant demand and growth potential of Chinese distribution markets has been driven by a number of key factors including:

- World Trade Organization related policy changes;
- a strengthening manufacturing sector;
- growth in export markets;
- 'Open Skies' aviation agreements;
- expanding domestic markets and investment.

Tax incentives and aggressive infrastructure development have been used to attract foreign investors to the Chinese market in development zones specified by the authorities, in either Free Trade Zones or Bonded Logistics Parks.

Geographically, distribution centres in China have been based in three regions: the Pearl River Delta (south), the Yangtze River Delta (east) and the Beijing Tianjin area (north-east). These areas are identified within the Chinese market as the primary hubs; secondary and emerging hubs are also identified (see Figure 4.4). Secondary hubs are those that are beginning to attract an increase in attention from international operators, and emerging centres are those that have strategically important locations.

Chinese infrastructure is receiving significant investment to support the rapid growth of the economy. Ports have played a vital role in the development of the logistics industry and will continue to develop with China's global manufacturing role. Excluding Hong Kong, Shanghai and Shenzhen rank amongst the largest ports in the country.

In terms of air transport, Hong Kong remains the most important link, primarily due to the large number of destinations served, the modern facilities and the efficiency of the operation. Shanghai, Beijing and Guangzhou are

Figure 4.4 China – main distribution centre hubs

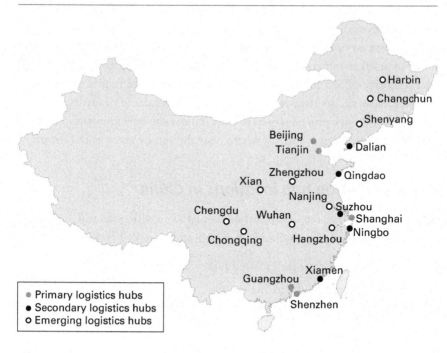

> • Primary logistics hubs
> • Secondary logistics hubs
> o Emerging logistics hubs

the three major air cargo hubs situated on mainland China. China is in the process of constructing a further 40 new airports across the country although air cargo growth is expected to focus on these four key hubs.

Inland waterway operations are centred along the Yangtze River, although use of this mode is restricted by low bridges. Rail and road networks are experiencing significant investment. Road is to be expanded from 41,000 kilometres to 85,000 kilometres by 2020, and rail from just over 70,000 kilometres to nearer 100,000 kilometres in the same period. Both networks are planned to expand into western China, although it could take up to a few decades to make an impact within the region.

The distribution market is forecast to see consolidation and a move towards out-sourcing. This, in turn, will create high demand for warehouses of higher standards and increased use of technology within the facilities. The use of warehousing is expected to incorporate value adding activities, a move away from traditional storage uses.

The locations of warehouses are focused in the three regions of the Yangtze River Delta, the Pearl River Delta and Bohai Bay (Beijing and Tianjin) with only 15 per cent of facilities located outside those. Shanghai alone boasts over a third of China's warehousing capacity.

Summary

This chapter has examined the impact that the centralization of inventory has had upon distribution strategies. It looked at the driving forces behind the location of distribution hubs, including geography, transport infrastructure links, economic and demographic centres of gravity as well as a range of secondary supply chain attributes. In specific detail, the key distribution locations in Europe, North America and China have been examined, looking at the reasons why they have developed and their future prospects.

Key points to consider:

- Distribution hub locations are dynamic, based on a range of decision-making criteria.

- As regions become more integrated, there will be more opportunities to supply multiple markets from a single location.

- In Europe, the Netherlands and Belgium will remain key locations, although as the EU's economic centre of gravity shifts east, many companies will adopt a multi-tiered approach to supplying an increasingly large market.

- In North America, Mexico's development as a near-sourcing market will accelerate the development of logistics hubs in the south of the United States.

- In Asia, the advent of the ASEAN Free Trade Zone and improving transport infrastructure will lead to the development of many more centralized hubs.

International freight forwarding

05

CHAPTER LEARNING OBJECTIVES

This chapter will provide the reader with:

- A definition and analysis of the freight forwarding industry by sector
- An understanding of the shipper decision-making process in terms of modal choice
- Insight into the levels of hyper-fragmentation evident in the freight forwarding market
- An understanding of the reasons behind the consolidation that has occurred in the industry through mergers and acquisitions
- The micro-economics that drive freight forwarding companies' revenues and profitability

The structure of the freight forwarding industry

A market definition

Freight forwarders play an important role in facilitating international trade, fulfilling a number of distinct functions. In basic terms, they act on behalf of exporters to buy and manage transportation services. These usually include air or sea freight, as well as the land transportation required to move the goods from the shipper to the port.

In its purest definition a freight forwarder owns no assets of its own, rather managing the transport and warehousing assets of others. However, in reality many freight forwarders are also involved in what could be termed 'integrated logistics'. One of the main reasons for this is that it enables companies to move from the commoditized buying and selling of carrier capacity to offering value added services, increasing what is traditionally a low margin business.

Clecat, the European forwarders' association, provides a comprehensive definition of the current forwarding industry. It states that 'Freight Forwarding and Logistics Services' include services of any kind relating to the carriage (performed by single mode or multi-modal transport means), consolidation, storage, handling, packing or distribution of goods as well as related ancillary and advisory services. The latter includes customs and fiscal matters, declaring goods for official purposes, procuring insurance and collecting or procuring payment or documents. Freight Forwarding Services also include logistical services with modern information and communication technology in connection with the carriage, handling or storage, and de facto total supply chain management. These services can be tailored to meet the flexible application of the services provided.

This definition draws little distinction between freight forwarders and global logistics providers, and indeed at the top end of the market this could well be the case. Companies such as Schenker, Kuehne + Nagel and DHL often combine logistics with freight forwarding services for global key accounts. For smaller customers there is no such crossover, with a more traditional approach to freight forwarding being adopted.

Customs brokerage

As well as buying and selling capacity from carriers, freight forwarders also play an important role in liaising with various customs authorities, acting on behalf of the exporter or importer. This is often referred to as 'customs brokerage' and includes the preparation of the requisite trade documentation as well as the payment of customs duties on behalf of the shipper. This calls for a knowledge of trade regulations, quotas and tariffs.

A customs broker will often also undertake bonded warehousing, which allows a shipper to defer payments of duties and taxes until a later stage in the sales process. For instance, it will be able to store imported goods until they are sold, at which time the duties become payable. This helps the shippers' cash flows.

Non-Vessel Owning Common Carriers (NVOCCs)

A specific type of operation exists in the sea freight sector known as Non-Vessel Owning Common Carrier (NVOCC). This is not only a term to describe a specific business function in the freight forwarding industry, but in some markets, mainly the United States, it also carries legal weight. In functional terms, an NVOCC buys space from a shipping line and then retails this space, usually to other freight forwarders, on a Less than Container Load basis (LCL). This provides a service to forwarders that do not have the necessary volumes to book a Full Container Load (FCL) directly with the shipping line. In many ways this is a similar service to that provided by airfreight wholesalers. NVOCCs buy the bulk space by entering into service contracts with ocean carriers that require the shipment of a minimum quantity of cargo throughout the year or the payment of damages.

The status of NVOCC is highly ambiguous, given that in function it resembles another form of freight forwarding, yet legally (in the United States for instance) it carries with it the specific responsibilities of carrier status. In Maritime Law, although an NVOCC accepts a 'carrier's entrustment' it is also charged with taking delivery and delivering cargo in the name of carriers, two contradictory principles. To complicate matters further it publishes tariffs and schedules in the same way as a carrier.

The ambiguity comes about as in Maritime Law the definition of 'carrier' does not depend on the criterion of 'having vessels' or 'not having vessels', but whether interested parties have a contractual relationship of transportation, and whether the party providing transportation service is liable for the transportation in accordance with the contract or law. From the perspective of global transportation practice, the NVOCC concept is only uniquely found in the US legislature, at odds with prevailing international transportation practice.

The status and definition of the NVOCC has been called into focus by attempts by China to create a regulated market. The authorities could either follow the US example and create a layer of regulation and administration dealing separately with freight forwarders and NVOCCs or adopt the internationally accepted pragmatic view that NVOCCs are a type of freight forwarder and should be dealt with as such. This latter approach would prevent confusion for new market entrants as to whether they should register as freight forwarders or NVOCCs.

Size is an important competitive advantage for NVOCCs. It gives them economies of scale in infrastructure, a wider range of routes and ability to obtain better load ratios for its containers. With these advantages, its current market position seems defensible and there is an opportunity to develop in the 50 per cent of the market served by forwarders using in-house provision and also to improve import market penetration.

Airfreight wholesalers

Although the major freight forwarders are able to buy and fill belly-hold space direct from the airlines on certain key routes, many smaller forwarders do not have the necessary volumes. Instead, a group of companies known as 'wholesalers' buy capacity, which they then sell on in smaller packages to freight forwarders. A wholesaler will act as a consolidator in much the same way as an NVOCC operates in the sea freight business. Wholesalers providing a 'scheduled' service are able to command competitive rates on behalf of their clients as they book regular space with the airline.

Modal choice by shippers

The decision by a shipper to use either air or sea freight is driven by four main factors (see Table 5.1):

- **The value of the goods.** If the transportation element of the final cost of the goods is small, say in the case of high-tech shipments, shippers can afford to send the goods by higher cost modes, such as air.
- **The time sensitivity involved.** Although the goods themselves may not have an innate high value, such as a spare part for a production line or a ship, the consequential loss that could be incurred by longer shipping times may itself be a factor in the choice of mode. This works equally well for documents and goods with short product lifecycles where there is a critical need to get to market.
- **The weight of the shipment.** The cost of transporting heavier weights usually precludes the use of air, either through cost, or through the constraints placed upon airfreight consignments by the size of capacity.
- **Product attribute.** Some consignments, such as some classes of dangerous goods, are not allowed to travel by air. This leaves a shipper with sea freight as its only option.

Although individual circumstances often drive the modal choice, it has been suggested as a rule of thumb, that a shipper will send goods by air only if the costs are less than 15–20 per cent of total value.

Table 5.1 Key factors in modal choice

Merchandise attributes	Airfreight	Sea freight
High value	Y	N
Time sensitivity	Y	N
Quick response	Y	N
Short product lifecycle	Y	N
High value : density ratio	Y	N
Dangerous goods	N	Y

Fashion goods can fall into either category, largely due to the needs of the shipper at the time. Most retailers will attempt to forecast needs far enough ahead to use lower cost ocean freight to move goods. However, if sales are stronger than predicted, airfreight can be used to replenish stocks albeit at a lower margin.

Fragmentation and consolidation

Freight forwarding is a highly fragmented market, characterized by small to very small companies. Low barriers to market entry allowed very small enterprises to enter the market and compete effectively with the major players, depressing margins.

This is despite the development of a small number of large companies that have sought to differentiate their products through intellectual capital and IT systems that provide visibility and coordination between the forwarder and the physical asset operators.

Larger companies can in theory also enjoy a competitive advantage through their scale. By being able to leverage their volumes on certain routes they can demand lower rates from carriers, which they are then able to pass on to customers. However, this advantage should not be over-emphasized, as smaller freight forwarders are able to use NVOCCs who consolidate volumes from different sources to achieve the same effect.

In order to gauge an idea of the level of fragmentation in the freight forwarding market, the Herfindahl-Hirschman Index (HHI) can be utilized. The HHI methodology applies a weighted system to market share data in order to determine the dominance of leading players. Using a scale of 0 to 10,000, a value of below 1,000 indicates an 'un-concentrated' market, while a value of between 1,000 and 1,800 indicates a 'moderately concentrated' market. If the number is above 1,800, the market is said to be 'highly concentrated'.

Using this technique, the sea freight forwarding market was found to have an index value of 227 in 2015. Air cargo was even more fragmented with an index of 187. This indicates a fragmented market with high levels of competition. Despite a large amount of M&A activity, there is little evidence of increasing consolidation in the sector. This is perhaps a little surprising bearing in mind the acquisitive role of large forwarders such as DHL, yet it only serves to highlight that despite their clear position as the biggest forwarder in airfreight, they hold a very modest overall proportion of the market.

Figure 5.1 compares the competitive nature of the road freight, air cargo and sea freight market segments with the much more concentrated UK contract logistics market.

Figure 5.1 The freight forwarding Herfindahl-Hirschman Index

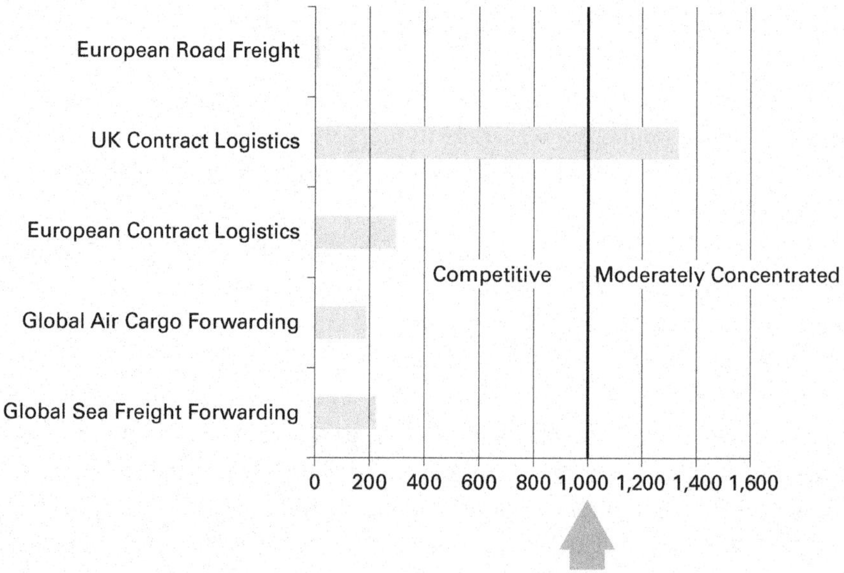

SOURCE: Transport Intelligence (2016)

The restructuring of the freight forwarding sector

The last few years have seen considerable mergers and acquisition activity as all the major logistics companies have sought to increase their presence in the global forwarding market.

The highlights of this trend are:

- The purchase of Exel by Deutsche Post. Exel itself was the product of a merger between contract logistics company Exel and forwarder Ocean Group (including MSAS). Deutsche Post had already acquired a number of other large forwarders, notably Danzas, AEI and ASG.

- Deutsche Bahn's acquisition of German forwarder Schenker and US forwarder Bax Global.

- UPS's acquisition of two US forwarders, Fritz and Menlo (formerly Emery).

- CEVA's acquisition of EGL.

- DSV's acquisition of UTi Worldwide.

The reasons behind these different purchases vary to a degree by company, but have a unifying logic in reflecting the trends in the market for freight forwarding. For example, DP DHL created out of its acquisition of both Exel and Danzas a logistics division that combines the ability to move large volumes of freight both by sea and by air, using its forwarding capability, with the road transport and warehousing capabilities of its contract logistics business. This is also the case with Kuehne + Nagel, which has aggressively built up its contract logistics/road freight network in order to complement its freight forwarding business.

Essentially, what these companies are trying to do is: increase market share by offering more integrated services; and improve margins by offering more sophisticated services.

There is another aspect to the strategic trends in the freight forwarders market. As in the case of UPS, a number of express parcel companies are trying to claim part of the business that has traditionally been undertaken by freight forwarders. This is particularly the case in airfreight services for the electronics business, but is also seen in other sectors.

Integrators v freight forwarders

Airfreight forwarders have seen their market share eroded over the last three decades by the emergence of the four major integrated express operators: DHL, UPS, TNT and FedEx. Their development has been aided by current supply chain management requirements, namely fast, reliable movement of goods underpinned by information technology. Originally, forwarders in Europe believed that integrators would provide little threat within the context of a complex multi-country trading environment, and would therefore largely be constrained to the United States. However, this proved not to be the case and the integrators proved extremely able to compete in Europe even before the advent of the Single European Market in the early 1990s, which did away with customs barriers.

One of the main problems for the freight forwarders was that as their 'asset-light' business model relied upon contracting with carriers they lacked the control that integrators could exert over their own vehicles and aircraft. This gave them considerable advantages:

- The integrators were able to introduce track-and-trace technology at an early stage.

- They guaranteed capacity on their own aircraft, whereas forwarders' consignments were often 'bumped' (not flown) if a carrier had overbooked.

- Quality control could be ensured.

The hub-and-spoke networks that were operated by integrators allowed them to offer daily services, rather than less frequent consolidations ('consols') on a point-to-point basis.

As mentioned, the integrators' use of their own aircraft meant that they were not dependent on belly-hold freight capacity supplied by the main airlines. Airfreight until recently was never given particularly high priority by the main air carriers who would base their network strategies on passenger demands rather than on freight, which was seen as a bi-product. Although this sometimes benefited forwarders as freight was priced on a marginal cost basis, it also meant that there was no long-term or consistent freight strategy in place. Speed and reliability can suffer where freight is subordinate to passenger requirements.

The result of competition from international express carriers led to the loss of the highly lucrative parcels for freight forwarders. Since then they have been forced to focus on heavyweight goods; on consignments that do not fit the integrators' need for high levels of standardization (for example, dangerous goods) or on price.

However, in recent years the major forwarders, in conjunction with the largest air carriers (such as Lufthansa, Air France) have fought back against the integrators. The airlines have introduced guaranteed time definite services that have allowed their clients, the forwarders, in turn to provide their clients with a more reliable service. Advances in technology have allowed forwarders to increase the level of visibility with which they can provide the shipper irrespective of who owns the transport and logistics assets. This has reduced the competitive advantage of the integrators.

'Disintermediation'

The term 'disintermediation' was coined in the 1990s to describe the process of removing third parties from the client–supplier relationship and applies to a range of different industries. Specifically related to the airfreight sector, the term applies to the potential removal of freight forwarders from the relationship between shipper (manufacturer or retailer) and the carrier.

The concept has attracted much discussion over the last decade, although there is no sign that it will be adopted. This is in stark contrast with the air passenger industry where many travel agents have been marginalized especially in the low-cost, short-haul sector. Airlines such as easyJet and Ryanair in Europe have adopted a 'direct' sales approach through telephone or internet sales, thus eradicating sales commission.

When one airline, KLM, was rumoured to be developing a direct sales approach with some major shippers (such as Philips) it attracted widespread criticism from freight forwarders, its existing clients. Afraid of alienating its client base, it backtracked, and there has been little sign that other airlines would develop a similar approach.

The power of the freight forwarders in the airline industry contrasts with the situation in the sea freight sector. Here shippers are accustomed to going direct to the major shipping lines.

Freight forwarding market dynamics

Essentially, a freight forwarder acts as an intermediary in the market between shipper and carrier. Their business model depends on their ability to buy capacity and sell it at a profit. This means that the fortunes of the freight forwarding sector are directly affected by supply issues in the shipping and air transport industries as well as underlying demand from shippers.

The freight forwarding market is counter-cyclical, which means that in times of economic downturn it is able to enhance profits, even though total revenues weaken. This is because as volumes weaken in a recession, the carriers (either shipping lines or airlines) have excess capacity, which allows the freight forwarders to drive down rates, whilst passing on only a proportion of these savings to the shipper.

As the economy picks up, carrier capacity starts to tighten and rates subsequently harden. Although the forwarder finds it difficult to pass on all these rate rises to its clients, its profits in absolute terms increase due to increased volumes.

Of course, there are times when this supply/demand pattern becomes asynchronous especially in the air cargo sector. Supply is not just influenced by the demand for cargo as a large proportion of goods travel in the belly-holds of schedule passenger flights. This means that supply can be affected by socio-political events (such as the SARS virus or terrorism) that reduce movements of passengers, rather than by the economic cycle.

In sea freight, the dynamics are slightly different although the fundamentals are the same. In theory, capacity takes longer to bring on stream, due to the time it takes to build ships. Therefore, for long periods of the economic cycle there is often under-supply, due to shipping lines' inability to accurately predict demand, followed by over-supply when a large amount of extra capacity is introduced. Owing to the time lag, this often occurs after the peak in demand, flooding the market, and resulting in a collapse in rates. Of course, in reality it is often more difficult to work out patterns of supply and demand (see Figure 5.2).

The air cargo sector is also highly cyclical but even more volatile than shipping. It relies on the shipment of high-value goods such as high technology and luxury items, which are dependent on the global economy. When there is a downturn in the economy, investment in new technology and sales in prestige goods are cut, with a significant impact on volumes.

Figure 5.2 provides an illustration of the relationship between carriers and freight forwarders throughout the economic cycle. It tracks demand, supply and the impact on forwarders' gross margins. This latter metric is most important for forwarders as it strips out the amount paid to carriers and is a better indicator of their performance.

Gross Margin = Gross Profit/Net Revenue

Net Revenue is Invoiced Turnover (but not including duties and taxes).

Gross Profit is Net Revenue less Fees Paid to Carriers.

Gross Profit is sometimes referred to, confusingly, as 'Net Net Revenue' as it is Invoiced Turnover less duties and taxes, less Carrier costs.

Figure 5.2 Theoretical counter-cyclicality in the freight forwarding sector – Scenario 1

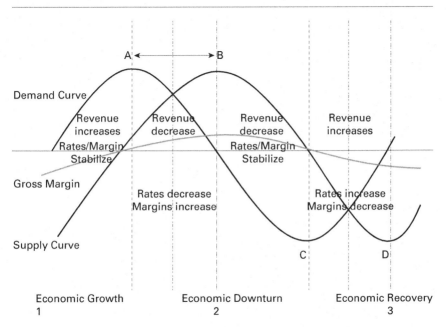

During a period of economic growth (1), demand and supply increase. In this particular 'normal' scenario, capacity and volumes are assumed to be growing at a similar pace, which means that rates and margins are stable.

However, as economic growth starts to slow (as the cycle enters its second phase at A), supply continues to increase. The reason for this (as outlined above) is that the carriers do not have access to 'perfect' market intelligence. Therefore, their decision making as regards whether to bring on or take out capacity lags the actual market situation. The effect of this for forwarders is that gross margins start to increase, although revenue growth slows as volumes and rates drop. This part of the cycle demonstrates forwarders' 'counter-cyclical' business model, which is one of the sector's key strengths.

At point B shipping/airlines have realized that they need to adjust their capacity and supply declines. Rates and forwarders' margin start to stabilize.

At Point C, the economy has reached the bottom of its cycle and demand once again picks up. However, due to the lagging effect, supply continues to be taken out of the market, meaning that rates harden and forwarders' margins drop. The latter bottom out at Point D, when supply (capacity) is brought back into the market. During this time forwarders still benefit from rising volumes.

It should be noted that the closer Point A is to Point B, the lower the amplitude of change in forwarders' gross margins (in other words the flatter the curve will be).

Another scenario is shown in Figure 5.3.

Figure 5.3 Theoretical counter-cyclicality in the freight forwarding sector – Scenario 2

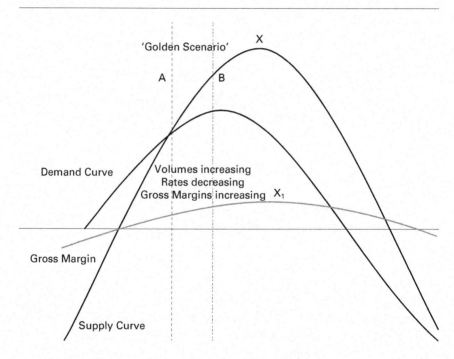

Here, the capacity and demand curves are further out of alignment. Supply (Point X) peaks higher and later than the peak in demand. This creates a period of time (between Points A and B) during which volumes are still rising, but are being outstripped by supply. This means that rates are falling, forwarders' gross margins are rising and so are their revenues. It could be termed a 'golden scenario' for forwarders.

Note, the peak of forwarders' gross margin occurs at X_1 relating to the peak in supply (rather than that of demand).

Market data supporting the counter-cyclicality model

Testing this theoretical model is more difficult, not least due to the difficulty in finding reliable and accurate market data. However, evidence does exist to support this hypothesis of counter-cyclicality.

The demand curve in Figure 5.4 is generated using estimates of annual container throughput (TEU) growth; the supply curve is generated by using estimates of available slot capacity growth (TEU) provided by market analysts, Alphaliner. The gross margin figures (year-on-year change in terms of

Figure 5.4 Demand, supply and gross margin in the sea freight sector (YoY growth)

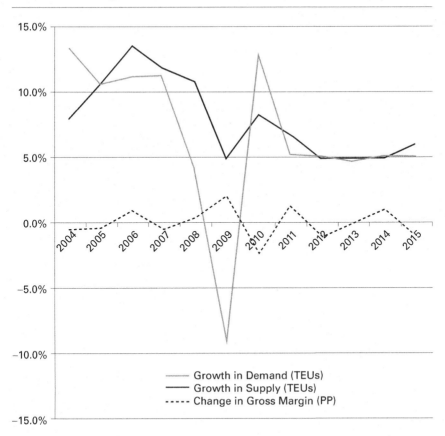

SOURCE: Alphaliner/Kuehne + Nagel (2016)

percentage points) are sourced from global forwarder Kuehne + Nagel, one of the few to publish financial data for this entire period.

The first observation that can be made is that demand in terms of container throughput follows economic development patterns, with growth slowing throughout the 2000s before going into reverse in 2008 and 2009 when the global recession took hold. It also shows clearly the 'V' shaped recovery that took place in 2010 and the dip in 2011 as the market growth moderated.

Supply actually tracks demand more closely than the theoretical model would suggest. However, it is the data from 2008 onwards that best illustrates the lagging counter-cyclicality of the sector.

As demand falls heavily in 2008 and 2009 after years of growth, shipping lines are not able or unwilling to remove capacity from the market. As a result, rates fall, and as already detailed, forwarders' margins rise. In 2010, demand recovers, but shipping lines are still wary of introducing more capacity as they have made major losses in the years prior. This results in soaring rates and falling forwarder margins. In 2011, the pattern is not so clear. It is true that growth in demand can be seen to drop but hardly sufficiently, it might be thought, to result in the extraordinarily low rates that were evident in the market. However, the falling rates that were observed had a highly positive effect on forwarders' gross margins.

It can also be seen that gross margin does not change by the same magnitude as either gap ratio or rates, both of which are much more volatile. Instead, it moves within a band of +/–3 percentage points showing that forwarders are not able to 'profiteer' in times of weak demand/high capacity, but nor are they as badly affected when shipping rates soar.

In 2015, demand growth once again was weak and shipping lines continued to add capacity into the market with new-build 'mega-ships'. Rates have dropped and, consequently, forwarders' margins have increased.

Future forwarding sector performance

As we have seen, forwarders' gross profits are directly influenced by the gap between demand and available capacity in the market place. Derived from this supply/demand relationship, of course, are freight rates.

To show this relationship between rates and gross margins more clearly, Figure 5.5 tracks gross margin (indicated on the right-hand axis) and annual average shipping rates between Asia and Europe (US $ per TEU). The gross

Figure 5.5 The relationship between rates and gross margin

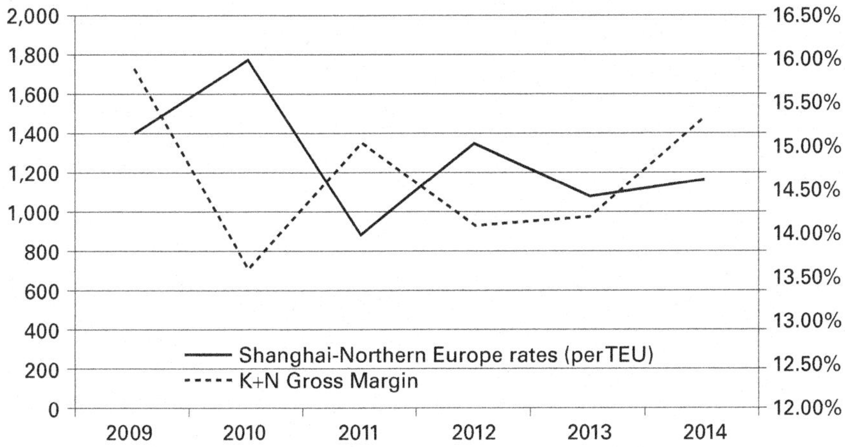

SOURCE: Transport Intelligence (2015)

margin figures used are those of freight forwarder Kuehne + Nagel, which derives a major part of its business on these tradelanes.

The figure shows in sharp relief what would be expected throughout a period of economic volatility. As volumes recovered in 2010, capacity was tight with average rates rising significantly. Consequently, Kuehne + Nagel's gross margins fell. In 2011, the economic slowdown caused demand to fall again, the gap ratio rose, leading to a fall in rates and an increase once again in gross margins. A rebound in 2012 had the opposite effect. Since then, continued weakness in rates has meant an upturn in gross margin.

In terms of counter-cyclicality and profitability, the air cargo sector performs in the same way to the sea freight sector.

Freight forwarders' profitability

As has been mentioned, freight forwarders are remarkably resilient in terms of profitability. Although margins undulated slightly over the period of the recession and beyond, this was within a range of 4.0 per cent to 4.8 per cent (see Figure 5.6). This is despite the considerable volatility in revenues that was seen over the same period.

However, there is a considerable range in the profitability of the leading freight forwarders. Expeditors achieve operating profit margins of around 10 per cent, whereas at the other end of the scale a number of companies operate at margins between 2 per cent and 4 per cent. It is difficult to identify

Figure 5.6 Freight forwarders' moving average operating profits

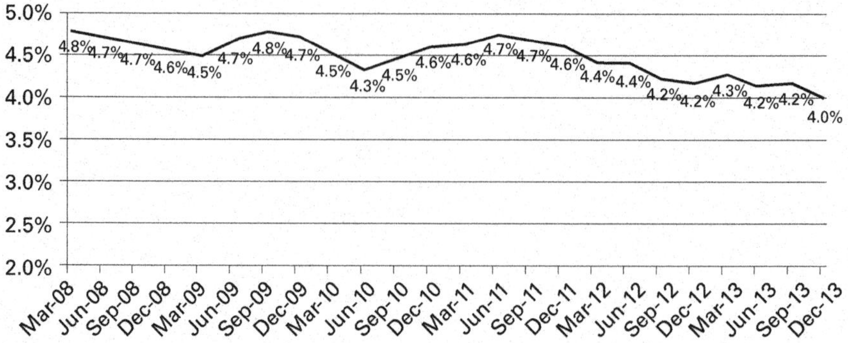

SOURCE: Transport Intelligence (2015)

one single reason for the diverse range of profitability; given the companies all perform similar functions in the same markets. Some suggestions, however, are listed below:

- Management and staff. Freight forwarding relies heavily on the ability of staff to buy and sell effectively. It needs well-experienced and high-quality personnel who are motivated and well managed.

- Buying power. Buying power in the industry is important. A freight forwarder with large volumes can buy better rates from a shipping/airline. However, the freight forwarder then has a choice. It can either benefit itself from the lower rates by not passing them on fully to shippers. Or it can use these lower rates to grab market share, by operating at lower margins.

- Overheads. Some companies will be better at operating with lower overheads than others – and this will include offices and IT. In many respects this comes back to the quality of the management making decisions on investment.

- Tradelane exposure. Forwarders that operate on the main tradelanes face heavy competition, whilst those that have built up a customer base on more niche lanes, or providing certain speciality services or knowledge, have the ability to charge a premium.

Summary

The international freight forwarding sector has been a key beneficiary of the trend towards the globalization of supply chains. Although still highly fragmented, the industry has undergone considerable consolidation over the past 10 years and this chapter described the main reasons for the acquisition activity. It also looked at the dynamics of the sector, its structure and examined how forwarders benefit in an economic downturn as well as during periods of growth.

Key points to consider:

- The high levels of fragmentation in the forwarding sector and low barriers to market entry and exit make the industry very competitive.
- As regions become more interlinked and integrated, international flows of goods will increase, continuing to drive growth in the international freight forwarding sector.
- Freight forwarders will remain targets for acquisition by other logistics companies to provide end-to-end international services to clients.
- Mergers and acquisitions will continue to increase the geographic scope of forwarders' networks, especially into Asia and Africa.
- Robust profitability even in the face of falling volumes will attract investment owing to the defensive nature of the sector, although the long-term migration of air cargo volumes to lower cost sea freight may have a detrimental impact on freight forwarders' yields.

Contract logistics

06

CHAPTER LEARNING OBJECTIVES

This chapter will provide the reader with:

- A description of how the contract logistics industry has developed as a response to higher levels of out-sourcing by retailers and manufacturers

- An understanding of the tendering process and the types of relationship that exist between logistics service provider and customer

- Insight into the strategic goals of logistics companies, attempting to develop higher value services and deeper customer relationships forged on intellectual capital rather than transport assets

- An examination of how collaboration between supply chain partners at a vertical and horizontal level can bring about economic and environmental benefits

Emergence of a global industry

The emergence of the contract logistics industry is driven by the level of development in an economy or, more specifically, the sophistication of its supply chains. As the world's economy continues to evolve through the development of global supply chains, the spread of contract logistics is being accelerated.

'Out-sourcing' has traditionally been perceived as the driver of the contract logistics sector. Large corporations have focused on 'core-competencies' and in many cases this has not included logistics. Many large retailers and manufacturers have sought to rid themselves of transport and warehousing assets, although to begin with (and still the case for some companies) many have been unwilling to lose control of the management of their logistics. This out-sourcing trend has been complemented by the need to manage global supply chains, resulting in a new structure to the logistics industry. Many logistics service providers' clients now look to them to provide management capabilities as well as transport and warehousing assets.

Globalization of industry has inevitably led to a globalized contract logistics market. Supply chains for many product types now stretch across the world driven by the dynamic of different value adding processes taking place in a diverse range of countries. This has had an enormous impact on logistics.

Company logistics systems are now not only more important strategically, but the nature of activities has also changed. The geographic reach of supply chains demands logistics concerned as much with coordination as access to physical resources. Issues such as inventory management have become more complex with product spread across world trading routes.

One of the salient characteristics of the larger LSPs in the sector has been their attempt to integrate freight forwarding into their business model. This is not new with companies such as the former Exel combining the two types of business in the late 1990s in order to serve customers in emerging production locations. None the less, this trend has accelerated with most major contract logistics companies having a freight forwarding business as well.

The origins of the contract logistics sector are quite parochial. Owing a good deal to specific market conditions in the UK in the late 1970s and early 1980s it grew, in part, out of the wish of grocery retailers and fast-moving consumer goods producers to improve return on capital.

However, it has since undergone a transformation. Although grocery retailing has remained important to the sector, a major driver of the business in the 1990s was the automotive sector in both Europe and North America. Yet this remained largely based on national industries. Large German car manufacturers approached the business of buying logistics services in a different manner from, say, Ford based in the UK. France was different again.

Towards the end of the 1990s this structure began to change, driven by the changes in supply chain management. Increasing numbers of Original Equipment Manufacturers (OEMs) in the automotive, electronics and also consumer goods sectors began to open plants in new production locations in Asia Pacific and Central Europe. Faced with underdeveloped transport markets they approached the existing 'third party' logistics companies to help them with logistics in these new locations. This started the trend towards a globalized contract logistics market.

Over the past few years the market for contract logistics has spread aggressively into parts of the world where previously it had been absent and these new markets are the major driver of growth.

The automotive logistics market is a good example of the change. Ford, for example, has developed its production facilities in areas such as South America, Turkey or South East Asia over the past 10 years. Although it has had assembly plants in countries such as Brazil for several decades, it has sought to improve the logistics operations in these plants by adopting the types of systems it has developed in its European and North American operations.

Key to doing this was bringing the LSPs it was using in Europe and North America into South America. So when Ford opened its new Brazilian plant at Camacari, Bahia in Brazil it brought in Exel (now DHL Supply Chain) to manage the plant's logistics. It is notable that this is an unusually comprehensive and close relationship. This illustrates that large customers such as Ford are more reliant on big LSPs in locations such as Brazil than they are in Western Europe and North America.

This trend has accelerated in the past decade and is very likely to continue to do so. The automotive sector may be a pioneer in terms of entering new markets, but it is being closely followed by other sectors. The Consumer Goods' sector regards emerging markets as being key to their present and future growth. However, the logistics infrastructure in many of these markets is poor.

Consequently, big manufacturers are receptive to global LSPs entering markets in the Middle East, Indian subcontinent, parts of South East Asia and to a lesser degree China, in order to support their businesses in the regions. This is particularly the case if LSPs construct physical infrastructure, notably warehousing, which is often in short supply. Other sectors are developing almost as rapidly, with electronic goods being a prominent sector.

The nature of this type of emerging market growth favours the bigger LSPs. They have the resources required both to establish a presence in these markets and they offer the depth and breadth of service that the big customers in these markets require.

The benefit of this market development for big LSPs is substantial. Not only are they offered the potential for much deeper – and therefore more profitable – relationships with customers, but they also have less competition. Markets in Western Europe and North America are highly competitive with the bigger LSPs often under pressure from mid-sized LSPs operating within their domestic economy. This pressure is markedly less in many emerging markets.

There is a tendency for some mid-sized LSPs to 'piggy-back' into new markets on big customers. An example of this is the German LSP Schnellecke, which has expanded into China on the back of Volkswagen business. This is possible when the client is willing to provide sufficient assurance of a contract to support the development of physical infrastructure.

Selecting the right logistics service provider

Supply chain services have been out-sourced for some time with contract distribution developed throughout the UK in the 1970s and 80s, with retailers leading the way. Initial out-sourcing was designed primarily to consolidate deliveries.

Choosing the right out-sourced logistics provider is one of the most critical steps that a manufacturer or retailer can take. It is now accepted that competitive advantage is achieved by having the best supply chain rather than just the best product and the consequences of getting it wrong can be catastrophic. Although the wider public only usually gets to hear about the success stories, there have been some well-documented supply chain disasters which have resulted in product left in warehouses rather than on the shelves.

In such cases it is the logistics provider that usually gets the blame, although the true responsibility must lie with the client. It is, therefore, not surprising that where experienced logistics suppliers do not exist (for example, in southern Europe) shippers are not keen on relinquishing control of a critical part of their business. Even in highly developed markets such as the UK, some specialist activities are still kept in-house as logistics suppliers have yet to develop the competency to deal with them.

Perhaps the most important part of the out-sourcing process is trust, as without it the relationship between client and supplier becomes adversarial and strained. In the worst case, the supplier will then start hiding mistakes, or the client will start to stretch the scope of the contract without advising the supplier.

The level of the logistics supplier's involvement will influence the point at which it is introduced into the sales process. Many clients will use a consultancy to undertake supply chain re-engineering, and then manage the tender process to find the logistics company with the best fit to the solution which has been developed. This type of approach often relegates the logistics providers input to providing rates for volumes on certain routes, with price a major factor in the decision-making process. For this reason many of the larger logistics companies are shunning the tender process as it diminishes their value add, and hence reduces their margins.

Some of the more proactive suppliers aim to contact potential targets at the beginning of the sales process, demonstrating the benefits that they could bring to the company in terms of inventory reduction.

This will also impact upon the type of contract that the client agrees with the supplier. Logistics companies can potentially make higher margins where there are elements of risk and reward in the makeup of the contract. However, when such agreements are made it is essential that they are backed up by objectivity and transparency of key performance indicators (KPIs). A breakdown of trust is inevitable if there is protracted wrangling over whether targets have or have not been met by the logistics supplier.

Most out-sourced contracts lie somewhere in between, with one of the biggest decisions for the client being whether to choose a dedicated or shared user solution. This will depend not only upon the volumes and scope of the operation, but also on the level of specialization required. For example, security is a major issue in certain high-value electronic sectors.

Having defined the overall out-sourcing strategy, the client is in a position to review the wide variety of suppliers in the market. The metrics against which they will draw up a potential shortlist range from the 'show-stoppers' to the 'nice to have'.

One of the first issues that the client will look at is the financial standing of a potential supplier. Given the critical nature of the logistics function to the client, it is essential that the logistics provider has a strong balance sheet, particularly in today's difficult economic environment. A company that has financial troubles is more likely to focus around its own problems than the needs of its clients. In a worst case scenario the failure of a logistics supplier could be catastrophic to its client.

Allied to this is the robustness of the supplier's management structure as well as the key points of contact that the client will have with the supplier. Communication will be fundamental to the success of the contract in overcoming the inevitable teething problems and it is important that the logistics supplier can demonstrate that it has in place the necessary systems for issue resolution. These must be backed up by commitment from senior management and assurances as to long-term allocation of account managers. Changing key personnel regularly is disruptive to the running of the contract, and is usually indicative of deeper rooted problems of staff turnover.

Another priority, albeit not completely essential, is the level of experience which the logistics supplier has in the client's sector. This provides a level of reassurance to the client that the supplier will not have to go through a learning process at their expense. It also means that the supplier will understand their needs and will be offering a similar price to that which is offered to its competitors. However, this is not necessarily the only option for clients. If they want to go beyond matching the performance of their peer group, they may be tempted to work with a logistics company with expertise in a different sector. This can introduce new levels of innovation and cost saving to a sector that may have become overly complacent. An example of this was the way in which Ford worked with UPS in the United States to bring the same level of efficiencies to the distribution of finished vehicles as barcoded packages.

A look 'behind the brochure' is also a prerequisite especially with multinational contracts. Few logistics suppliers are in a position to offer consistent levels of service across a range of geographies, despite claims. The client should look at the level of resources that the supplier has in each country; where applicable the agreements that it has in place with subcontractors or agents, and if feasible actually visit the operations and facilities on the ground.

Technology is also an important factor in making an out-sourcing decision. Many companies look to their logistics suppliers to provide them with the latest technology, which will save them from having to make the investment themselves. However, there is evidence that over the last five years technology has become less of a competitive advantage for logistics suppliers than it was. The number of companies with sufficiently competent IT capabilities has grown as the cost of the technology has reduced. Companies with highly specialist IT needs (a large multinational, for example) will often opt to keep the capabilities in-house to reduce reliance on a supplier. This will enable them to disengage more easily from a supplier at the termination of a contract.

Cultural issues must also be addressed in the out-sourcing process. The logistics supplier must demonstrate an awareness and understanding of the business philosophy of the potential client. Sensitivity to different working practices and the sharing of the same priorities is essential in making the relationship work.

Finally, and to many clients most importantly, is the issue of cost. However, although surveys continue to show that price is still the major factor in awarding contracts, undue emphasis on this element is misplaced. The potential for making savings throughout the total supply chain far outweighs squeezing the transport and warehousing element of the logistics system. Losing focus of other issues outlined above such as quality, innovation, technology and operations can be counterproductive. It can also reduce the process from a highly strategic exercise providing the company with competitive advantage to purely a cost-cutting exercise delivering short-term benefits only.

Financing contracts

One reason behind a company's decision to out-source its logistics to a third party is the desire to take assets off balance sheet and thereby free up capital to be invested in other areas of its business. This is not the case in every contract, as for instance many manufacturers and retailers actually prefer to own the distribution centres, whilst contracting out the activities (and the labour force). This decision is primarily taken for reasons of control, as it facilitates disengagement at the end of contracts. However, many other companies welcome the opportunity to effectively sell off these logistics assets.

A transfer of assets effectively means that the logistics provider becomes a provider of capital to its clients, a role to which it is not necessarily suited. The logistics provider is limited in the level and cheapness of funds it can provide to its client, and there are other specialists in the market who are much more competitive in terms of financing. For example, for vehicles, the truck manufacturers themselves have major finance divisions and for warehousing there are companies such as ProLogis and Goodman. LSPs now usually work in partnership with these specialists, effectively out-sourcing this element of its business in the same way as their clients have out-sourced their logistics requirements.

However, when the client requires it, logistics providers are able to take on this role as provider of capital, even though it will be more expensive than some other options. The industry as a whole has become more sophisticated in this role, especially at pricing the cost of capital into new contracts and making sure that when logistics assets are provided they limit the level of exposure. An example of this is making the lease of distribution centres co-terminous with contracts, reducing the level of assets on their balance sheets.

Logistics providers are still required to invest working capital in contracts, however, and this typically results in contracts being 'front-end loaded' with costs as shown in Figure 6.1. The costs incurred prior to the contract and at the outset will include elements such as information technology, supply chain solution design, project teams, facilities investment, etc.

Figure 6.1 Contract lifecycle costs

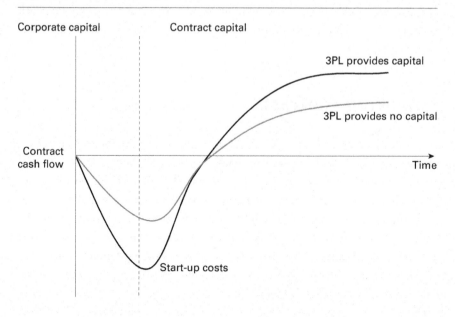

The greater these costs the longer the contract needs to be in order to pay back the investment and make a reasonable level of return. This is not so necessary where an open book contract is agreed, as these costs, and other running costs, are paid for directly by the client. However, where a closed book contract exists, the onus is on the logistics supplier to balance the risk and reward successfully. As also illustrated in the graphic, when the logistics company provides capital it should be seeking a greater return than if it did not.

Sales cycle times

Sales cycle times vary considerably depending on whether a logistics provider takes a 'product' or 'project' approach. A product, which has easily identifiable attributes, a repeatable format and a set price, should have a low sales lead time. An express parcel service or shared user network is an example of the product approach. Effectively, the client makes a decision to trade off flexibility and customized solutions against speed of implementation, and a lower price.

The project approach requires a much longer lead time to come to fruition. The client decides that its needs are so specific or of a magnitude that rules out sharing common attributes with other clients of the logistics provider, that it requires the development of a dedicated, customized solution. Owing to the size of the revenues involved in such a deal many logistics companies are keen to win such 'big ticket' contracts. However, there are many risks involved in pursuing this option rather than choosing to focus on selling low sales cycle time products.

One of the greatest risks is that the actual contract price does not fully reflect the true cost of all the resources that have been spent on winning the deal. In some cases it can take two years or more from point of first contact with the client to implementation of the logistics solution. In the intervening period teams of sales, finance, administrative, consultancy as well as implementation personnel will have worked on the deal in its various forms and iterations. Over such a long period it is inevitable that some key figures on both the client and provider side will change, which increases the likelihood of key elements of the solution requirements also changing. This increases the possibility of 'scope creep' (that is, changing parameters of the operation) and this has to be effectively managed by the logistics provider.

However, this form of sales approach is still preferred by many companies to the tendering procedure that many manufacturers and retailers adopt through the use of consultants. By working with the client at the very outset of the deal, the logistics provider has far more say in the eventual outcome, and it is able to develop value added elements which will increase its margins. Also after a long period of solution development it is unlikely that the client will be able to walk away from the eventual deal as this would mean starting from scratch with another provider and setting back implementation even further.

If their wish is to be able to pre-empt the tendering process, logistics companies need to have highly proactive sales forces which have been able to 'capture' the client at an early stage after it has made the initial decision to review its supply chain requirements. In order to assist with the targeting process, the most sophisticated sales divisions utilize financial analysis software, which allows them to identify potential clients who have the most to gain from supply chain innovation. Usually this takes the form of analysing the levels of inventory in a company's supply chain as well as cost of capital and comparing it with sector benchmarks. The logistics provider is therefore able to make a case for change and demonstrate the value that they can bring to the organization.

Contracts and relationships

One of the fundamental, perhaps defining, areas of contract logistics is the nature of the relationship between logistics service providers and customers. Relationships in this sector are very rarely on a fixed-price basis. Rather the contractual relationship between provider and customer can take several forms:

- Open book – this discloses all of the costs encountered by the LSP in fulfilling the contract and sets a fixed profit margin.
- Closed book – a set price for the contract is agreed and the LSP has to manage the costs.
- A compromise between the two (hybrid).

The management of these different contract types is fundamental to the success of any logistics service provider. In truth, although the above categories are extensively used to define business, contracts are very frequently bespoke to each customer and situation. For example, if an LSP has an existing facility in a locality, its cost structure is likely to be a competitive advantage and this may well be something it wishes to conceal from customers.

However, if a contract demands investment, it may wish to demonstrate to a customer the level of investment it is making, leading it to prefer an open book relationship. The success of any contract logistics provider really depends on its ability to manage this activity.

The variety of different business relationships results in a range of different operating profit margins. For instance, open book relationships often have very small margins (and limited upside for the supplier) as the LSP is not taking on much, if any, risk. The flip side of this is that neither do they have to invest in assets, which means that although profit margins may be thin, return on invested capital is high.

The corollary of this is that a closed book agreement may offer high margins if volumes are strong, but much lower return on investment as well as higher risks.

A 4PL relationship, as described below, may offer high margins as well as high returns on investment. However, the market for such services is relatively small, so profits in absolute terms will also be small, relative to the rest of the operations of the large LSPs.

Enhancing value through deeper relationships

Longer-term relationships between customer and logistics service provider afford a host of opportunities unavailable in a short-term, purely transactional relationship.

A major strategic goal of many transport companies has been to increase their engagement with clients and, as illustrated in Figure 6.2, deliver integrated logistics solutions that leverage their core-competencies, such as IT and intellectual skills.

Figure 6.2 Moving up the value chain

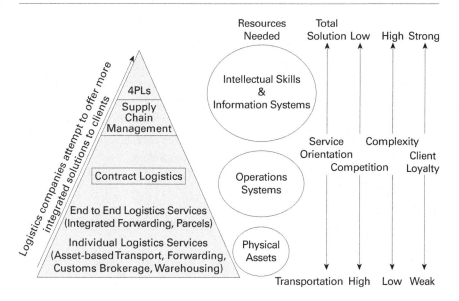

A deeper engagement allows a logistics company to better understand the needs of its client, and develop more innovative solutions. This, in turn, de-commoditizes its service offering, and increases its capacity to enhance margins.

However, one of the major challenges that asset owning logistics companies have to overcome is the innate tension between the need to utilize their assets efficiently, and the need to optimize a solution for its client. A 4PL, a term first coined by consultancy Accenture, was originally developed as a completely asset-free solutions provider, although the concept in its purest form has never really taken off. Most shippers expect their logistics providers to own assets although at the same time they are suspicious that the solution that they develop will be in the logistics provider's interest and not their own.

There have been some successful examples of 4PL relationships, but these have tended to be hybrid – a combination of the logistics providers' operations, assets, technology and networks together with a range of third-party providers. The case study below of Shell and Accenture is an example where a 'pure play' asset light 4PL arrangement has worked. The second case study, of UPS Worldwide Logistics, is an example of a logistics company developing a 4PL operation.

CASE STUDY   Shell and Accenture's 4PL partnership

Multinational oil and gas company Shell was seeking a new way to manage its upstream logistics due to a changing market environment, increasingly intensified materials requirements and a growing focus on the safety aspect of transportation. This required a greater visibility of its supply chain as well as planning and reporting capabilities. This was especially the case owing to the project nature of much of its needs, which meant that in many examples parallel logistics operations had been put in place run by separate logistics contractors.

These factors had resulted in:

- lost operational synergy;
- rising transportation costs;
- project delays;
- higher exposure to risk.

Shell engaged consultancy Accenture to design and implement a new model to support Shell's upstream logistics, which involved the use of a 4PL to manage a range of LSPs to undertake the execution.

Accenture undertook a project to analyse existing operations and shape an overall vision for Shell. The 4PL solution it developed became known as Logistics Management Services (LMS) within Shell. Accenture then helped Shell with the choice of 3PLs that would be used within the 4PL solution.

Part of the challenge was to build a single solution that would be flexible enough to meet the needs of local teams, bring together existing in-house expertise with the experience and knowledge of a 4PL provider and its LSPs.

The scope of the solution included meeting the needs of diverse projects around the world including the development of a drilling project in a remote gas field requiring the movement of large volumes and materials from China at short notice.

Benefits

Accenture claims that Shell was able to reduce logistics costs by up to 25 per cent through improved logistics utilization and integrated supply chain planning. It also saw higher service levels and reduced supply chain risk through better safety planning. Other benefits included the ability to leverage industry specialists to augment Shell's own experts and the implementation of better reporting and analytics.

CASE STUDY   UPS Worldwide Logistics

One of the earliest logistics providers to adopt the 4PL model was, perhaps surprisingly, UPS. Overwhelmingly known at that time in the 1990s as an asset-heavy parcels delivery company, management recognized that major opportunities lay in expanding the services it offered into other parts of the logistics industry. The company enjoyed strong customer relationships amongst a blue chip client base (albeit mostly in the United States) but it recognized that most flows of goods fell outside its parcels network capabilities.

Rather than attempting to build up a traditional logistics operation, thereby competing with market leaders such as DHL (at the time Exel and Tibbett & Britten), the company decided to focus on its strengths of brand, intellectual capital and information technology capabilities. A subsidiary, UPS Worldwide Logistics, was established at an arm's length from the parcels operation to provide neutrality, assuring customers that any solution developed would utilize the services of 'best-of-breed' logistics companies, most suited for the geographies or capabilities required, rather than funnel volumes through the network of UPS's parcels network.

Working for global companies such as Cisco and IBM, the proposition was highly successful. Developing cutting-edge supply chain visibility tools and managing a range of 3PLs (including administration such as quality management and freight payment), brought about significant cost savings (25 per cent +) in terms of transport spend and allowed customers to implement distribution centre by-pass schemes through merge-in-transit, drop ship and crossdock of shipments.

The operation was asset-light, which meant that there were high levels of return on investment for the parent company. However, there were also challenges. Many potential customers could not be convinced that UPS Worldwide Logistics would act independently of its parcel delivery sister-company. Also, for many used to the traditional 3PL business model, the concept was too difficult to come to terms with. Although in theory the benefits were obvious for both customer and logistics company, in practice the market was very small and the sales cycle lead time for selling and developing solutions very long (sometimes more than 18 months). This meant that although the 4PL business could be very profitable, it only ever remained niche, and for ambitious companies looking at making more of an impression in the global logistics market the model has remained incidental to their mainstream business.

Collaboration within supply chains – the role of a 3PL

The term 'collaboration' can be used to describe partnerships between different types of companies at many supply chain levels. However, in this context it refers to cooperative relationships between manufacturers, merging their shipment volumes and distribution networks to achieve a range of logistics' efficiencies, often facilitated by a contract logistics provider.

One of the most compelling reasons why collaboration is an important supply chain initiative is that it has been shown to bring fast and measurable benefits, and is relatively cheap – an important factor in a harsh market environment.

Within the warehouse environment, combining inventories can increase distribution centre utilization. It has been used to good effect when, for example, a supply chain re-engineering project has resulted in the reduction of stock held at centralized facilities. This then leaves an underutilized warehouse, which usually has to be disposed of, incurring property and employee costs. By inviting another manufacturer to share the premises, these costs are avoided and efficiencies are increased.

On the transportation side, there are also benefits. By co-loading shipments there are obvious synergies to be gained, especially where the product is being distributed to similar retail outlets. However, collaboration not only benefits warehousing and transportation operations. It can also enhance customer service by providing a critical mass, which allows increased frequency of deliveries. That is to say, shippers do not have to weigh up the benefits of increasing the number of consignments to customers against the cost of dispatching half-empty vehicles. Co-loading with a partner ensures that vehicle breakeven points are met.

The last major benefit in terms of bottom line is the leverage that shippers can gain in terms of negotiating freight rates. Consolidating shipment volumes can ensure small and medium-sized manufacturers can compete in the market on the same basis as larger rivals.

Collaboration also has important environmental benefits, which today must rank as importantly as financial and operational.

The European Commission has estimated that 30 per cent of the distance travelled by goods vehicles are with the truck empty. This equates to 33.5 billion euros worth of fuel and between 20 and 30 million tonnes of carbon dioxide. Collaboration has the potential to mitigate this enormous problem in a number of ways:

- reducing congestion by better utilizing the vehicles deployed;
- enabling modal shift by creating unit loads through consolidation of shipments;
- encouraging sustainable distribution networks and partnerships;
- reducing waste.

Collaboration works best if the products and distribution profiles of the collaborating companies are similar. Even if the products themselves do not need to be identical, it certainly helps if handling characteristics, lifecycles, inventory velocity and seasonality as well as environmental control and security needs are compatible.

Some examples of successful collaboration include the following:

- Global consumer goods giants Kimberly Clark and Unilever have collaborated to build a joint warehouse to supply retailers' distribution centres in the Netherlands.
- Reckitt Benckiser, Johnson and Johnson and Colgate-Palmolive manage a facility in Unna, Germany, to distribute goods on a shared user basis.
- In France, Reckitt Benckiser, Kimberly Clark and Colgate-Palmolive cooperate in another distribution centre operation.
- In the UK, competitors Goodyear Dunlop and Continental operate a tyre distribution centre in Birmingham managed by a 3PL. The project was driven by the manufacturers who realized the majority of goods were destined for the same dealers.

However, there are reasons why collaboration can be difficult to achieve in practice. It can be difficult to find suitable partners with whom to work. To aid the process, cross-industry forums have developed – such as ELUPEG – which foster discussions between manufacturers, consultancies and logistics providers.

For any partnership to be long-lasting, the allocation of the cost savings as well as any costs involved in establishing the venture needs to be seen to be fair. This will involve an openness which again may challenge many companies.

Although collaboration is considered to be a 'cheap' supply chain initiative, there may be investment needed, depending on the complexity of the relationship. For example, information and communication technology investments may be required, to enable data-sharing.

Finally, if a company sees its supply chain as a competitive advantage, then it may be best not to collaborate with a competitor. Collaboration will bring benefits, but also nullifies advantages. Therefore, whilst providing cost savings, it may well additionally improve a competitor's speed to market, customer service and inventory levels. In this case it may be better to collaborate with a complementary product manufacturer instead.

The role of the logistics provider in collaboration

A major challenge is finding a partner that can facilitate collaboration and act as an independent facilitator. The role, which can be undertaken by a logistics provider, may involve promoting the concept, identifying partners, quantifying the benefits, managing data (for confidentiality reasons as well as operational) and operations themselves.

If competing companies are collaborating there may well be anti-trust issues involved. And in fact this makes the role of the LSP even more important to act as a 'Chinese wall', as it might be termed.

CASE STUDY   Collaboration in practice

One example that can be cited, showing that the business model has implications for all sectors, is presently in operation in the Netherlands. Here, the Healthcare Logistics Forum (HLF) has been established for several years, including such companies as Abbott Laboratories, Boston Scientific and Baxter Healthcare plus 17 others.

The forum has already undertaken collaborative projects including bench-marking, consolidation and cold chain development. One initiative that has resulted from discussion in the HLF involves manufacturers located in the same area consolidating their line haul shipments to a carrier distribution centre.

Interestingly, the pharmaceutical industry is unlikely to embrace collaboration with companies from other sectors. The logistics requirements are precise, and include high regard for temperature control, supply chain visibility and security. The people dealing with pharmaceutical products need to be highly trained, and this mitigates against multi-sector shared user networks.

Therefore, in this case it makes a lot of sense to share the costs of specialized logistics and transportation operations with other companies in the same sector, especially when they are so high.

It can also be observed that pharma manufacturers see their competitive advantage lying with product differentiation rather than supply chain. Consequently, on this level, horizontal collaboration with a competitor also makes more sense.

In a different context, it has been suggested that in the future a 'neutral' healthcare logistics campus could be one way in which manufacturers and hospitals could combine to improve efficiency of distribution. This could be an excellent way in which healthcare budgets could be reduced, without compromising on product availability.

Summary

The development of the global contract logistics industry has come about due to the widespread adoption of the management concept of out-sourcing. This trend has been compounded by the increased importance of supply chain management to retailers and manufacturers. This chapter examined the way in which a logistics service provider is selected by a customer; the attributes a logistics company must exhibit; the typical sales process and the various commercial relationships that can develop. In addition, it looked at how deeper relationships can enhance value between customer and logistics supplier.

Key points to consider:

- Although the contract logistics industry has its roots in the UK retail industry of the 1970s, it has now spread throughout the world and has been adopted widely in all other sectors and markets.

- It has allowed road hauliers in particular to develop stronger and deeper links with customers, moving away from transactional relationships to ones that are more contractual and value adding.

- The market is growing strongly in developing markets, although a dearth of Western sophisticated providers in these regions has put a drag on its development.

- Logistics service providers who want to maximize value from their solutions should proactively approach customers before they get to the competitive tender stage.

- There is a risk to many providers in the retail and consumer sector that margins will be eroded by contract 'churn' as customers focus on logistics cost reduction.

European road freight

07

CHAPTER LEARNING OBJECTIVES

This chapter will provide the reader with:

- A segmentation of the European road freight sector, in terms of service provision, type of goods moved and asset ownership
- An analysis of the business models employed and their respective strengths and weaknesses
- The link between road freight output and economic growth
- The cost structure of a typical road haulage company
- An analysis of the links between the cost of oil, profitability and company failure
- A definition of cabotage and its impact on the European market

The structure of the European road freight industry

The European road freight industry can be segmented in several different ways. The following are some of the most common.

'Own account' and 'hire and reward'

Also known as 'in-house' and 'third party' this categorization draws a distinction between road haulage carried out by a manufacturer or retailer for its own products on its own vehicles and that undertaken by a professional provider for a range of clients. This distinction was previously recognized by many countries in law with own account operators having a lower regulatory burden than hire and reward.

In Europe, the latest Eurostat figures show that for most of the key European countries own account operators comprise between 15 and 30 per cent of the overall market, with hire and reward operators providing the remainder. By far most own account haulage takes place on a local basis (less than 50 kilometres) with specialist haulage companies undertaking movements with a longer average distance. For international movements, their share of the market is in excess of 90 per cent.

The out-sourcing trend for transport varies on a country-by-country basis. Germany has shown the highest out-sourcing growth rates. Since 1999 the number of vehicle tonnes/kilometre undertaken in-house has dropped by 21 per cent. However, in the UK and in Spain, the reverse is true, with the in-house market growing.

There are several reasons why companies retain control of their own transport fleets. In some cases it is because management views haulage as a key competence or at least too important to entrust to a third-party haulier. There are also times when their needs are highly specific and specialist vehicles or operations are required (for example, some types of chemicals or fragile goods such as sheet glass). However, the most frequently cited reason is that on many occasions deliveries can be undertaken more cheaply by an in-house fleet rather than by an external hire and reward operator.

Conversely, there are many benefits from using a third-party haulier. Asset ownership is transferred, reducing the level of investment in a function that many companies believe to be non-core. Road hauliers can also bring with them expertise in information technology and people management. Using a shared network rather than dedicated will also bring benefits in terms of cost reductions.

Segment by operation

Less than Truck Load (LTL)/groupage networks

Less than Truck Load (LTL) operators (also known as groupage operators) undertake the collation of consignments from a number of different sources to make up a full vehicle load. Services often depart on a set schedule, and therefore it is down to the operator to sell capacity on the vehicle in much the same way as a scheduled air cargo carrier sells space on its aircraft. LTL services take place on a point-to-point basis, with distribution of the consignments taking place from the destination hub. The market is highly competitive owing to extreme fragmentation and, consequently, margins are low. Asset intensity can be low, due to the predominance of using sub-contractors to undertake line haul (or 'trunking') although some investment is required in facilities.

A more recent development has been that of national and European networks. These largely replicate the systems used to move parcels, except they are capable of moving much larger weights. They work on a hub and spoke system, with local hauliers delivering consignments into regional hubs. Shipments are then moved between hubs, usually overnight. The advantage of using a network rather than a point-to-point system is the increased frequency that they provide. However, they require a critical mass of consignments to be viable and this has favoured the major players such as Schenker and DHL Freight.

The development of European road freight networks has come as a response to a number of macro-economic trends. The Single European Market (SEM) has enabled the seamless movement of goods crossborder and this has allowed the network concept to develop. Prior to the removal of border controls, customs delays were endemic, which resulted in unreliable transit times. Secondly, the SEM has enabled manufacturers to establish pan-European distribution models, which have reinforced crossborder supply. Networks with intensive coverage can also provide a way in which to mitigate the effects of the European Working Time Directive (WTD). Driving time will be reduced, which will require shorter trip distances between delivery points.

Full Truck Load (FTL)

A Full Truck Load is defined as any consignment that fills a whole truck. Operators usually undertake the movement of truckloads on a point-to-point basis, direct to the customer from the consignor. This requires less sophistication of operation, as there is less administration and fewer clients moving larger loads. Many of the larger players offer both services to clients.

In between LTL and FTL there is a further classification of Part Load or Semi-Truck Load (STL). This bears more of the characteristics of the FTL model than LTL, with each vehicle undertaking a small number of drops.

Segment by speciality

Further segments exist by categorizing the road freight market by speciality equipment:

- temperature controlled (for example, refrigerated, frozen and thermo);
- bulk (for example, liquid, powder);
- air cushioned (for example, high-tech sector);
- finished vehicle transporters.

In each of these cases, a distinct industry segment has developed with highly specialized operating practices. This provides some level of differentiation from the rest of the market, to some extent reducing competitive pressures.

Segment by geography

Road haulage can be further segmented on the basis of the geographic scope.

Intra-regional and local transport

Most road haulage takes place on this basis under 50 kilometres.

Inter-regional or national

Fewer goods volumes are moved on a region-to-region or national basis. This, therefore, requires a (relatively) more sophisticated groupage or part load operation to make operations economically viable.

International

Only a small volume of consignments are shipped internationally. Prior to the Single European Market, international shipments required documentation, which increased complexity and administration. Now barriers to market entry are very low in terms of technical capabilities, and this has encouraged hauliers from Central and Eastern Europe to take market share (especially when bidding for return loads).

Segment by consignment attribute

The parcels sector is increasingly important to the transport industry, not least with the emergence of e-commerce. The sector is dealt with in more detail in Chapter 8.

Parcel (<35 kilograms)

There is no single definition of a 'parcel' in terms of weight. However, materials handling equipment in sorting hubs is designed to move shipments less than around 35 kilograms in weight. There are also difficulties off-loading heavier consignments by hand.

Pallet (unitized shipment <35 kilograms)

The pallet has revolutionized the movement of goods in the road freight sector in much the same way as the container did for the shipping sector. It is a convenient way of unitizing goods in a form that facilitates movement by materials handling equipment (for example, front lift trucks).

In recent years, 'pallet networks' have developed using advances in materials handling technology to treat pallets in much the same way as parcels. The UK has been at the forefront of this trend, which is now spreading throughout Europe. The result has been the development of hub and spoke operations, with next day delivery the industry standard.

Segment by service attribute

A further method of defining the market is by the level of service that can be offered by road hauliers for either parcels or freight. Supply chain compression has driven trends towards same and next day delivery.

Express (day-definite or time-definite)

Express companies usually undertake to deliver consignments by a specified day and even by a specified time. In Europe and domestically, 'express' usually means next working day. Some companies have a more stringent definition: to qualify as express it must be delivered in the morning of the following day.

Standard (non-time-definite)

Where price is more important than time, delivery is usually on a non-specific two to three days basis or longer and the service is also referred to as 'deferred' or 'standard'.

Segment by company size

Smaller trucking companies make up most of the market, particularly in terms of the number of vehicles owned. Most individual truck operators are small firms, either operating as 'owner-drivers' or owning fewer than 10 vehicles.

Although they are exposed to most aspects of the market, their position is quite different from the medium and larger companies. It is rare for them to have direct contact with large customers. Rather, they rely on the larger companies as intermediaries. Indeed, it is difficult for many of the owner-drivers or small companies to fulfil the requirements of customers, in terms of systems development.

To a greater or lesser extent, the smaller companies are increasingly a physical asset resource for the large network transport providers to draw on. This structure has emerged, in part, due to the willingness of these smaller companies to accept low returns on their assets. Traditionally, the supply of truck capacity from smaller providers has outstripped demand for their services, pushing down returns. Whether this will continue is unknown. The poor margins from the provision of physical trucks services has led to low wages and poor conditions, and the logical extrapolation is that the supply of smaller companies will decline. This has not happened yet, but there are some signs that it could happen in the near future.

Figure 7.1 Size of transport and warehousing enterprises by employment (EU27, 2011)

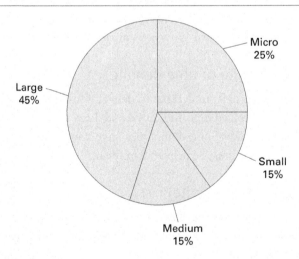

SOURCE: Eurostat (2012)

Segment by level of asset ownership

The road freight market can also be divided between asset-owning companies ('road hauliers') and those that manage subcontracted road hauliers ('ground freight forwarders'). Although in most cases there is some element of crossover between the two categories, the market forces affecting each are very different.

There are arguments both in favour and against asset ownership. Many of the largest companies such as DSV and Schenker decided specifically to reduce the number of vehicles that they own in order to utilize subcontractors. There are a number of reasons for this, which have become compelling in recent years.

For those companies that have pursued the asset-light approach, the benefits are:

Flexibility

One of the major benefits of using a subcontracted fleet is the increased level of flexibility that this allows. If a company is able to build a large supplier pool it is better able to match supply against demand. This means it is always able to cope with peaks in demand without the need to maintain a fleet of vehicles that are underutilized at certain times of year.

Employee costs

With the increase in the payroll and social costs associated with employees, haulage companies have been keener to use self-employed subcontractors. This limits the company's liability in respect of a whole range of regulations and responsibilities including holiday entitlement, working hours, tax as well as redundancy and severance pay.

Asset costs

A further compelling reason for the use of subcontractors is the positive effect on companies' balance sheets. Asset-light companies are able to provide a much higher return on capital employed, as subcontractors' operating costs are regarded as 'above the line', a factor which is very important for many shareholders. The subcontractor effectively provides the capital on behalf of the contracting company. Although in theory the subcontractor should be able to build the cost of the capital into its pricing, there is little doubt that in practice this does not happen.

Maintenance and repair

As part of the responsibilities of the subcontractor, the roadworthiness of their vehicle must be ensured in order to comply with legislation. Any downtime whilst the vehicle is off road is cost absorbed by the subcontractor.

Counter-cyclical model

As mentioned above, for the asset-light model to work effectively, there must be a large pool of suppliers that can be tapped by the contractor. With very few barriers to market entry and exit this pool has been augmented in recent years especially in times of economic downturn. With high levels of unemployment in many countries, the prospect of self-employment with the relatively low investment in transport assets required has allowed this model to flourish. What is more, contracting companies have benefited from the low levels of commercial awareness of these new market entrants. With relatively few exceptions, owner-drivers are less able to build into their pricing the full life costs of their vehicles including depreciation. Most are more likely to set their prices too low in a bid to win business rather than at the rate that the market will actually stand. Likewise they are less able to respond to increasing costs, which often erode whatever profits they are making. Finally, they are likely to work for an income that they would never sanction from a formal employer whilst not placing funds in reserve for the renewal of the vehicle at the end of its life, maintenance costs or even tax liabilities.

Inevitably, this basic inability to deal with commercial reality leads to a high turnover or 'churn' in the supplier pool as businesses become non-viable. However, whilst those dropping out are replaced by new owner-drivers at a comparable rate, the subcontracted model will continue to operate.

As a corollary to this situation, the costs of subcontracting rise during times of economic upturn. Subcontractors become scarcer as higher-paid employment is available elsewhere, and therefore rates rise leading to what has been termed a counter-cyclical market. This is discussed at greater length below.

Business risk

One of the risks to using subcontractors is the possibility that the end client may approach the subcontractor directly. Although this is unlikely to happen where the contractor has sufficiently differentiated its offering from its smaller suppliers (as in the case of the large European networks such as Schenker and DHL Freight), this is a constant problem for local or regional operators.

For those companies that have invested heavily in assets, there are also benefits.

Availability of supply

One of the greatest benefits is the reliability of supply, which can be ensured through the ownership of vehicles and employment of drivers. Subcontractors may work for a number of other clients and will not necessarily be available whenever required. (The best asset-light operators will utilize a large pool of suppliers with an element of built-in redundancy). At peaks of demand there is more likely to be a problem with supply as subcontractor capacity will be at its lowest.

Reliability of supply

For many companies to make a profit, the asset-light model relies on 'burning out' suppliers who do not pass on the full costs of their operations. This can result in vehicle failure or longer than necessary downtime. Companies that run their own vehicles can ensure that sufficient maintenance is carried out or, in fact, have their own in-house workshops.

Quality of personnel and vehicles

The role of the driver is crucial to how a company is perceived by its clients and to the public at large. Companies can ensure that their workforce is fully trained to appropriate levels as regards both driving skills and customer contact. The state of the vehicle being used is also important as regards how the brand of the contracting company is perceived.

Route knowledge

Although transport telematic systems have grown in sophistication, any haulage companies rely on the knowledge of their drivers to ensure fast and efficient navigation on a local, national or regional basis. Maintaining this level of training is easier when drivers are working consistently on the same routes. This is certainly possible with subcontractors, but it requires developing longer and deeper relationships with them.

Asset utilization

Companies that employ multiple drivers have the opportunity to more efficiently utilize their transport assets by ensuring longer periods of vehicle usage. This can be achieved by using several drivers for a single vehicle, ensuring round the clock usage after any one driver has used up the allotted working time.

Cost of capital

In the late 1980s, there were double-digit interest rates, which meant that repayments on money borrowed to invest in assets were very high. Occurring at the time of dramatic falls in volumes, this led to large numbers of corporate failures driven by companies' inability to downsize quickly enough. However, in recent years interest rates across Europe have been at historic lows, which has meant that owning or leasing vehicles has become much more attractive. Large companies have been able to acquire capital for investment at a more competitive rate than smaller subcontractors, providing them with one of the few economies of scale apparent in the industry.

Defensive business model

Those companies with their own fleets are less vulnerable to the impact of tightening capacity on prices during increases in volumes. Whilst asset-light companies end up being squeezed between their suppliers and clients unwilling to absorb the full cost of price rises, owned-fleet operators are not so badly affected in terms of margin erosion.

Of course, in reality, many road hauliers and ground-based freight forwarders operate a mixture of the two models. Subcontractors are used to augment owned operations, called in on an as-and-when-required basis.

European road freight market landscape

As detailed above, the road freight sector is not one single structure. Rather, it is divided up into a number of different segments that may overlap, yet operate distinctly different patterns and serve different customer types.

The big players in the market are the international network transport providers. These are generally described as 'less-than-trailer' providers, although most of them also provide 'full load' services. Fundamentally, these companies are characterized by the use of extensive pan-European networks of cross-docks, which enable truck capacity to be optimized. These include DSV, Kuehne + Nagel, DHL, DB Schenker, TNT and XPO Logistics.

Establishing such networks is demanding in terms of capital, increasing the entry barriers to the sector and making it very difficult for smaller companies to compete. Essentially, these companies offer economies of scale, to complex patterns of freight. The offer of higher frequency services and small batch sizes, at an economic cost, is highly attractive and these types of services are gradually winning market share. These companies tend to be less active and competitive in national and regional markets, where smaller, medium-sized carriers are better able to compete.

Generally, networked providers use smaller truck operators as subcontractors, to supply trucks for their system. In many cases, more than 90 per cent of vehicle capacity is provided by these subcontractors. The attraction of using subcontractors is the ability to work assets hard, as well as flexibly. In effect, it exploits the over-supply of trucks and the willingness of smaller companies to get poor returns on their assets.

Medium-sized trucking companies are markedly different. Although they may offer networked services covering smaller geographies, the structure of their business is often focused on 'full load' services. These tend to serve medium to large customers, with a demand for services of a higher quality and larger scale. For example, large OEMs may have extensive supply chains that require a dedicated service that is sufficiently sophisticated to provide visibility in consignment tracking or integrity of materials handling.

Road freight is one of the most fragmented sectors of the transport and logistics market. The large supply of owner-operators and smaller providers, with tiny overheads and margins, limits opportunities for market dominance by big players. The economic crises of the past few years have made operating in a challenging market exceptionally tough, particularly for small/medium-sized players although larger players have shown more resilience.

Drivers of growth

Much research in the past decade has been dedicated to analysing links between road freight sector output and economic performance. As part of their sustainable transport policies, governments in Europe have been keen to find ways of breaking the link between economic growth and road freight output. However, according to research carried out by Transport Intelligence, comparing GDP and tonne/kilometre growth over the last seven years, there is still a fairly strong correlation, as can be seen from Figure 7.2. Road freight is usually measured in 'tonne kilometres' as, by combining the weight of freight lifted with a distance coefficient, it gives a truer indication of industry output than purely weight or distance alone.

1 tonne km = 1 tonne × 1 km

Figure 7.2 Year-on-year economic growth (GDP) and road freight output
(tonne kilometres)

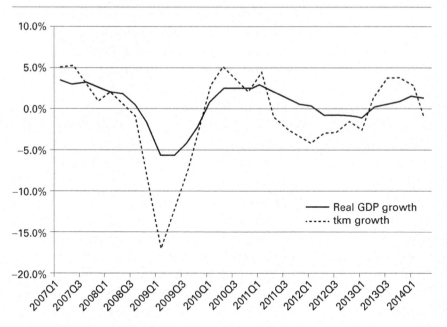

SOURCE: Transport Intelligence/Eurostat (2016)

One of the problems with the broader data, is that they cover areas of the economy that are not intensive users of road freight. Banking is a good example of this and is a sector that contributes to the volatility seen in the wider GDP numbers. An even better correlation is seen when looking at the activity levels of sectors of the economy that are likely to be major users of road freight, such as the manufacturing and construction sectors (see Figure 7.3).

Another important driver of the freight industry has been transit traffic. This has been due to the advent of the Single European Market and then the accession of the Central and Eastern European countries to the EU. This increased considerably the level of transit traffic, not least because manufacturing became integrated on a regional rather than national basis. Increased production in countries such as Poland and the Czech Republic was often fed by tiers of suppliers located elsewhere in the EU. Centralization of stock holding also became a key supply chain strategy, and this balance of inventory versus transport has characterized the European logistics industry for the past two decades.

Not all markets have been so affected. At the periphery, the UK, for example, has largely missed out on the impact of transit traffic.

Figure 7.3 Manufacturing and construction growth and road freight output (tonne kilometres)

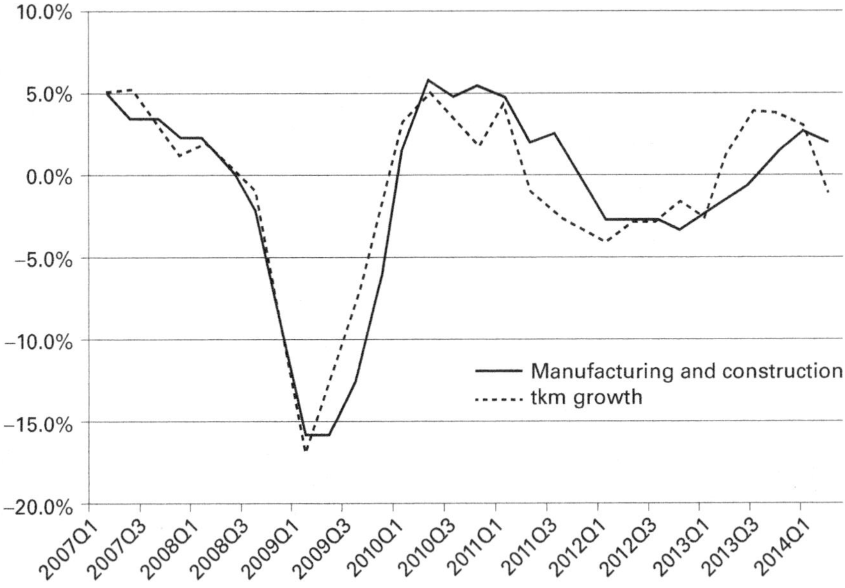

SOURCE: Transport Intelligence/Eurostat (2016)

Cost structures

Even in economies with high labour costs, fuel generally comprises a greater proportion of overall costs than those related to the driver (see Figure 7.4). This could vary if fuel continues to fall very significantly. However, it is important to note that diesel attracts very substantial non-deductible taxes, which can mitigate any price fall. It should also be noted that these numbers were generated before the major fall in oil prices at the end of 2014.

Costs do vary, to a degree, around Europe. For example, toll costs in Italy and France are more substantial than those in the UK and Germany. Of greater importance is the impact of lower labour/driver costs in Central European economies. These costs, both direct and indirect, are often around, or less than, half of those in Western Europe.

The differences in cost profile are important for understanding market structures. Western European truck operators have superior access to their home markets, where these higher costs can be sustained. However, international routes, along with the related cabotage activities seen in Central Europe, are more competitive (as discussed below).

Figure 7.4 Average cost structure per truck 2013 (Germany)

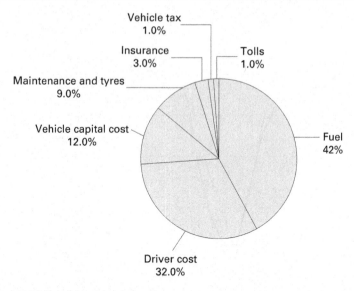

SOURCE: Comité du Routier Nationale (2015)

Road freight rates

Using a Road Freight Price Index provided by Eurostat, it can be seen that European road freight rates have surpassed the peak seen in 2008, just prior to the recession-related downturn (see Figure 7.5). Rates have steadily increased since the worst of the economic crisis but plateaued and even dropped in 2015, due, no doubt, to the ongoing economic weakness in the region.

Fuel costs constitute an important proportion of freight transport operators' costs. Since the lowest point of the recession in 2009 there has been a steady increase in the cost of diesel. The UK remains the most expensive market, 25 per cent more costly than Spain. The impact of the falling world oil price on European diesel pump prices can be seen in Figure 7.6.

It is generally assumed that rising fuel costs are not helpful for road freight operators, as they find it difficult to pass on these charges to customers. Generally, the increases are handled better by the larger players,

Figure 7.5 Road Freight Price Index – EU (28)

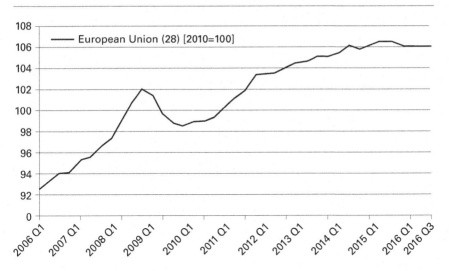

SOURCE: European Commission (2016)

Figure 7.6 European diesel prices

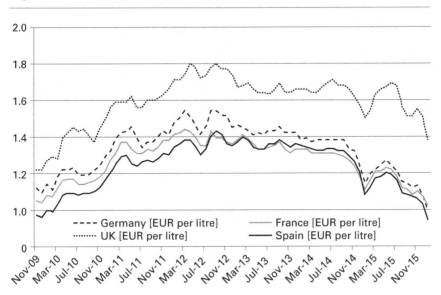

SOURCE: European Commission (2016)

Figure 7.7 The link between fuel costs and freight rates

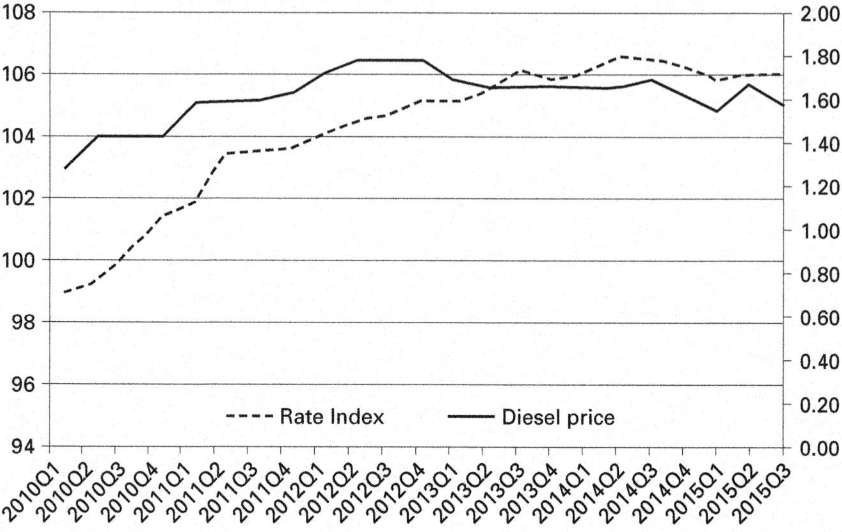

SOURCE: Transport Intelligence (2016)

many of whom have agreements in place, which result in surcharges being passed on directly. Smaller players either do not have these mechanisms in place or do not have the bargaining power to increase their rates in line with fuel pump costs.

One way in which it is possible to test how well freight operators are able to pass on fuel cost increases to their customers is by examining the correlation between fuel costs and rates (see Figure 7.7). If rates rise in line with changes in the price of diesel it could be concluded that freight operators are successfully passing on these costs to their customers. In fact, from the high correlation (0.78) this does indeed seem to be the case.

This is not to say that freight operators do not bear any pain. There are significant cash flow implications (especially for medium-sized or small players, which have to outlay significant sums of money upfront for diesel fuel). The greater the proportion of their cost base that fuel makes up, the larger the problem, as it can take up to 90 days for a haulier to recoup from customers the amounts paid out.

However, despite this, as we shall see in the next section, fuel costs do not play a significant role in company failures.

Profitability and company failure

The rising cost of fuel is one of the biggest political issues that transport operators and governments face. In the UK it was the reason for a wave of fuel strikes in the early 2000s, with operators making the point that increases in the oil price through market forces and taxation were driving companies out of the market.

However, in reality there seems little evidence for this. Using official company failure statistics from the UK government and a diesel pump price index there does not seem to be a link between fuel costs and company failures (see Figure 7.8). The correlation coefficient is −0.4, which indicates a negative correlation. A strong positive correlation would have been expected if indeed the price of oil were a major factor in transport company bankruptcies (that is, an increase of diesel would be expected to result in an increase in company failures).

In reality, the reasons behind company failure in the sector are far more complex. For example, many road freight operators are highly leveraged, leasing road transport assets or borrowing finance to buy them outright. Hence, fluctuations in interest rates have far more of an impact.

Figure 7.8 Index of company failures and diesel fuel price

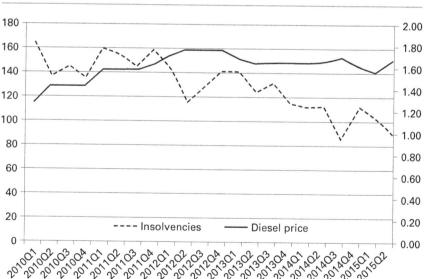

SOURCE: Transport Intelligence/Eurostat (2016)

The present low interest rate environment may well be one of the key reasons why company failures are around half of what they were six years ago.

In addition, research has shown that there is a strong link between the level of freight volumes, operating margins and bankruptcies. In the present economic environment, volumes are reasonably robust, which combines with low interest rates to create a benign market for road freight operators.

The reasons for this are clear. Freight operators are able to make money once a 'breakeven' point has been reached on each vehicle or on a network. This breakeven factor is, of course, influenced by input costs and freight rates. Research seems to show that operators are good at managing the breakeven point by passing on costs to customers through higher rates. However, they are less able to control volumes, especially when the industry is impacted by wider economic crisis. This seems to be the major reason behind fluctuations in profit margins.

Frustratingly, visibility on the profitability of the rest of the sector is minimal. In keeping with the fragmented nature of the road freight supply side, medium and small companies are frequently privately owned. This makes it difficult to assess the success of the various business models. Indeed, inadequate visibility is probably an internal issue for these companies. Setting accurate pricing structures that reflect the cost of assets has to be key to their business model, yet it is questionable whether many participants actually do this. Indeed, it is the low yield on fixed assets (trucks) that smaller companies receive that is causing large network providers to rely on subcontracting transport services to such a great extent. It is likely that smaller providers only receive a return at the cost of capital on their assets (which in many cases are leased), whilst other cost drivers are also charged at less than could be delivered by the larger companies. There is a strong possibility that the highly fragmented nature of the road freight market not only drives down the costs to an economic equilibrium, but even goes beyond this, to deliver a de facto subsidy to freight buyers. That the margins of the large providers are still so modest in these conditions, strongly illustrates that the market is ruthlessly competitive.

There are deviations to this model. For example, Norbert Dentressangle (now XPO) operates a higher proportion of own account vehicles and its margin is better than many others (see Figure 7.9). However, this is in part to do with good design of routes, for example between the UK and France.

Figure 7.9 Profit margins of selected road freight networks 2014

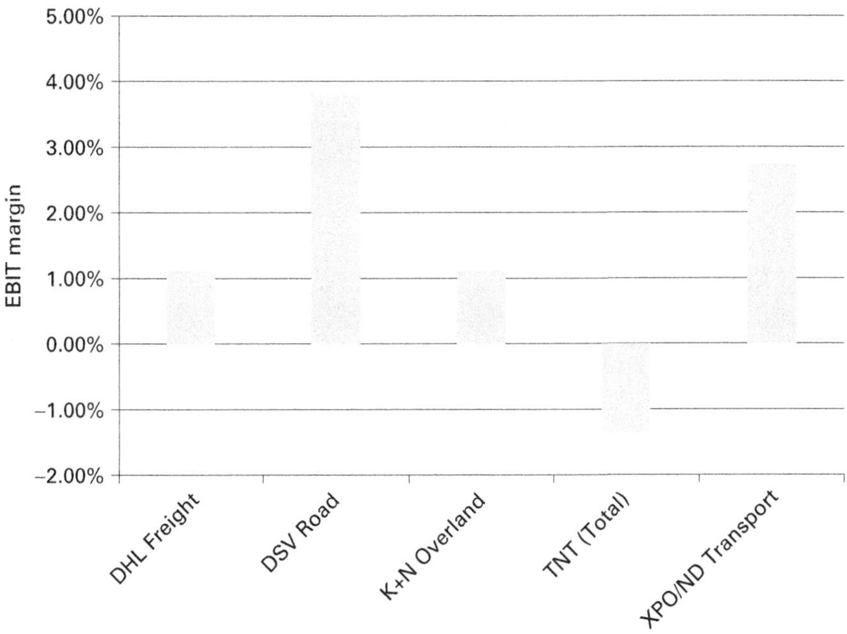

SOURCE: Company Annual Reports (2015)

Cabotage

Road freight in Europe is highly regulated, and drivers living and working in one country do not have the right to work in another European country. However, 'cabotage', which is the ability of drivers from outside one country to collect a load and deliver it within that country, is permitted. This is limited to drivers carrying three loads in seven days. After that they must return to their home country. Despite these restrictions, it is quite an important activity in the sector, as it supports the economics of international routes between economies.

Much cabotage is carried out by Central European drivers exploiting their lower costs in the domestic markets of Western Europe. It is, therefore, unsurprising that Germany has the largest cabotage market, in terms of volume. Smaller economies, such as Belgium, also offer opportunities, owing to the level of transit cargo. Despite the UK's open market and level of international traffic, its geography mitigates against a high level of cabotage. This is also the case in Spain.

Figure 7.10 Eurostat estimates for percentage of total road freight market accounted for by cabotage in major markets (2011)

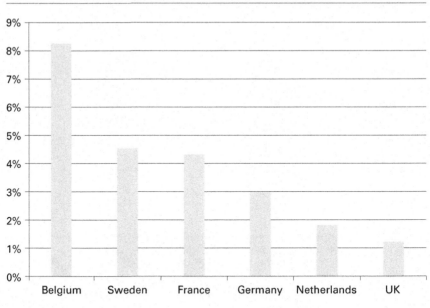

SOURCE: Eurostat (2014)

Summary

The growth of the European road freight sector is linked very closely to economic development. With the centralization of inventory holding and the internationalization of supply chains, road freight has become very important to manufacturers' and retailers' logistics strategies. This chapter looked at the structure of the industry – segmenting it by type of operation, levels of service or commodities moved. In particular, it examined the differences between asset-heavy and asset-light operating models and also addressed the issue of profitability and company failure – a key problem for the industry.

Key points to consider:

- There is a very strong link between demand in the road freight sector and economic output, although at one point in the mid-2000s statistics had pointed towards a 'decoupling'. This has long-term environmental policy implications for the future when the European economy starts to grow again.

- Increased integration of European markets and the consolidation of production and supply will lead to the enhanced growth of international road freight.

- This will also mean that transit traffic will become more of an issue for countries located in the centre of Europe as manufacturing moves to the periphery of the region.

- Research shows that despite the general assumption that road freight operator company failure is linked to the cost of fuel, this is not the case. Far more important to the sector are interest rates and economic output.

- Asset-light road freight forwarders will be impacted in terms of quality and profitability by the reduction of available subcontractors (the 'supplier pool') should a future recession lead to more company bankruptcies.

Express parcels 08

CHAPTER LEARNING OBJECTIVES

This chapter will provide the reader with:

- A history of the global express parcels industry
- Market definitions and an analysis of the industry's structure by individual segment
- An examination of the leading companies in the market and their respective business models
- A breakdown of the sector's cost structures and the drivers of its revenues and profitability
- Case studies of DHL's failed entry into the US domestic market and the acquisition of TNT

The origins of the express parcels industry

The express parcels industry has grown rapidly over the last 30 years. At the outset it fulfilled a need for faster, more reliable services, which also provided customers with an increased level of supply chain visibility. Its ongoing success has been based upon the systemic changes that it has been able to facilitate in global manufacturing and its associated supply chains. Whilst it has led the way in the modernization of the transportation sector, as much as in attitudes as in technological and process developments, it has enabled and benefited from trends such as globalization, e-commerce, lean inventory management, Just-in-Time and customization of mass production.

Its impact on the global freight industry has been dramatic. Freight forwarders, which had until the 1970s enjoyed a monopoly on the control of international freight movements, rapidly lost market share in the lucrative small parcel sector to the express parcels companies. In Europe, international and domestic freight haulage companies and groupage operators also lost out to cheaper and faster express parcels companies.

The express parcels industry is widely acknowledged as having been developed in the United States by companies such as UPS and FedEx. This was aided by the development of a country-wide interstate system (from 1956), deregulation of the air industry (1978) and interstate trucking laws (1980 and 1994). FedEx was the first company to introduce the hub and spoke model which revolutionized the way in which parcels could be distributed around the United States in a fast and economic way.

In Europe, TNT's UK operation is generally credited with creating the first next day parcels service back in 1980. Prior to this, three to four day parcel services had been the standard. TNT was the first company to utilize advances in communication technology to create a flexible, national network. Across Europe development of the industry has taken place at different rates, complicated by the regulatory nature of many of the markets. Until liberalization, which in some cases is still ongoing, the post offices controlled much of the market for parcels and the express industry had difficulty in breaking through the monopolistic regime.

Since the origins of the industry, the market leaders – UPS, FedEx, DHL and TNT – were generally known as the 'Big 4'. As time went on, it became increasingly clear that TNT lacked the resources to compete on the same terms as its three other rivals. Although it made efforts to expand globally, some of the acquisitions it made were ill-judged and instead of enabling it to compete more effectively, the result was falling profitability. This inevitably left it exposed to acquisition with UPS being the first to make a bid for the company, eying up its strength in the European road and parcels market. When this was blocked by the European Commission on competition grounds, FedEx eventually stepped in. It seems inevitable that this deal will proceed, meaning that the 'Big 4' will shrink to the 'Big 3'.

Market definitions and structure

There is no single definition that encompasses the parcels and express sector. A wide variety of companies operate in the market providing services to a number of different segments. Over the last decade international air express operators have entered the domestic road-based market and ground networks have also started to provide international air services, often through partner companies.

However, it is possible to make some broad-brush definitions that relate to the following attributes of service and consignment.

Time sensitivity

Traditionally, there has been a separation in the market between 'parcels' and 'express' services. The most obvious differentiation between these services is the level of time sensitivity involved. Express companies usually undertake to deliver consignments by a specified day and even by a specified time. Domestically, 'express' usually means next working day. Some companies have a more stringent definition: to qualify as express it must be delivered in the morning of the following day, and even by a particular time. For users of 'parcel' services the time attribute is not as important, usually with cost being the overriding consideration. Delivery is usually on a non-specific two to three days basis or longer and the service is also referred to as 'deferred' or 'standard'.

The difference between these services has blurred in recent years and is no longer all that useful. Most parcels companies offer express services, and owing to improvements in systems, overall delivery times have become compressed.

In the United States there are more 'hard-wired' distinctions related to time sensitivity. UPS and FedEx both offer 'Next Day Air' and 'Deferred' (also air) package delivery services, which are categorized as 'Express' services. However, they also offer 'Ground' package delivery solutions that would be defined as 'Parcels'.

In Europe both DHL and TNT have sought to segment the market into 'Time definite/Day definite' categories and 'Economy', the former roughly relating to 'Express' and the latter to 'Parcels'.

The situation is complicated further when comparing international with domestic services. A two to three day delivery time for a package from, say, China to the United States would be seen as falling into the Express category. However, two to three day domestic delivery services would certainly not be seen as Express, demonstrating the problems related to trying to define a service by duration of transit.

Size of consignment

Traditionally, the maximum weight of a parcel (whether express or not) is usually considered to be about 31.5 kilograms (70 pounds). This is an estimate of the maximum weight that can be handled by one man. This was important to ensure that the standardized procedures that are essential to the profitable running of a network are maintained. A large reliance is placed on the quick and efficient collection and delivery of parcels as well as the automated sortation at a sorting centre or hub. Parcels that are non-standard, too heavy, out of gauge, or with other attributes that require specialist handling (such as hazardous, perishable, etc) diminish the overall efficiency of the network. Such consignments are often termed 'non-compatible' and either attract a heavy surcharge or are refused.

However, definitions have evolved over the years and now the main integrators segment their volumes in different ways. TNT regards anything under 50 kilograms as a parcel (over is freight) whilst UPS and FedEx use 68 kilograms and DHL 70 kilograms.

This is a sign that the integrators have been able and willing to penetrate further into what was once considered to be the 'freight' segments.

At the other end of the scale, express companies have been keen to prioritize volumes of documents. They take up little room on board a van or airplane relative to the revenue that they can generate. They also require comparatively little handling, which can be more easily automated. They can be collected and delivered by smaller capacity vehicles that do not require highly trained staff (thereby reducing costs) and are quicker and more flexible than larger vehicles. This allows greater volumes to be processed in a single day.

Business to consumer (B2C)/business to business (B2B)

This is one of the key differentiators between post offices and express or other parcels companies that specialize predominantly in business-to-business deliveries. An express or parcels company will typically operate on a door-to-door basis providing services to business clients.

Although in recent years many companies have started to offer B2C services ('home delivery'), these have specialist requirements owing mainly to the fact that it is often impossible to effect a delivery as, unlike businesses, many people are not in during the day to receive goods. A non-delivery will impact on the efficiency of an operation as it will either require redelivery or else follow up by a customer service agent. In many cases procedures have not been designed for this eventuality.

Post offices, on the other hand, have established systems that can deal with non-delivery of consignments, usually by leaving a parcel at a local post office. Their dense networks of local drop-off points provide them with a competitive advantage over other companies that can only take the undelivered consignment back to a regional depot.

Many large B2C operators have been spun off (or in some cases are still owned) by large catalogue, and more latterly, online retailers.

International/domestic

The express and parcels industry is broadly defined by domestic, regional or international destination. Although in many cases the operations are similar, for instance with hub and spoke networks, there are some major differences. Domestic express services are normally road based whereas international express can require multi-modal transport. Domestic or regional operations are highly competitive owing to the lower barriers to market entry. The international air express operators, often owning or leasing aircraft, use their scale and resources to offer higher levels of services over longer distances. Some companies, such as TNT, use a further segmentation, segregating the intra-European market (where it is market leader) from intercontinental volumes.

The difference between the prices that a domestic parcels player can charge and those of an international air express operator are significant. The average revenue per piece for the packages that UPS moves domestically in countries such as Germany is around US $7. Its corresponding revenue per piece for international parcels is around US $35.

Express market leading companies

In the last five years, boundaries in the market have become blurred as express operators, parcels companies and post offices have started to compete against each other in order to offer clients a full service portfolio. For express companies, lower value parcels business is also a way in which to increase utilization of transport assets and resources. To European parcel networks such as GLS or DPD, express consignments offer higher margin volumes at premium rates.

The air express operators who actually own or lease the airplanes that carry the consolidated parcels or documents between corresponding hubs, are known as 'integrators'. This is due to the way in which they have been able to seamlessly integrate all the various transportation segments by controlling the assets. Globally there are four integrators that are able to operate in this way:

- DHL;
- TNT;
- FedEx;
- UPS.

Although they are well known for their branded air operations, most cross-border movements in Europe occur by road rather than air. In conjunction with major air hubs, they also operate hubs that feed major ground networks. In general, any shipment that has an ultimate destination of less than 800 kilometres (500 miles) will travel by road. However, in the Asia Pacific region, air is very important due to the insular nature of many of the markets and the lack of quality road infrastructure. This is gradually changing with TNT leading the way in building an Asia Pacific road network. Road is obviously less time efficient, but considerably cheaper.

The four integrators have developed different strengths. FedEx and UPS have traditionally focused around the delivery of documents and packages under 5 kilograms, whereas DHL has based its service around document delivery. TNT Express on the other hand has focused on heavier weight freight, which may be to its advantage. Pressure from electronic substitution will be stronger at the document end of the scale, affecting DHL more than the other carriers.

The alternative to owning the air transportation assets is to utilize those of the established air carriers such as Lufthansa, British Airways, Air France or KLM within a multi-modal solution. As an attempt to provide an alternative to the integrators most of these carriers now offer time-definite services of their own with 'flown-as-booked' guarantees. Although these are not retailed to the consumer market, they allow companies such as Chronopost, the subsidiary of French Post Office, La Poste, to compete more effectively.

Express operating model – hub and spoke

All the major European (and global) express and parcels companies operate hub and spoke systems, which enable them to provide comprehensive regional and global coverage through the economies of scale that it provides. The system works through consolidating smaller volumes from local markets at a central hub and then trunking them to a selection of global gateway hubs, usually regionally based, where the process is managed in reverse (see Figure 8.1).

Figure 8.1 Express hub and spoke systems

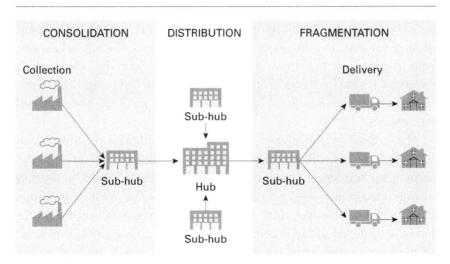

As an example, TNT utilizes nine sub-hubs (Northampton, Paris, Frankfurt, Helsingborg, Milan, Hanover, Brussels, Nuremburg, Madrid) and one main hub in Arnhem, Netherlands. Consignments are collected from the hinterland of each sub-hub, consolidated and then transported to Arnhem. Here they are de-consolidated, sorted and dispatched to the corresponding sub-hub where the reverse process takes place.

One of the benefits of the hub and spoke system is that it allows optimum utilization of assets and capacity across the network. The alternative, line haul between city pairs, is not as efficient and although may be quicker in terms of transit times, will be less appealing to clients owing to the lower frequency of service or higher costs.

One of the downsides of the network solution is that when volumes become weaker, the maintenance of a frequent service, and the fixed assets required to maintain hub and sorting operations, can make the entire network unprofitable.

Express economics

Cost structure

The global express industry is dependent on the development of comprehensive networks spanning regions. As with any form of network, this means that a substantial proportion of costs are fixed due to the investment in hubs and the servicing of fixed routes. TNT estimates that 85 per cent of an air network's costs are fixed compared with 65 per cent of the costs of a ground network. Consequently, substantial economies of scale exist in the industry, making volumes and pricing essential to the success of a network. A network requires a critical mass to make it profitable, over and above which incremental parcel volumes result in higher margins. Conversely, the capital expenditure required for fixed cost networks compounds the impact of falling volumes.

The industry is also highly labour intensive, although the automation of some hubs has reduced this dependence to a degree. Labour costs can account for two-fifths of sales. In the case of UPS in the United States, they account for as much as 65 per cent of costs, mainly due to the dense nature of its network. However, there are significant variances dependent on the business model used. Many companies out-source to subcontractors much of the long-distance trunking between hubs, and others use a franchise system, thereby taking many employees off the payroll. In FedEx's ground network, for example, which subcontracts out much of its transportation requirements, only 22 per cent of costs are employee related, whilst 43 per cent is purchased transport. Its air express operations are far more dependent on in-house staff, with 45 per cent of costs employee related.

Profitability

There is a wide variance in the level of profitability across the various express and parcels segments. This is due to a mix of asset utilization, cost control, pricing discipline and – importantly – a willingness of customers to buy high-yielding products (such as air over road).

Table 8.1 shows the profits of some of the major express players.

Table 8.1 Profitability of major express companies 2014

Company	Operating margin
UPS	9.3%
FedEx	5.8%
TNT	−1.3%
DHL	10.1%

SOURCE: Company accounts (2015)

The difference in performance of UPS, DHL and FedEx on one hand and TNT on the other is stark. TNT's low margins have made it vulnerable to takeover, as evidenced by UPS's abortive acquisition attempt in 2012 and FedEx's acquisition bid in 2015. DHL has managed to turn around its performance over the past decade by shutting down or disposing of loss-making domestic express operations – particularly in the United States.

The link between express parcels and economic output

Demand in the express sector is closely tied to performance of the overall economy. During the economic downturn volumes in the international express sector plummeted as customers switched from premium express to cheaper standard or deferred alternatives.

In order to retain the spend of migrating clients, companies such as FedEx have aggressively developed lower value ground operations in the United States to compete with the market leader UPS. However, the migration to lower value products at the same time as falling volumes has a multiplying effect on the revenues of the express companies.

Growth in the international express industry shows particularly strong correlation with growth in trade. Figure 8.2 shows international package revenue growth for UPS and US export growth data. When testing the linear relationship between the two variables for the period 2009 to 2015 a correlation coefficient of +0.99 is derived, indicating a very strong positive relationship.

Figure 8.2 Comparison of US exports and international parcels revenue

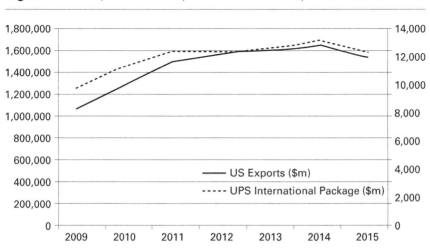

SOURCE: World Trade Organization (2016a)/Company Accounts

It is believed that when world trade finally rebounds, the value of trade will increase faster than volumes, which will favour higher value express products. The global express industry is also able to reach into emerging markets where trade is fastest growing, especially in sectors such as healthcare, spare parts and the movement of documents.

Long-term trends in the express sector

The growth of the express industry has been driven by the trend towards Just-in-Time manufacturing techniques. This has led to the increase in the demand for flexible, frequent and more reliable delivery services, which removes the necessity to store inventory on hand. It also allows the end user to source goods from remote locations, reducing costs. The development of sophisticated information and communication technology has given customers the ability to track and trace their consignments wherever they are geographically. This has allowed manufacturers to plan production with more certainty, integrating the express companies into their supply chains.

In summary, the success of the express industry has been based upon providing manufacturers and retailers with the following benefits:

- Speed. By transporting the product more quickly to the customer the shipper benefits from:
  - lower sales-to-cash cycle time;
  - lower total supply chain inventory levels;
  - better customer service.
- Reliability. Tracking and tracing technology, combined with guaranteed service levels, allows clients to plan schedules with confidence.
- Global service. Most parcels and express operators offer worldwide services, either through their operations or with partners.
- Price. The market is highly competitive both on an international and domestic basis. This provides the shipper with a number of alternatives and consequently value for money.

Key developments in the express industry

CASE STUDY DHL in the United States

One of the biggest events in the express parcels sector of the past decade was DHL's ill-fated venture into the US domestic market. Such was the magnitude of the losses involved that it is worthy of a section in its own right. The episode has shown up many of the difficulties of breaking into a mature market already dominated by two strong players – UPS and FedEx.

Back in March 2003, as part of its global expansion strategy, DHL bought the ground operations of the USA's third largest parcel carrier, Airborne Express, for $1.05 billion. The air operations were spun off owing to regulatory reasons. The acquisition was fought tooth-and-nail by UPS and FedEx who tried to block the deal in the courts, at the same time vigorously lobbying Washington.

DHL carried on in the face of this opposition. Management said that the company could not claim 'global leadership' until it succeeded in the United States. However, losses were heavy right from the start despite the integration of DHL and Airborne and attempts to cut costs. Operational issues impacted upon DHL's attempts to be seen as a low-cost alternative to UPS and FedEx, and the company started to lose market share from around 8 per cent at its height.

In 2008, the decision was finally made to pull out of the domestic segment of the market. In total, the amount spent by the company in establishing a domestic presence in the United States is estimated to be around 7.5 billion euros, including DHL's losses, reorganization costs and the expense of buying Airborne.

The episode was a disaster for DHL, and it has only been able to survive owing to its extraordinarily large resources, and the profitability of its express operations elsewhere in the world. DHL still operates international services to the United States, but it is likely that the experience also prompted it to pull out of other non-performing domestic markets, such as those in France and the UK.

CASE STUDY   UPS, FedEx and TNT

TNT's low margins and its relative lack of resources have made it a target for acquisition by its US rivals. European competitor, DHL, would not have been allowed to make a bid for the company by competition authorities and no new market entrant has come forward, leaving the way open to firstly UPS and then FedEx.

In 2012, UPS made a bid to acquire TNT, which many had felt was too small to compete effectively in the international express sector, and which had come under pressure for many years from its shareholders to improve its share price. The logic was to combine TNT's strong European ground network with UPS's global scale. The deal was eventually abandoned in 2013 in light of the likely veto by European competition authorities.

What appeared to be a straightforward – if rather large – deal to acquire TNT Express was made much more complicated by the behaviour of the European competition authorities. That UPS abandoned the bid, despite the hurdle of a 200 million euros termination fee, illustrated the magnitude of the obstacles that UPS perceived it was faced with to make the takeover work.

The negotiations revolved around the competition authorities of the European Commission. The logic of its objections appeared to focus on the number of competitors in the marketplace. The Commission hinted that the removal of TNT Express would reduce the level of competition in the express parcels market. In suggesting remedies for this problem, they were drawn into dismembering the TNT and UPS network, a task which was doomed to fail as such assets are only worth anything as part of a network.

In 2015–16 FedEx had more luck convincing the European Commission it should be allowed to take over TNT. FedEx's weaker position in Europe was the deciding factor, especially in terms of express road freight.

The purchase represents a big stride forward in deepening the globalization of the FedEx business. FedEx has strong presence in intercontinental traffic but its profile in markets such as China or continental Europe bears little relationship to the depth of business it has in the United States, characterized as it is by a strong 'last mile' operation and a leading road freight network to complement its core air express franchise.

When in possession of TNT, FedEx will have a bridgehead to expand into Europe to develop what might be seen as a sort of 'FedEx Ground Europe' or 'FedEx Freight Europe'. But realizing it will be difficult. Europe is not one coherent market. Even neighbouring markets such as Britain and France are very different, with different types of customers and providers. Traffic flows are often fragmented and follow patterns different from the United States.

Certainly, the UK and German e-retailing markets are very advanced and growing quickly but with that comes a ferocious level of competition. Another big problem is that TNT Express is orientated towards the 'business-to-business' market not the consumer 'last mile' segment.

TNT Express does have a strong presence in networked road freight, being one of the largest hauliers of crossborder consignments and especially strong in less than pallet load business. However, this is both a fiercely competitive market and not very profitable. International 'Less-than-Trailer Load' services may be the most dynamic part of the road freight market across Europe but that is not saying much. In the United States, FedEx – and UPS – have been able to create a road network that in part replicates the sorts of efficiencies seen in the air express 'hub and spoke' system. Doing that across Europe would be ambitious but hard. Rivals, including Deutsche Bahn Schenker, Gefco and indeed DHL will insist that they have already built such systems.

Summary

The emergence of the express parcels sector has allowed manufacturers to deliver goods to customers in a fast and efficient way, as well as providing supply chain visibility. It has underpinned many of the inventory-reducing management techniques that have been introduced and facilitated globalization. This chapter examined the origins and structure of the industry as well as the hub and spoke operating model used by the leading express companies. It also researched the links between economic and trade growth and market development as well as outlining some of the key developments in the sector over the past few years.

Key points to consider:

- Internationally the market is led by four main players: DHL, TNT, UPS and FedEx (soon to be three once FedEx has acquired TNT). Domestically, however, the industry is much more fragmented with many companies competing on very small margins.

- The demand for fast and trackable deliveries has grown, as manufacturers implement supply chain management practices designed to reduce inventory whilst improving customer service.

- Volumes are essential to the network models employed by the express parcels operators due to the high level of fixed costs employed.

- Profits for the international express operators can be high, owing to the high barriers to market entry. However, TNT has struggled to compete with the other three rivals, and this left it vulnerable to takeover.

- The link between economic growth, trade and parcels volumes, means that the express parcels companies are well placed to take advantage of any economic recovery.

Air cargo   09

CHAPTER LEARNING OBJECTIVES

This chapter will provide the reader with:

- An explanation of the importance of air cargo to international supply chains and the global economy
- A brief history of the air cargo industry from its origins
- A description of the various roles fulfilled by players in the sector and their importance
- An identification of the leading air cargo operators
- The importance of integrators and the disruptive impact on the air cargo sector

Development of the air cargo industry

Air Cargo is an integral element of many manufacturers' and retailers' global supply chains, allowing companies across a range of sectors to operate in lean inventory environments. Air cargo operations enable fast, frequent and predictable transit between many parts of the world as an increasing number of companies out-source to remote locations.

From an early stage of the airline industry's development, the spare hold space on passenger flights was used to carry freight. Since the early days of commercial flying, mail has also been transported on aircraft. As those aircraft became bigger, more efficient and more reliable, a wider range of goods was carried and freight volumes increased. Dedicated freighter aircraft and combined freight and passenger aircraft started to appear as volumes grew. In the 1970s, a new industry, using air transport to provide express parcel deliveries, emerged and its major players – FedEx, UPS, DHL and TNT – have become household names.

Decreasing product cycles for high-value, high-tech goods have made fast delivery to market essential. Perishable commodities, such as foodstuffs or flowers, can be delivered into markets on the opposite side of the world in perfect condition. Periodicals can be delivered to readers worldwide while still current. Local companies have been able to develop into global traders, allowing consumers to buy all types of goods from any part of the world. In this respect, the air cargo sector has played an essential, although understated, role in the development of the global economy. Its continued development is key to the ongoing success of globalization.

The early years of air cargo

Air cargo services grew very rapidly during the 1960s; in fact, faster than passenger growth over the same period. This rate of growth slowed considerably in the early 1980s, although it was still around 9 per cent per annum. The early growth was centred in the United States and on transatlantic routes and the European and North American airlines were the dominant players until the mid-1970s.

Before the 1960s, airfreight was considered as a way of filling spare capacity on what were essentially narrow-bodied passenger aircraft. The high rate of growth in the 1960s, together with the introduction of wider-bodied passenger aircraft, provided the opportunity for many airlines to generate income from air cargo. Where cargo volumes exceeded the capacity available in passenger aircraft, there was an incentive to introduce scheduled all-cargo services. All-cargo aircraft enabled more unit loads and consignments to be carried and when these services were introduced they had the effect of further stimulating demand. The increased use of specialized handling equipment speeded up the movement of freight and the turnaround of aircraft. All-cargo aircraft were also able to fly at night to schedules that would not be suitable for passengers. This led to shorter freight transit times as well as adding extra capacity.

As the growth in the North American and European markets slowed in the 1970s, the Asian markets began the pattern of growth that continues to the present. In parallel came the rapid development of the East Asian and Pacific regional airlines – Korean Air Lines, Singapore Airlines, Cathay Pacific, Japan Airlines and China Airlines – which are now all among the top 10 cargo airlines in terms of route tonne kilometres (RTKs).

Cargo charter

Cargo charter airlines have existed from the early days of the industry and their development accelerated briefly in the 1970s, benefiting from freedom to operate outside bilateral agreements and the growing deregulation of freight operations to and from the United States, UK and some other European countries. This growth was curtailed as the scheduled airlines began to take cargo more seriously with more flexible and competitive pricing. The latter were able to offer considerably more freight capacity as they introduced wide-bodied passenger aircraft on an increasing number of routes. Added to this was the restriction of charter operations by developing countries aiming to protect the interest of their own national airlines in the freight market.

Today, charter cargo carriers operate as an integral part of the industry carrying regular as well as specialist loads.

The integrators

The most significant development in the airfreight business has been the rapid development of the express sector. Express parcel services were pioneered by Federal Express (FedEx) in the United States. FedEx identified the requirement for door-to-door and overnight transport, which at that time was not normal practice in the airfreight industry for either documents or urgent small parcels. Instead of selling on the basis of weight and price, convenience, speed and reliability became the principal product features. The express parcels sector in the United States boomed during the 1980s with courier and express parcels companies following the Federal Express example and setting up their own air operations. By the 1990s, an international sector had emerged offering the customer a single provider of ground transport, air transport and the related clearance and documentation services. The providers of these services became known as integrators.

Market growth

The relationships between economic indicators and air cargo volumes have been well evaluated by several bodies including Airbus and Boeing. There is a consensus view that air cargo market growth is closely related to economic development, tending to be higher.

The market for airfreight is most commonly measured by tonnes carried or revenue tonne kilometres (RTKs) – in other words, the sum of the revenue-earning cargo carried multiplied by the number of kilometres for which it was carried. This last measure is sometimes expressed as FTKs (freight tonne kilometres) or in the United States, in miles.

Figure 9.1 Global air cargo industry output

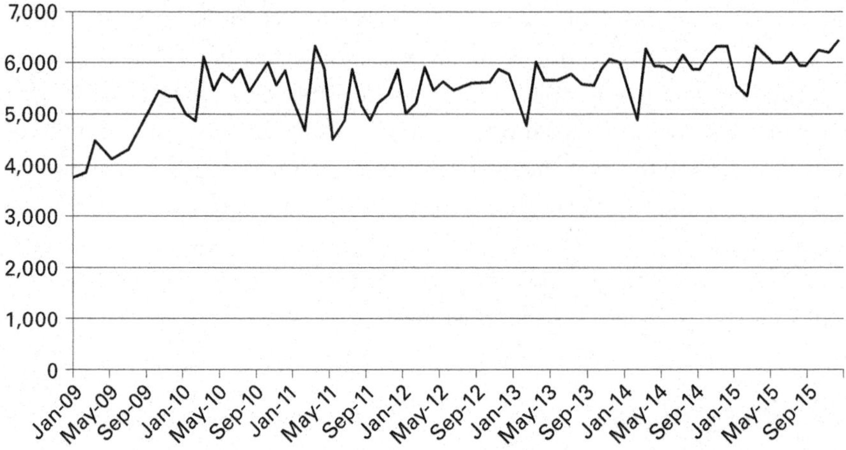

SOURCE: Airports Council International (2016)

Market volumes in tonnes are measured by the Airports Council International and are shown in Figure 9.1. The chart shows that since the rebound from the economic downturn in 2008–9 there has been gradual growth, despite the recent loss of long-haul traffic to maritime channels.

Industry players

The air cargo industry involves many different types of organizations providing shippers with a range of interrelated air cargo services. These organizations include government bodies, privately owned concerns or hybrids with a mix of state and private ownership. These operations function in a highly competitive market.

Airlines

Airlines provide and fly the aircraft in which air cargo is carried. Airlines range from the national passenger-carrying airlines to small operators with one aircraft. A description of the main types of airline is as follows:

- Scheduled operators provide air cargo capacity principally in the belly-holds of passenger aircraft. Some also operate freight-only aircraft on dense cargo routes. They principally work on behalf of freight forwarders, express operators (including integrators) and national post offices.

- Freighter operators operate freight-only aircraft and do not provide passenger services. Within this group are the larger airlines that carry all types of freight; specialists that concentrate on a particular type of freight or a particular route, and freight charter operators. Freighter operators give priority to the demands of the air cargo business and are able to operate on key airfreight routes at times that satisfy customer demand.

- Integrators are operators that provide complete door-to-door services for the customers. Part of their service offering is the airfreight component of any transit and these operators are now some of the largest airlines in the world.

- Passenger charter operators do not figure as major players in the air cargo market. Charter operators primarily operate on holiday routes. As with scheduled operators, they offer very limited freight capacity principally to forwarders, usually through general sales agents.

Within the airline sector there are a range of trading arrangements relating to aircraft ownership and operation. Some operators purchase their aircraft and operate them; others enter long- or short-term lease agreements with other airlines or aircraft owners. These can be on the basis of a dry lease (aircraft only) or wet lease (crewed, maintained, etc). There is also a great deal of trading between airlines to enable them to balance demand and cover a wider range of routes and share facilities.

Airline alliances

No single airline can cover all routes and all destinations and 'alliances' of airlines have been formed. These alliances are mainly aimed at passenger operations where shared terminals, bookings, through bookings and transfer facilities provide advantages. There are, nevertheless, similar advantages in cargo systems. The three major groups are the Star Alliance, the oneworld Alliance, and the SkyTeam alliance.

Integrators

Four major express parcel companies, DHL, FedEx, UPS and TNT, all operate their own fleets of freight aircraft and in their own right are some of the largest airlines in the world. As they combine the roles of freight retailers, wholesalers and carriers they are known as integrators. They normally contract directly with the shipper and provide a door-to-door service, usually using their own road and air network, handling and transit warehousing facilities.

The integrators started as express operators but have steadily increased the scope and scale of their offering until today they provide a full range of logistics services. In doing this they have taken market share from freight forwarders, first in the lucrative document and small package sector and then further up the size range. They now compete increasingly directly with freight forwarders and the airlines in order to maximize the capacity on their line-haul routes. However, whilst there is a degree of disintermediation, integrators are also reliant on freight forwarders to provide them with additional loads.

Airports

Airports provide the infrastructure to the sector, charging landing fees and parking fees to airlines and charging rent to service companies for cargo transit sheds, etc. A major cargo hub will have sophisticated handling equipment, trans-shipment facilities, customs clearance arrangements and ground delivery arrangements. Typically, there will be a number of on-site providers of these facilities and many of the major airlines and integrators have their own dedicated cargo facilities at their main base and other airports of strategic importance to them. Smaller airports will offer a lower level of provision with fewer, and sometimes just one, providers of services at that location.

Cargo flights are often run overnight or at off-peak times. This is for the benefit of shippers, for which an overnight delivery is often required, and for the airlines, which can more easily obtain landing and take-off slots at congested airports.

For many airports, noise and other environmental issues are increasing concerns, particularly in relation to night flights. For this reason, many cargo airlines are making increasing use of airports where there are fewer restrictions. The integrators have been the leaders in this trend in moving their hubs to airports where they can operate for 24 hours per day without restriction. One example of this is the move by DHL from Brussels, where there were an increasing number of regulations being placed upon night flying, to Leipzig where there are none.

Airfreight forwarders

Freight forwarders provide a service to manufacturers and other businesses that have a requirement to move goods internationally. The forwarder's role involves receiving or collecting consignments from customers and arranging transportation and documentation to either the destination or to a foreign airport.

General sales agents (GSAs)

General sales agents are utilized by many airlines as a marketing channel, to sell airfreight capacity on their behalf. These organizations are normally used in geographical regions where it is not economically viable to set up a dedicated sales and marketing operation.

Transit warehouse operators

Transit warehouse operators provide a transit handling service for airlines and forwarders. Their function is to receive cargo from the aircraft, de-palletize and deliver to truck or vice versa where customs clearance is required.

Customs brokers

A customs broker is an agent that arranges inbound customs clearance. This role is usually undertaken as a service provided by a freight forwarder.

Air trucking companies

Air trucking companies specialize in collecting and delivering goods between a shipper's premises and airport transit warehouses. These tend to be specialist companies with the appropriate security clearances and access to 'secure' areas.

Air truckers also provide road transport between airports. This need arises when freight is trans-shipped from one airport to another, either for onward shipment or, particularly in Europe where trucks are used as a substitute for aircraft, usually to a schedule.

Express operators

Express operators provide services for the movement of documents and small packages, where the timescales for transit are measured in hours, in contrast to forwarders whose transit times are generally managed in days. The largest of these are the four integrators previously described.

Logistics providers

For many years, the integrators have provided an 'end to end' service for the delivery of parcels. As supply chains become increasingly complex, many organizations are looking for a provider that will provide the equivalent 'end to end' service for their supply chain and to which they can out-source supply chain management.

Services such as this are often branded 'logistics solutions'. They are provided by many of the major forwarders, most of which also have strong logistics capabilities; integrators that have developed strategies to offer logistics solutions, and others including '4PL' (fourth-party logistics) companies that provide supply chain management but subcontract all the transport warehousing and handling services.

The air cargo chain

Figure 9.2 illustrates the air cargo shipping process using traditional exporters, freight forwarders, air truckers, warehouse companies, etc.

The exporter will typically book the shipment with a freight forwarder, which then manages the remainder of the process. Some freight forwarders have assets and facilities for carrying out some of the processes in-house, but many out-source all services.

The forwarder would typically use an agent at the destination to make the arrangements for customs clearance and delivery to the recipient.

There is a tendency for the major players in the business to expand the scope of their operations so that they are carrying out more of the functions in the chain themselves. This means that many of the asset-owning forwarders, whilst not integrators, are offering a more integrated service.

Figure 9.3 illustrates the process if the same consignment is shipped by an integrator. The integrator deals with the sender of the consignment, uses its

Figure 9.2 Air cargo processes: Traditional air cargo

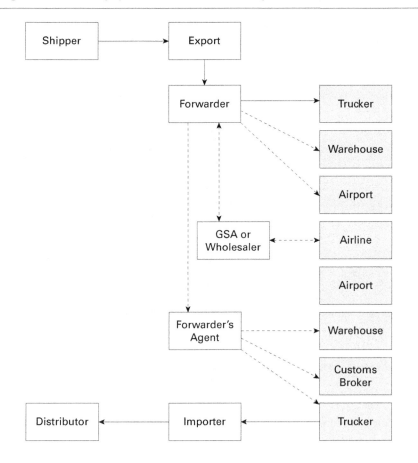

own resource to provide all the various steps in the cargo chain and delivers the consignment to the recipient. As can be seen from the diagram, the possession and control of all the resources needed to make a shipment means that there are fewer steps in the otherwise very long chain of companies involved.

There is also a tendency to encroach into areas previously dominated by other operators. For example, DHL is now actively selling airfreight solutions on its European Air Transport network. In the 'reverse direction', Lufthansa has recently begun to offer customers (forwarders rather than manufacturers) a time-definite express parcel and document service, taking advantage of the higher growth rates in that sector.

Figure 9.3 Air cargo: Integrator process

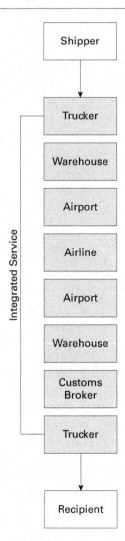

Cargo types

Most airfreight volume today is 'general' freight. This includes goods ranging from plant and equipment to cosmetics. International express comprises about a tenth of overall air cargo. There is also a specialist airfreight charter sector catering for special needs and regular shipments. Within each of these sectors, there are many specialisms such as heavy lift capability, refrigerated transport, cut-flower transits, etc. The largest volumes of commodities moved in rank of importance are:

- capital equipment;
- intermediate materials (that is, electrical components);
- computers;
- express parcels;
- refrigerated goods;
- consumer products;
- fashion goods.

Freight aircraft

Cargo was originally seen as a means of filling spare hold capacity on passenger aircraft. As the market has grown, aircraft partly or wholly dedicated to the carriage of cargo have been brought into service. This is particularly the case in the North American market in which more than half the world's cargo aircraft are presently deployed. Airbus estimates that 50 per cent of the world's air cargo is now carried in dedicated freighters, with the remainder carried in the belly-holds of passenger aircraft.

With a substantial proportion of the cargo fleet deployed in North America, the main aircraft types are those with payloads of up to 60 tonnes, which are well suited to operations between North American cities. Many of these narrow-body or medium wide-body jets are converted passenger aircraft. This market segment is driven by express carriers, to whom the balance between the lower cost per tonne achieved by larger airplanes and the schedule flexibility of smaller airplanes is important.

Capacity on passenger flights has been expanding, especially as greater numbers of highly cargo-compatible airplanes, such as the 777-300ER, enter the global fleet. This increase in capacity will inevitably have an impact on freight rates, especially with the global economy so weak.

For intercontinental movements of goods there is likely to be a shift away from older designs towards larger wide-bodied jets as these are regarded as being operationally more convenient, with the integrators being cited as an example of a type of user that needs bigger aircraft with extended ranges.

Air cargo routes

The major air cargo routes are those centred on North America, Europe and Asia and the major flows were east–west or west–east between and within these areas. Figure 9.4 indicates the major flows, the largest being between Asia and North America and Asia and Europe. In recent years, air cargo flows between the China and the Middle East, Africa and Latin America have been growing quickly.

Figure 9.4 Major air cargo routes by volume

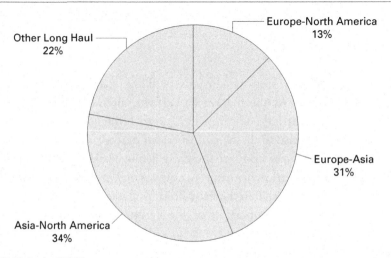

SOURCE: Boeing (2015)

Leading air cargo operators

In 2014, the 10 largest cargo airlines in the world carried more than 85 billion revenue tonne kilometres (RTKs). That group comprises two integrators (FedEx and UPS), seven scheduled passenger airlines and one specialist freight airline (Cargolux). The volumes expressed in million route tonne kilometres are set out in Figure 9.5.

Figure 9.5 Top 10 air cargo carriers (freight tonne km)

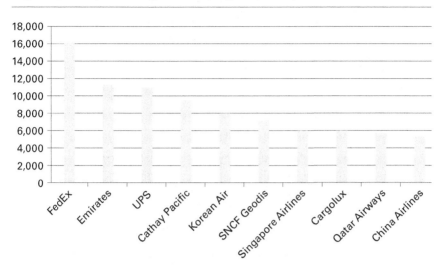

SOURCE: IATA (2015)

Summary

Although the air cargo sector has been hit hard by the economic downturn of the past seven years, it is still an essential element in many consumer, high-tech and pharmaceutical supply chains, not to mention perishable goods. This chapter tracked how the air cargo industry developed from its early days in the 1960s, when it was considered purely a method of filling spare capacity, to the multi-billion industry it is today. It examined the structure of the sector, outlining the complex relationships in place between airlines, forwarders, airports and sales agents to name just a few of the parties involved.

Key points to consider:

- Although the largest air cargo volumes remain centred on Asia, Europe and North America, niche markets are developing fast between China, the Middle East and Latin America.

- Capacity on passenger flights has been growing with the introduction of wide-bodied jets. This has placed pressure on cargo rates that are already weak due to lower volumes.

- Air cargo volumes have been hit by the migration to lower cost sea freight as customers prioritize economy over speed in the difficult economic environment.

- Express parcels are an important part of the airfreight volume mix. High-tech goods, cut flowers, perishable fruit and vegetables, apparel and capital equipment are some of the other major commodity types shipped by air.

Container shipping

10

CHAPTER LEARNING OBJECTIVES

This chapter will provide the reader with:

- A history of the container shipping sector and its development
- An analysis of the micro-economics of the industry and the decisions affecting capacity and their impact on shipping rates
- An analysis of the industry's structure, identifying the various players involved and their functions
- A discussion of the cooperative and competitive relationship between freight forwarders and shipping lines
- Analysis of the changing character of tradelanes as a result of economic development in emerging markets

The origins of the modern industry

The shipping industry underwent a transformation in 1956 with the voyage of the first container vessel, the *Ideal X* from Newark, New Jersey. Since that time the major proportion of goods moving by sea (with the exception of bulk) have been unitized in standard size boxes. This has created major efficiencies in terms of loading, unloading, storage and onward delivery of products. Intervention in, and interruption of, a consignment's movement has been minimized. It is estimated that just over half of seaborne trade in terms of value is moved by container ships, although still under a fifth in terms of volume – the rest either being bulk or general freight – 'break bulk', as it is known.

In turn this innovation had a major impact on the global economy. The falling cost of transport made it possible for manufacturers to source goods from remote locations on a much larger scale, despite barriers to trade such as tariffs. This has led to the globalization of industry and directly to the interconnected world in which we live today.

The size of container ships has risen rapidly over the last decade, in line with shipping lines' desire to optimize efficiency. The average vessel size in terms of Twenty Foot Equivalent Units (TEUs), a standard industry metric, has grown from 2,417 TEUs in 2007 to around 3,800 TEUs in 2015. In 2005, the largest container vessel was the MV *Colombo Express* at 8,800 TEUs. In 2016, the MSC *Oscar*, *Oliver* and *Zoe* were estimated to be over 19,000 TEUs.

The increasing size of container ships has had a major impact on ports, as many can only dock at the major gateway ports, such as Rotterdam in Europe, or Port of Long Beach/Los Angeles in the United States. Ports have had to invest in large new cranes and information technology software in order to be able to load/off-load the thousands of containers carried by each ship in an efficient and timely manner.

Shipping economics

Despite this revolution, the shipping industry has remained highly vulnerable to cyclicality. The most recent example of this was in the last recession of 2008–9, which occurred after a long period of economic growth.

One of the reasons for this is the relationship between supply and demand. In normal conditions, supply – fleet capacity – cannot be switched on overnight. For new-build ships, there are lead times of between two and four years and these long lead times mean that orders placed in boom periods can be delivered after the peak has passed.

In other words, for long periods of the economic cycle there is often under-supply, due to shipping lines' inability to predict demand accurately, followed by over-supply when a large amount of extra capacity is finally introduced. This means that shipping lines' revenues are hit by the 'double whammy' of falling rates (due to over-capacity) and falling volumes (due to weak economic demand). As good load factors are essential for shipping lines to make money, when they fall beneath the breakeven level, losses are very quickly racked up.

The shipping industry is regarded by many to be driven by derived demand (that is, the faster economies and trade grow, the higher the growth in container volumes). However, as mentioned above, there is very much a two-way relationship with the fall in transport costs stimulating economic activity. It can be speculated that during the 1970s, when containerization of goods was still being adopted, these cost savings had most impact (a paradigm shift, as it may be termed, from high- to low-cost transport).

There has been much research undertaken on the links between demand, shipping rates and capacity. In general, it can be concluded that an increase in volumes and increase in rates has a positive impact on new orders of ships and, consequently, on fleet size (and hence capacity). One piece of research claims that as a determinant of growth in capacity, volume growth is more important than rate growth.

However, the situation is more complex than might first be assumed. Shipping lines have the option, in times of tight capacity, of extending the lives of ships (increasing 'broken up' age) and vice versa. They can also speed up or slow down the rate at which their ships move around the world (the latter, so-called 'slow steaming'). There is also the option of slowing the rate at which new-build ships are brought into the market, although in an upturn the reverse is not true.

These discretionary decisions make it difficult to gain an insight into the market based on quantitative data alone. Consequently, forecasting of rates is impossible, even though at first sight this should be theoretically possible.

During the last recession, large amounts of capacity were taken out of the market as ships were laid up and many shipping lines adopted 'super-slow steaming' speeds. It was estimated that up to 10 per cent of the world's fleet was taken out of operation in one way or another. This capacity was brought back into the market gradually as the market improved, allowing the shipping lines to improve revenues and profits. This is in contrast to the more usual 'step change' in capacity growth caused by the introduction of new-build ships alone.

In 2015, container shipping growth was just 2.2 per cent. With capacity anticipated to grow by 7.7 per cent in 2015, the disequilibrium in the market was extreme. To put it into context, Drewry's own measure of the relative balance of container vessel capacity and cargo demand was at its lowest level since the recession year of 2009 – a score of just 91, with 100 implying equilibrium (Drewry, 2015). This resulted in the collapse of shipping rates.

Looking ahead, one major worry for the sector will, of course, be any rebound in global oil prices. According to the Bunkerworld Index (BWI), the price of fuel in October 2015 was approximately half the price it was in October 2014, a major buttress to profits. But the weakness in demand-side growth is the latest reality that liners are coming to terms with. Perhaps most worryingly, emerging markets have failed to deliver their usual boost to world trade in 2015. According to the Netherlands' CPB, seasonally adjusted month-on-month export volume growth has averaged –0.5 per cent in 2015, and five out of eight of its monthly growth estimates are negative. If emerging markets do not recover some of their lustre, then further cuts to demand forecasts may well have to be made.

The structure of the shipping industry

The container shipping industry is characterized by three key attributes:

- it has a high level of fixed costs;
- there is little difference in the types of service offered;
- it is highly concentrated, with a few shipping lines accounting for the majority of market share.

Although the shipping industry was once regarded as a simple commoditized, point-to-point transport activity, this is no longer the whole story. The sector is now characterized by a complex ecosystem of interrelated parties and processes.

Shipping lines

Shipping lines can either choose to service a route using their own vessels or collaborate with other shipping companies. Most lines choose to share their capacity on the key routes. Managing space in this way mitigates the financial risk of capital investment, and allows them to invest in larger ships to create scale economies, whilst ensuring a frequent service for shippers. However, alliances can be difficult to run not least because different shipping lines have different service levels and pricing structures.

Collaboration in terms of capacity has, in fact, always been an industry practice, through what were termed 'conference' arrangements. Agreeing rates amongst the partners was also widespread, although this has now been outlawed in Europe following the implementation of anti-trust legislation. Formal conferences where rate-setting still takes place remain in several other geographies including the United States, Japan and Singapore.

In a tough economic environment, conferences seem to be making a comeback. Maersk and MSC are part of an alliance called '2M'; it is believed the French-based CMA CGM will align with COSCO (China Ocean Shipping Group), Evergreen and OOCL in a new conference (CCEO). This will weaken another conference, the 'G6' alliance, which was hit by the loss of NOL/APL, which was bought by CMA CGM in 2015. This network would then be in a position to rival the combination of Maersk and Mediterranean Shipping Lines, particularly on the largest trades.

The CCEO would have a capacity of between 2.5 and 3 million TEU, as compared with the G6, which has around 1.7 million TEU. This would imply a considerable restructuring of the container shipping sector. The heightened capital utilization theoretically offered by such an alliance would inflict greater pain on smaller lines who are already suffering from the ferocity of the market. Consequently, the likelihood of them going out of business would increase.

This may not be good for shippers. The power of the largest lines appears to be increasing and the smaller lines may be disappearing. If such a trend continues customers will be faced with fewer options in purchasing shipping services whilst the pricing power of the big container lines will inevitably drive up prices.

Ports

A port is an important node in the supply chain. It acts as a point of loading as well as a trans-shipment hub. With one of the major trends in the industry being towards larger ships, the number of ports that can receive the latest Post-Panamax vessels (that is, ships too big to transit the Panama Canal) has fallen. Thus, the industry is more reliant on 'feeder' services, which provide the 'spokes' to the port's hub. Barges play an important role in this system, as does intermodal freight.

In Asia, Hong Kong and Singapore are important trans-shipment/hub ports and are retaining their importance despite the growth of ports, for example, in the Pearl River Delta of China. Some shipping lines, such as Maersk, operate their own feeder services. Others work with specialist lines.

Terminal operators

Terminal operators work within a port, often on a long-term lease. The largest terminal operators are able to bring the latest technology, both in software and in handling equipment; operations knowhow; and large-scale investment, which a port on its own would not have access to.

The ability to load/off-load container vessels in a timely manner is a key competitive advantage for many ports. Shipping lines are very sensitive to delays to service schedule and this is one of the key criteria on which they will choose their ports-of-call.

Intermodal freight

With the growing importance of visibility and velocity in supply chains, the role of intermodal freight in the shipping process has become more critical, not least the ability of road and rail services to interconnect seamlessly and quickly with sea freight operations. This goes as much for ports in Asia, where most goods originate, as in Europe and North America, the gateway ports to the main consumer markets. This has led to high levels of investment over the years, especially in rail infrastructure links, which circumvent heavily congested roads.

Container relocation

One of the most challenging problems that the shipping industry has faced is the imbalance in the flow of containers around the world. With most goods consumed in the West, but manufactured in the East, empty containers need to be repatriated. On one hand, containers are expensive to build, buy or lease, and repair. On the other, moving 'empties' is costly in terms of back-haul or idle storage.

There are opportunities for shipping lines to work more closely with road, rail and other intermediaries to reposition containers.

Consolidation in the shipping industry

In a quest to increase economies of scale, the shipping industry has in the past seen plenty of acquisitions. Maersk was one of the main protagonists, building a position that would then allow it to price competitors out of the market. Sealand, Safmarine and finally P&O Nedlloyd were bought, producing a giant with annual revenue of US $50 billion. However, the last of these – P&O Nedlloyd in 2005 – proved disastrous.

The integration of the purchase of P&O Nedlloyd was handled badly, with Maersk spending 2.3 billion euros on the Anglo-Dutch container shipping company, but failing to gain any market share from the business. These problems were compounded by internal issues around Maersk's IT systems. Since then, it has been content to grow organically.

Over a third of container shipping capacity is operated by just three ship-ping companies according to Paris-based analysis company, Alphaliner (see Table 10.1). The clear leader remains Maersk with more than 3.0 million TEU. Next largest is Mediterranean Shipping Line (MSC) with 2.69 million TEU, with the third largest CMA CGM 1.82 million TEU.

Table 10.1 World's largest container ship fleets (TEU) 2015

Shipping line	Fleet capacity (TEUs)
Maersk	3.00 m
MSC	2.69 m
CMA CGM	1.82 m
Hapag Lloyd	0.94 m
Evergreen	0.93 m
COSCO	0.85 m
China Shipping (CSCL)	0.69 m
Hamburg Sud	0.65 m
Hanjin Shipping	0.63 m
OOCL	0.56 m

SOURCE: Alphaliner (2016)

These three have a clear differentiation in terms of size, with the next largest container shipping line, Hapag Lloyd, half the size of CMA CGM. Below this group, the companies are generally regional operators, although they may serve individual global routes.

This differentiation by size is not a clear trend, however, as Maersk suffered a loss of market share after its takeover of P&O Nedlloyd. In contrast, MSC has more than doubled its market share in the past decade, whilst CMA CGM has almost tripled its share.

Despite reluctance to make acquisitions over the past 10 years, there is plenty of speculation about industry consolidation in the near future. Already French shipping line CMA CGM has acquired Singapore's NOL/APL.

One of the reasons behind the talk of a new wave of acquisitions is the hyper-competitive nature of the shipping market, fuelled in part by Chinese state-owned shipping companies. There is also speculation about a merger of the three largest shipping lines: NYK, Mitsui OSK Lines (MOL) and 'K' Lines. This merger would create the world's fourth largest carrier, with 7.5 per cent of the world's total fleet, just behind CMA CGM. In a sector that appears to be increasingly driven by economies of scale, this is a powerful logic.

Ship size

Increasing ship size is an essential element in ensuring that shipping costs on a per TEU basis are kept low. The first post-Panamax vessel was the MV *Regina Maersk*, launched in 1996 at 6,400 TEU. Within 10 years the MV *Emma Maersk* was launched with a capacity estimated to be around 15,500 TEUs. Now, however, ships as large as 22,000 TEUs are on the order books, so-called ultra-large container ships (ULCCs) or Malaccamax (the maximum size that are able to transit the Straits of Malacca).

The size of the new vessels means that they can be used only on certain main lanes, such as China to Europe. This excludes whole continents such as Africa. These geographies will be served by the ships that would previously have worked the East–West routes. It also means that trans-shipment will become more important, adding time and cost to shipments from these developing regions.

Freight forwarders v shipping lines

One characteristic of the global shipping industry is the relationship between freight forwarders and shipping lines. Forwarders are both shipping lines' customers as well as their competitors, vying for the volumes of the major shipper companies such as Walmart or Ikea.

The major forwarders have been very proficient in providing global shippers with end-to-end supply chain solutions. They are widely believed to have better customer service and IT systems that have been designed to provide requisite levels of visibility. The largest forwarders have huge buying power, and can be major customers in their own right; hence, they are able to provider retailers and manufacturers with very competitive freight rates.

For these reasons it is believed that forwarders have managed to increase their market share over the past decade – 'owning' more customers than ever. The overall global container trade has increased from roughly 55 million

TEUs in 2000 to more than 130 million TEUs in 2015. Forwarders account for about a third of these volumes.

Key growth lanes

The shipping industry, in terms of volumes of containers shipped, is now dominated by intra-Asian trade, which accounts for around one in three containers shipped. For several years the importance of China–Europe and China–United States volumes has been declining. One of the main reasons for this is the development of virtual manufacturing networks, which have spread right across the whole of Asia. Japanese manufacturers, for example, have looked to un-bundle and out-source parts of their production to lower cost manufacturers, not least in China. Now that China's manufacturing is getting more expensive, there has also been some migration of manufacturing to lower cost producers elsewhere in the region.

Table 10.2 Containerized trade by route 2014

Main Lane East–West	30%
Secondary East–West	14%
Intra-Regional and South–South	40%
North–South	17%

SOURCE: UNCTAD (2014)

The past few years has seen strong growth on so-called 'non-main lanes' including North–South (that is, from North America to South America and Europe to Sub-Saharan Africa), and China–Africa and China–Latin America. This latter growth had been fuelled by Chinese investment in the extractive industries of developing countries. Such growth has been running in the high single digits, according to some authorities, compared with low single digits on more established routes. According to UNCTAD, the total container trade on main tradelanes is estimated to have grown by 9.0 per cent between 2007 and 2014, while trade volumes on secondary routes have expanded by 45 per cent during the same period.

One thing is clear: much more complex, sophisticated patterns of trade are emerging as a result of a nexus of new demand-driven trends. These also include the rise of the Asian consumer, which has meant the region has become a destination as well as an origin for containerized goods. This has been positive in terms of rebalancing supply and demand, with many more fully laden container vessels destined to Asia than before. This will eventually impact on prices, with 'backhaul' rates (that is, Europe to Asia, for example) coming more into line with 'headhaul' (Asia to Europe or United States).

A further positive trend for the sector is the migration to containerized shipping of commodities that have traditionally been carried by other forms of transport. Many manufacturers of high-tech goods, for example, which once would have used air cargo extensively, have in the economic downturn adjusted their supply chains to take advantage of slower, but cheaper, shipping. Also, some commodities are being shifted to containers from bulk shipping (such as foodstuffs and raw materials) where the economics of such a move allow.

One trend that may well impact on the traditional mainline trades is the effect of 'near' or 're-shoring' of manufacturing in the West due to rising costs in Asia and supply chain risk fears. It is still too early to judge whether it will have a material impact on shipping volumes, but it is certainly of concern to many shipping lines.

Summary

The advent of the first container ship 60 years ago led to a revolution in the way goods are moved around the world. The reduction in unit costs and the improvement of delivery times, which containerization brought about, facilitated globalization and directly allowed China, the largest beneficiary, to grow into the global economic powerhouse it is today. This chapter looked in detail at the emergence of the sector; its structure in terms of the various players involved, from shipping lines to terminal operators; how the industry has consolidated; and what impact the increase in ship sizes will have on the industry.

Key points to consider:

- Ship sizes are growing rapidly as shipping lines seek to increase economies of scale. However, the number of ports capable of taking these 'post-Panamax' size vessels is decreasing, leading to fewer direct calls.

- There have been many acquisitions in the industry, although not all of these have been handled well. A third of shipping capacity is operated by just three shipping lines.

- Shipping is highly cyclical and prone to 'boom and bust' with shipping lines historically poor at controlling the supply of capacity onto the market due to aggressive ship-building strategies.

- Slow-steaming policies, first implemented from an environmental policy perspective, have allowed shipping lines to more effectively control capacity although rates are still highly volatile.

- Freight forwarders are taking market share from the shipping lines owing to their more customer-focused approach and end-to-end supply chain solutions.

The European rail and intermodal sectors

11

CHAPTER LEARNING OBJECTIVES

This chapter will provide the reader with:

- An explanation of the importance of the European rail and intermodal sector in terms of environmental policy

- Its strengths and weaknesses compared with road freight haulage

- A definition of the industry and analysis of its various segments and market sectors

- Insight into the importance of the sector to automotive manufacturers

The European Commission (EC) believes that rail – and the way it interacts with other transport modes through intermodality – is highly important to the future of the European transport industry. A White Paper published by the EC in 2011 on the transport sector stated that the challenge was to ensure structural change to enable rail to compete effectively with road freight and take a significantly greater proportion of medium and long-distance freight. To do this, considerable investment would be needed to expand or to upgrade the capacity of the rail network (EC, 2011).

The White Paper accepted that freight shipments over short and medium distances (less than 300 kilometres) would, to a considerable extent, remain on trucks. However, over longer distances intermodal freight could become economically attractive for shippers if efficiency could be improved. According to the paper, the EU needs specially developed freight corridors 'optimised in terms of energy use and emissions, minimising environmental impacts, but also attractive for their reliability, limited congestion and low operating and administrative costs'.

In many respects the need for such statements reflects the lack of progress seen in the intermodal sector over the past few decades. Road is, and will remain, the mode of choice for most shippers. However, given the environmental priorities that have been set by governments and administrators, this form of transport has achieved significant political importance, even if out of proportion with commercial realities.

The reason why there has been a push, at least at governmental level, for greater use of rail is evident from the European Commission's assertion that whilst 1 kilogram of fuel is needed to transport 50 tonnes of goods 1 kilometre with a truck, the same amount of fuel can move 97 tonnes by rail and 127 tonnes by ship. However, it is estimated that intermodal transport represents only a small proportion of goods transported in Europe – somewhere between 2 per cent and 4 per cent of the total, although it is increasing by about 10 per cent a year.

What is intermodal transport?

The European Conference of Ministers of Transport (ECMT) and the United Nations Economic Commission for Europe (UN/ECE) have put forward the following definition: 'Intermodal transport [can be said to take place] when the major part of the journey is by rail, inland waterways or sea, and any initial and/or final legs carried out by road are as short as possible.'

Intermodal transport involves the carriage of freight using specially designed cargo-protecting units that can easily be swapped between several transport modes (for example, road, rail, inland waterways, sea, air). The advantage of utilizing this method is that it reduces cargo handling, and so improves security, reduces damages and loss, and allows freight to be transported faster. It avoids unloading and reloading of individual items but results in a lower overall payload due to the duplicated load-bearing elements of the rail vehicle and the load-carrying units. As a transport system, intermodal business tries to combine specific advantages of otherwise competing transport modes to achieve an overall gain for all partners involved. In some countries, road vehicles used mainly for intermodal transport get a tax redemption and these may carry a heavier load, thus commercially compensating for the higher dead weight of the units carried.

Intermodal terminals are the transfer points and are designed to take into account the very different properties of the transport modes involved. For example, road with single load-units carrying intermittent traffic flows, as compared with transport by trains based on timetabled transport of consolidated loads. Some major ports have developed advanced freight terminals and good rail or inland waterway links that integrate the different modes of transport efficiently.

Europe's longest lorry trailer-carrying railway freight service started operating commercially in 2007. The 1,060 kilometre-long 'piggyback' transit line transports trailers from Bettembourg in Luxembourg to Boulou (near Perpignan) in the south of France, close to the Spanish border. The rail service needs about 14 hours to make the journey so not only does it reduce road congestion and cut journey times (down from around 20 hours) but it also reduces transport costs. Echoing the drive-on capability of EuroShuttle – the train carrying cars through the tunnel under the English Channel – the Bettembourg-Boulou rail-freight line allows lorry drivers to load their trucks directly onto the train using a system of pivotal rail trailers.

Generally, freight benefits from the ability of different systems to operate together, particularly for container traffic, ship to rail. The role of combined road-rail transport in easing road congestion, for example, on the main north–south routes across the Alps to some extent depends on rail's ability to impact on infrastructure development. For example, Switzerland has developed its rail network with rail-friendly policies that have promoted a modal shift from road to rail. Rail now accounts for two-thirds of the volumes carried by Switzerland's trucks and trains, and Switzerland aims to reduce the number of trucks on its roads further.

Who does what in intermodal transport?

Demand side

Companies involved in buying and managing services from rail/intermodal operators include:

- Shippers: Directly or sometimes on their behalf contracts are signed for the movement of cargo between locations. The shipper is the owner of the cargo.

- Forwarders: The forwarder calculates the best option for moving the cargo; decides the service required as well as handling all administrative procedures such as customs and freight document processing.
- Ocean shipping lines: Shipping lines buy services in order to move containers to inland clearance depots on behalf of their customers. The shipping lines not only ensure that their customers' requirements are met but also have to ensure that their container fleets are fully utilized.
- Logistics Service Providers (LSPs): LSPs manage or own assets including warehouses, cross-docking platforms, container freight yards, storage areas and not just transport equipment.

Supply side

Companies involved in providing services within the complex intermodal ecosystem include:

- Terminal operators (TOs): TOs trans-ship loading units between the various long-haul transport modes such as trains, shortsea vessels, inland barges and, of course, road. Their main assets are trans-shipment equipment as well as short-term storage for the loading units.
- Rail, barge and shortsea transport providers: These operators handle the movement of the loading units between terminals via rail, inland waterway or sea routes. Assets are railway traction as well as wagons, barges and shortsea vessels.
- Road transport providers: Within the intermodal process they operate trucks for local haulage between the relevant terminal and the consignor or consignee.
- Intermodal transport operators: Intermodal operators obtain transport and trans-shipment services and either offer door-to-door or terminal-to-terminal transport. In addition, they also are able to assume the commercial risk of selling transport capacity from the transport providers as well as attempt to optimize the use of their own transport services.

Public supply side

Other parties involved in the process include:

- Infrastructure providers: Rail infrastructure providers (usually owned by governments) maintain the track, assign capacity (slots, pathways, etc) to users and decide access charges.

- Port authorities: Not only do they manage the port area but in addition they develop services and facilities for trans-shipment, transport and often other logistics services.

- Regional local government: Their role is similar to ports and they are frequently involved in logistics parks, often with the express aim of developing and encouraging intermodal services and facilities.

How is the market structured?

It is not unusual for providers to have activities involving more than just one aspect of the intermodal process. This means that the industry comprises not only highly specialized providers but also those that cover all functions from logistics planning through to transport operation. This has resulted in a diverse market with traditional providers operating alongside more hybrid providers, in a wide variety of partnerships and cooperations.

As a result, six market segments have emerged, all with slightly different aims and participants, and driven by differing market demands. However, there are many overlaps between segments; for example, it is often the case that the shipping lines and forwarders are each other's customers. Equipment used to transport and trans-ship is used by all the providers regardless of the segment, and many of the original road-rail operators now also handle containers.

The six segments are:

- carrier haulage;
- merchant haulage;
- seaport terminals;
- railway operator;
- continental shortsea;
- continental rail-road.

Carrier haulage

Often shipping lines have the responsibility for carrying the goods into the hinterland ('line haul'). These costs are high in comparison with ocean movements over much longer distances. It is not unusual for shipping lines to have a stake in seaport terminals, which enables the lines to optimize the end-to-end supply chain. This becomes more relevant as the size of ocean-going vessels increases with the continuing consolidation in the shipping industry itself.

In addition, shipping lines have also taken stakes in inland terminals particularly where these are the only point of entry for the hinterland. These terminals are often logistics centres optimizing not only cargo consolidation but also container logistics, particularly where they can be combined with container depots to minimize empty runs, thus improving productivity.

Some shipping lines handle shortsea feeder services themselves, but most of this trade is handled by independent feeder operators with their own or chartered vessels.

When still independent, Sealand and P&O/Nedlloyd founded the intermodal operator ERS (European Rail Shuttle) mainly because shipping lines were dissatisfied with the existing services being offered. By 2003, ERS (now owned by Maersk) had also entered rail operations itself, giving the shipping line owners full control over trans-shipment and hinterland transport in and out of some of Europe's ports.

Merchant haulage

In this case it is the shippers, forwarders or LSPs that are responsible for carrying the goods (and restitution of empty containers) from the seaport terminal to the customer based in the hinterland ('merch haul'). This is traditionally associated with forwarders who have the specialized knowledge in intercontinental trade along with customs and administration skills.

In this market there are more providers and the average actual transport requirement is less in comparison with the ocean shipping lines' 'line haul'. As a result vertical integration with seaport terminals is less likely, with a few of these providers linking only with feeder terminals.

Within the inland waterway segment both LSPs and forwarders are often owners or shareholders and often act as intermodal transport operators. Some of the forwarders are also involved in shortsea feeder services and as a result are able to offer a more comprehensive hinterland and overland transport.

Seaport terminals

Along with the consolidation that is taking place in the shipping industry, a considerable amount of horizontal integration is occurring amongst seaport terminals. Today many of the largest container terminals serving the shipping lines are part of providers such as Hutchison Port Holdings, PSA and DPW.

By offering a network of terminals it makes it easier to coordinate and integrate supply chains on a global scale for customers as well as providing operational flexibility in handling demand and in spreading risk. The widening of the scope of the offer on a global scale has allowed the terminal operators to increase productivity utilizing their terminal management and developing ICT skills. It is often the case that these operators also take shares or stakes in inland terminals as well as intermodal hinterland transport services.

Railway operator

Historically, rail providers have been in a dominant position for providing hinterland transport, particularly when the European rail market consisted of national monopolies and integrated infrastructure, terminal development as well as terminal operations. It was not unusual for these rail companies to have shares in seaports.

As the rail market underwent reform and liberalization, infrastructure and operations were separated and freight operations were transferred to new operating providers. This opened the market for new intermodal transport providers bringing with them different types of providers and cooperation. This increased competition between rail and intermodal providers has not prevented new intermodal services being developed jointly, but the mix of parties varies greatly.

Continental shortsea

These services are provided by ferry, Ro-Ro or container operators and the market tends to be concentrated on a few larger providers centred on the North Sea, Baltic and the Mediterranean. They tend to focus on this only, leaving other aspects of freight forwarding and overland transport to their customers. Some have their origins as ferry providers with road transport operators as their customers. Most of the door-to-door operators began life as freight operators in shortsea shipping, who extended their services either into the hinterland or a full range of logistics services.

The scale of operations of a Ro-Ro provider often dictates that a terminal is dedicated to a single provider with ownership of the port terminal usually remaining with the port authorities. It is unusual for container operations to be the domain of the shortsea provider.

Continental rail-road

Most of these types of intermodal operators were founded by road and rail companies, with the latter always having a minority share. Railways provided traction, trans-shipment services and often wagons, whilst road providers (or forwarders) had access to the customer as well as collection and delivery services. This meant that any additional development of logistics services was usually provided by the road companies and not the resulting alliance of the two. This development was of mutual benefit: road providers had access to large-scale rail transport and the railways access to cargo flows.

As the intermodal market opened up so other logistics providers entered the market and started their own intermodal operations. Often these were neither owned by nor associated with rail companies and these additional services became strategic assets that could be integrated with their existing logistics services such as road transport, warehousing and storage as well as other added-value offers.

Who decides what to use?

When transport management is out-sourced by the shipper, the choice of mode is often left to the logistics provider, albeit some may express a preference for a particular supply chain solution. Whenever logistics service providers are involved with their own assets they try to increase their returns by utilizing them to their full optimization, and intermodal services are offered as part of a portfolio of integrated services. They become very much part of the decision-making process and big influencers as to which services best suit the shippers' requirements.

Other intermediaries, such as forwarders who have little or no assets, manage transport for the shipper with a different agenda. They are interested in maximizing the margin above the actual procurement cost, albeit within the constraints set by the shipper. Intermodal transport is often utilized because of the potential to cut costs.

Shipping lines are often attractive to shippers as they can, in many instances, provide hinterland routes as well. Intermodal fits well into this because it adds to the overall scale of port terminal operations, thus providing additional opportunities for hinterland traffic and inland terminals.

Rotterdam is Europe's largest port. As such the strategy that is in place to deal with the distribution of containers throughout its European hinterland is highly important.

In response to the growing pressure of congestion on roads around the terminal, the Dutch government invested US $6.1 billion in the development of a freight-only rail line connecting Rotterdam to Germany – the Betuwe Line. The project also involved the creation of two dedicated rail service centres rationalizing previous operations in the port and run by a private company. A shuttle service links these two service centres with 100 TEU capacity per shuttle.

Using the Betuwe Line, a daily shuttle links 37 European destinations with Rotterdam with a total capacity of 7 million TEU per year, although the line is not confined to container traffic – chemicals and bulk dry are also important.

Overall intermodal rail in the Netherlands has been eclipsed by intermodal barges. Rail accounts for just 5 per cent of volumes to Rotterdam compared with 48 per cent by inland waterway. However, destinations such as Italy will benefit most from the rail link.

Internationally, 15 per cent of cargo moving to Germany through Rotterdam goes by rail; this compares with 13 per cent of volumes to Belgium and 14 per cent to France.

Largest domestic intermodal operators

According to the UIRR, the industry body representing the leading inter-modal operators, German company Kombiverkehr is the largest national player (that is, not including international shipments) in terms of tonne kilometres. It is followed by the largest players in Italy (Cemat) and in France (Novatrans). Taking into account purely international shipments, Kombiverkehr is still the largest intermodal player. Swiss operator Hupac is the second largest followed by Italy's Cemat. Both these players are very active in the transalpine market.

Intermodal solutions in the automotive sector

The rail market has played a very important part in the distribution strategies, both inbound and finished vehicle, of all the major vehicle manufacturers (VMs). The automotive industry, unlike geographically dispersed light industry, is still focused around major industrial plants, which are large enough to support investment in railheads and have the necessary level of volumes. However, changes in the industry over the last 20 years have meant that even in one of the last remaining heavy industries, rail has become increasingly marginalized.

Rail is inherently less flexible than road freight, and this became a major problem when VMs started to implement JIT supply chain management techniques. Manufacturers moved from the stochastic flows of components, to a model based on more frequent deliveries in smaller batch sizes. Inventory holdings have also been reduced, making delivery times more critical. Rail's reliability issues have therefore become another reason why volumes have been driven from rail to road.

In Europe especially, rail has not been able to benefit from the trend towards centralization of production in fewer plants. It may have logically been assumed that rail's competitive advantage over longer distance against road would have given it an edge, especially as production has migrated to the peripheries of the European Union (that is, Spain, Italy, Central and Eastern Europe). However, the fact that Europe's railways continue to operate largely as nationalized and domestic focused organizations, mitigates against efficient international operations. There are also practical problems, such as difference in rail gauges in Spain and the rest of Europe. Russia has the same problem.

There is a much larger market for intermediaries in the United States than in Europe, focused on the intermodal sector. Forwarders such as Yusen Logistics and the Hub Group, working with the railroads, guarantee capacity, recommend rates and routes.

The US railroads have also been much more proactive in developing services, especially on the inbound distribution side. Norfolk Southern runs a 'JIT rail network' for both GM and Ford. It works with a partner, Innovative Logistics Group, to provide daily milk runs from JIT rail centres in all the key hubs. Norfolk Southern also works with Penske Logistics for Ford, developing new services and more efficient rail equipment.

CASE STUDY Intermodal logistics strategies of Europe's leading auto manufacturers

PSA Group Peugeot-Citroen

The handling of finished vehicle logistics from both PSA brands is handled entirely by French logistics subsidiary, GEFCO, which uses a mix of rail and road transport, with most trunk routes for the movement of vehicles being by rail. For example, although GEFCO does not use the Channel Tunnel to move finished cars into the UK, it does use rail in order to move cars to its central storage area in the English Midlands.

GEFCO also benefits from exploiting its relationship with French railways (SNCF). It has a major intermodal business, which is built upon the scale of traffic moved by GEFCO for Peugeot-Citroen, giving it access to an infrastructure and – just as importantly – a relationship with the state-owned SNCF.

Ford

Ford has been traditionally a heavy user of rail services, although it has moved away from its reliance on rail. Firstly, it redesigned its finished vehicle logistics operations out of Cologne and Saarlouis. These are now heavily reliant on barge traffic to Vlissingen and Antwerp. Secondly, it has redesigned much of its finished vehicle movements from other plants to use shortsea shipping. Major product flows to Scandinavia, UK and countries in the Mediterranean now use shortsea shipping rather than rail. This not only reflects annoyance at poor service from national rail systems in France, Italy and elsewhere, but also a greater concern for reliability and transparency from finished vehicle logistics providers.

Volkswagen

The origins of Volkswagen lie in its German Wolfsburg plant. Located in the centre of Germany, the plant dates back to the 1930s when it was built around rail transport. As a consequence Volkswagen Group in Europe is still a heavy user of rail services. VW Logistics' operations in Germany rely on a structure of 'Gebeitspediton' (area transport) at its core. This is a series of logistics companies who use road transport to collect materials from VW's component suppliers. These components are then loaded onto trains at rail terminals and taken to the relevant VW Group plant. For the distribution of finished vehicles the process is reversed. The main exception to this is the delivery of components from suppliers located near to assembly plants, which use road transport. The companies used to doing this are dominated by German LSPs, notably Schenker.

DB Cargo is fundamental to the 'Gebeitspediton' operations. This system covers a high proportion of components supplied to VW Group as VW has less supplier park developments than are seen at other VMs. Even bulky items such as seats and interiors are drawn-in from suppliers some distance away (for example, much of the seating for the Golf is now sourced out of Belgium). Transport into VW Group plants outside Germany is more complex, but generally the same system is used, with plants in Poland, Spain, Czech Republic and Slovakia being heavily reliant on rail freight.

General Motors

In the past few years, GM's European rail activity has been rationalized. Its supply chain, particularly for inbound, has a very localized 'Gebeitspedition' system, which generally delivers around 70–90 per cent of all components. However, as GM's production geography has changed, the supply chain has stretched. Some suppliers, even of major engine components, are only located near one plant. As GM 'flexes' its production schedules a need has arisen to move components between plants. To do this GM has once again moved to use rail services, creating a dedicated daily 'block-train' travelling between its plants in Spain, Belgium, Germany, Austria and Hungary. The volumes moving on this service are quite substantial and illustrate that GM frequently looks to rail to achieve economies of scale in logistics.

For finished vehicles again a 'Gebeitspedition' system, with local road-based car-carriers interfacing with rail trunking services, is used. This service has been consolidated to achieve the highest volumes possible. Across Europe GM uses GEFCO as its 4PL, allowing it to combine its volumes with competitors such as PSA Peugeot Citroen.

Renault-Nissan

Renault's inbound logistics is dominated by road freight with the close location of suppliers precluding other options. Outbound still has a strong rail element, particularly between Spain and France, but also within France. The company, however, has sought to reduce its exposure to rail transport for long-range trucking movement of finished cars as rail was found to be too unpredictable and lacked 'transparency'. This has led to the increased role of shortsea shipping.

BMW

In terms of modal choice, BMW shows a substantial preference for rail over road. In large part this is due to political pressure in Germany and Austria against road transport. Rail is used both for inbound material flow, but even more so for the movement of finished vehicles. Whilst local and some 'trunk' movements are still made by road, long-distance markets are increasingly served by rail. Large rail traffic includes:

- vehicles for export to the UK and non-European markets;

- Mini exports from Oxford, UK, through the port of Purfleet, UK;

- vehicles to Italy and other southern European markets by rail from its assembly plants.

The trend towards rail transport in Germany and certain other western European countries is likely to continue.

For inbound, the question is more complex. As ever there is a trade-off between the capability of rail to handle high volumes of material and the flexibility of road freight to handle smaller batch quantities. In a slight departure from the norm, engines from the Hams Hall engine plant are moved to Germany by road. However, much of the rest of BMW's other major component flows within Germany and between plants use rail.

Mercedes Benz

Mercedes Benz is a more modest user of rail than the other German VMs. The fewer production locations and lower volumes mean that suppliers tend to be located nearer to assembly sites and therefore the need to move large quantities of inbound materials over long distances is less.

The important exceptions to this are the movement of finished vehicle and components for CKD exports out of Germany to non-European locations via the ports of Bremerhaven and Hamburg. Bearing in mind the proportion of production exported from its German assembly plants, this is an important aspect of Mercedes Benz's overall logistics activity. The company has collaborated with Deutsche Bahn to create new designs of covered rail wagons that facilitate more efficient use of rail for finished vehicle distribution to the German ports, within Germany and into other European markets. Like most European VMs, MBPC feels under pressure to increase its use of rail as opposed to road freight and it is assumed that projects like this will continue.

Summary

In Europe, legislators have placed a good deal in faith in the ability of intermodal rail services to reduce road freight traffic in line with environmental goals. Intermodal services are efficient over longer distances, but the sector has been blighted by its structural complexity and problems with national rail freight operators. This chapter described the way in which the sector is organized, outlining the various parties involved with intermodal movements of goods. It also examined how intermodal solutions have been successfully integrated into automotive supply chains.

Key points to consider:

- A key problem for the sector is its complexity and the number of parties involved in comparatively simple movements of goods. This compares poorly with the flexibility and simplicity of the road freight sector.

- Ports and shipping lines can use intermodal services as a way of moving containers quickly into their hinterlands (to 'inland ports' such as Duisport), avoiding congestion in and around the port area.

- Intermodal solutions can be made to work in 'heavy industries' such as automotive. However, even here, modern supply chain management policies call for small, frequent delivery schedules, which is at odds with the intermodal operating model.

- The European Commission is working on making certain key 'freight corridors' more efficient in order to increase the competitiveness of long-distance intermodal services against road.

Supply chain technologies   12

CHAPTER LEARNING OBJECTIVES

This chapter will provide the reader with:

- Explanation of the various types of supply chain management software and the differences between planning and execution systems

- A detailed overview of transport (international and domestic), warehouse and trade management systems and how they interrelate

- An overview of the changing nature of supply chain technologies due to the development of cloud-based systems

- An examination of freight exchanges, control towers and the latest developments in the sector, driven by the needs of e-commerce operations

Owing to supply chain trends such as Just-in-Time, remote manufacturing, increased inventory velocity, proliferating SKUs, omni-channel strategies as well as the need to meet ever-increasing customer demands, the supply chain has become a massively complicated environment.

The threat to manufacturers and retailers is clear. Unless managers are able to achieve visibility within their supply chains, overcoming traditional functional silos and coordinating sales, production and logistics efforts, they risk escalating inventory levels, diminishing customer service and the inability to react to supply chain disruption.

Technologies have developed to meet these changing needs and are now a critical element of any well-functioning supply chain. Although the range of functionalities that these technologies have been designed to address is diverse, essentially their role is to provide accurate information, which enables managers to make better decisions, whatever the complexity of the supply chain.

What is supply chain management software?

Supply chain management (SCM) software can be broadly divided between those applications that focus on supply chain planning (SCP) and those that focus on supply chain execution (SCE).

Supply chain planning systems are designed to relate demand forecasts for products with the coordination of supply, schedule manufacturing and provide the relevant data for metrics for performance analysis. This ensures the optimization of inventory and the relation of marketing and sales effort to production and logistics in a close collaborative effort.

Supply chain planning itself can be subdivided between 'strategic' and 'tactical'. At the highest level, a manufacturer or retailer will try to work out its requirements for facilities, distribution channels and inventory holding locations over a two to three year (or more) period.

At a tactical level, the company will typically plan, during its annual budgeting process, sales targets, materials requirements and labour.

Typical tasks undertaken by SCP software include:

- network planning and design;
- capacity planning;
- scenario planning and real-time demand;
- manufacturing planning.

At its most basic level, SCP software allows a planner to look at aggregated customer and sales office orders and then match these against the manufacturing schedules and capacity. At this point, orders can be allocated 'intelligently' to the best factory or supplier based on lowest cost production and available resources, including inventories, transport and lead times.

Whereas SCP systems are designed to give managers a long-term time horizon (years and months in advance) and operate at a strategic and tactical level, SCE systems are much more operational, allowing supply chain tasks (such as in the transportation or warehousing functions) to be completed effectively in minutes, hours or days. In effect, SCP systems sit 'above' SCE, with information from each feeding into the other, establishing plans and then, after execution, providing insight into the effectiveness of the planning.

SCE software typically includes:

- transport management systems (TMS);
- warehouse management systems (WMS);
- inventory management systems;
- order processing.

As the supply chain touches every part of a business's function, SCP and SCE systems will necessarily interface with a range of other software types such as HR and Finance. Many software companies such as SAP, for example, provide SCP and SCE systems as part of a broader enterprise resource planning (ERP) system.

Figure 12.1 Supply chain management and execution levels

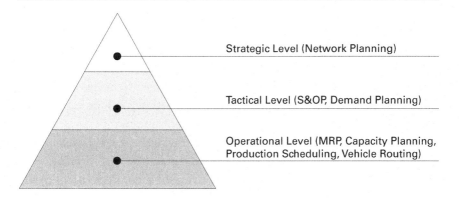

Supply chain execution systems

Transport management systems (TMS)

Whilst early transport management systems (TMS) were designed solely to manage the movement of trucks, facilitating loading, routing, pricing and costing, they have evolved significantly over the past three decades. In addition to these tasks, they can now integrate the management of a shipper's or logistics operator's vehicles with carrier and bid optimization, facilitate collaboration across departments, fleet management and a range of other functions.

For example, typically a TMS can now be used to tender out shipments to carriers in real time, resulting in significant freight cost savings. To allow the bidding process to take place, transport companies can be 'hooked up' to a system. This allows the shipper to tender out their business to pre-qualified carriers, ensuring that quality levels are ensured.

Freight payment is also an important feature of many TMS. Automation eliminates administrative activities related to the receipt of invoices from suppliers. A TMS can cover all aspects of transportation rates, including surcharges and discounts and make automated payments as well as reporting on costs. They typically hold a (global) database of rate cards from carriers against which bills can be checked automatically.

There are also some sophisticated systems that support 'spot pricing', enabling users to negotiate with various carriers, either via discounts from standard card rates or specifically negotiated deals. This capability illustrates how technology is mimicking the expertise of human operators and it will be inherent in many of the new Cloud services that are beginning to emerge.

Visibility and event management allows for shippers to manage exceptions throughout the execution of the shipment. This will include tracking planned versus actual milestones, diverting shipments, and where necessary expediting delivery. Even if the TMS is provided by a 'pure play' provider rather than a broad ERP provider such as Oracle, they will be expected to integrate seamlessly with other supply chain applications.

Beyond this, they also allow for shipment tracking as well as even vehicle tracking through GPS technology. Many are exploiting 'Geo-Fencing' capabilities to define specific routes and boundaries so that any deviations by the vehicle trigger alerts.

TMS are now far from being standalone. They will typically be integrated with enterprise-wide resource planning systems (ERPs), linking with warehouse management systems (WMS) as well as production and sales and marketing. In addition, they will also have to link with the carriers' systems (involving EDI and Web Services) and, if used, those of the 3PL managing warehousing and distribution.

In addition, they can be contracted by the shipper on an on-demand basis (software as a service SAAS) or bought outright if their volumes are high enough.

The benefits accrue not only from the savings in freight rates and the additional visibility that TMS can provide, but by being fully integrated into the shipper's financial systems, it can ensure greater accuracy of billing and an improved awareness of transportation costs. A further opportunity for users of TMS is the ability to consolidate multiple individual shipments into full loads, thereby optimizing flows of goods to individual customers or locations. This can even influence modal choice, with lower cost options being used.

For example, when Korean consumer goods manufacturer LG implemented a TMS in the United States it aimed to increase 'load fill' rates by 3 per cent and reduce transportation costs by 4 per cent. With more than 700 truckload movements a day, this would be a considerable saving. In fact, the company was able to reduce transport and distribution costs by 8 per cent as well as improve its customer delivery reliability to between 98 and 99.2 per cent. According to a consultancy, ARC research, TMS users can achieve average freight savings of 7.5 per cent.

The TMS has also gained in importance due to omni-channel strategies being employed by retailers. This has added additional levels of complexity within the distribution process and the reduction in shipment size has increased costs. It is more important than ever before to maximize efficiency. 'Green' agendas also require shippers and logistics companies to minimize their carbon emissions, which of course the use of TMS allows.

Along with many applications, TMS are increasingly migrating to the Cloud and this is bringing their benefits to shippers with much smaller transportation budgets. The set-up costs and implementation meant that TMS had most benefits for shippers with transportation spend of more than US $100 million. Industry analyst, Gartner, now believes that this has reduced to just US $20 million bringing sophisticated TMS within reach of a whole new 'mid-market'. The Cloud option means that the shipper can deploy fewer IT resources; there are no upgrade costs; it has easy connectivity resulting in low total cost of ownership.

Of course, TMS applications are widely used by much smaller trucking companies and the reducing cost of technology has made them ubiquitous for companies with only a handful of vehicles. These types of TMS traditionally had a much more limited functionality but even they now increasingly offer a greater range of services such as the ability to integrate with telematics (that is, vehicle tracking). Each country will have numerous, 'boutique' TMS developers either competing in specific niches which the larger providers do not see as cost effective, or at a lower price point for

'TMS-light' products. Many customers now insist that even their smallest transport providers use a TMS as this can then be integrated with their own systems.

Leading TMS providers

The market can be divided into three main types of provider: 'pure players', broad ERP providers who as part of their suite of products provide TMS capabilities, and LSPs who provide managed transportation services for their clients.

The leading providers include the following:

- Oracle;
- JDA;
- SAP;
- GT Nexus;
- Descartes;
- Kewill;
- Manhattan;
- Quintiq;
- Accellos (now Highjump);
- IBM/Sterling Commerce (now Kewill).

Kewill has transformed itself into a market leader through acquisition in the past few years including IBM's Sterling Commerce. It is believed that these 10 providers account for roughly 60 per cent of the market. There is a plethora of other smaller players, many nationally based, which do a really good job at providing solutions for specific markets. For example, Lean Logistics in the United States is seen as a market leader. However, it has faced challenges when moving out into a multi-country environment in Europe and Asia due to its lack of multi-modal capabilities, especially crossborder.

Other US providers include Transplace, TMW, inet-logistics, Logility and MercuryGate. In the UK Mandata is a major player.

There are some logistics providers that provide TMS capabilities for their clients. At the forefront of these is CH Robinson.

A further step in the development of TMS is the trend towards 'Control Tower' management systems. In theory these should allow a team of analysts to gain real-time insight into the performance of in-house and out-sourced logistics provision. In times when supply chain risk has been pushed up the corporate agenda, visibility and the ability to flex inbound and outbound logistics through agile decision making has become crucial. Control Towers can be implemented either by the shipper itself or through the use of a 4PL, which manages all other resources. As such DHL, DSV, Damco and a host of other leading logistics companies have been keen to develop their capabilities in this value adding sector.

4PLs or lead logistics providers (LLPs) have overall responsibility for coordinating and managing all of the parties used to operate the supply chain on behalf of the principal or supply chain owner. The key to managing anything of this nature, particularly on an international basis is supply chain visibility. This has been a critical necessity for many years and while some companies and operators claim they have it, very few really do. The global integrated carriers come closest, with their sophisticated track and trace capabilities, but these only work well when the entire supply chain operates within their realm, using their assets. In fact, the truth is that most global chains use a variety of logistics service providers, transportation service providers and others. As soon as the chain of custody of a particular order or shipment transfers to another party, the granularity of visibility changes.

A 'Control Tower' is, in essence, a multi-party visibility hub, which interconnects and interoperates with the information systems of all of the involved parties. These entities take a long while to set up and, depending on the technologies involved, require constant adjustment. At best, they can provide a central point for understanding the general location and status of the supply chain activity. They may also be able to provide the ability to go through the 'Control Tower' and drill down into a specific system for more detail. However, for the full concept to be realized, any information about any activity in the chain needs to be made available instantly to the appropriate parties across the supply chain. Technology is moving towards achieving this goal, but it is as much an operational and cultural challenge for the interested parties as it is a technical one, but one that must be addressed before the rewards of such a concept can be realized.

Warehouse management systems (WMS)

The warehouse management system is fundamental to the operations of any manufacturer, retailer or LSP. As well as supporting the day-to-day operations of a distribution centre, allowing for visibility of stock and, of course, therefore stock levels within the warehouse environment, it also allows for order management, processing and pick and pack, interfacing with a range of other business functions such as finance, customer service, sales and transport. As such WMS systems have to be able to interface seamlessly with ERP systems and material handling equipment as well as including 'deeper' functionality such as voice recognition, RFID and even virtual reality.

At the highest level, a WMS must be able to support sophisticated warehousing needs, including value added services, lot management, serial number tracking and product recalls. As with most supply execution applications WMS are increasingly being hosted in 'The Cloud' rather than 'on premises'. These 'Cloud' solutions also make it easier to support multiple warehouses on the same platform enabling inventory 'pooling'. Although some existing 'on premises' solutions can support multiple warehouses, they frequently involve additional hardware and licence costs.

A WMS must be able to capture data at every stage of the warehousing process. This includes the type and number of goods at time of receipt (as well as condition). It will then allocate the best location for the put-away or, if a cross-dock model is being employed, the other parts of the order it should be bundled with for immediate dispatch. The product's meta-data along with its storage location will be stored in a vast database.

When an order is received at a traditional distribution centre, the WMS will provide details to the pickers either in the form of printed-off bills, or through communication with the picker via pick-by-voice, pick-by-light or even through virtual reality glasses. The WMS will plan the most efficient route for the picker, which may involve picking by individual order, or where more appropriate, picking by batch. The order is then packed, labelled (with data from the initial order by way of the WMS), documentation generated, the order status updated and it then becomes ready for dispatch. At this point the WMS will alert the TMS and the next part of the order fulfilment will commence – in some cases an Advance Ship Note will be sent to alert the customer. At the same time as this, information will be transferred back up the supply chain, triggering decisions on stock replenishment, supplier and customer invoicing, packaging requirements, etc.

Although this sounds very simple in theory, the huge amount of data and variables involved require a very sophisticated solution, even in relatively small operations:

- Warehousing staff. The WMS manages and directs the pickers, order processors and other warehouse staff in the most efficient way. It also keeps records of their performance (such as number of picking errors) as well as time management.

- The meta-data related to each consignment are considerable. Through its barcode or RFID tag, each stock keeping unit (SKU) could have data concerning its type, weight, dimensions, sell-by date and storage restriction (such as perishable or hazardous) attached to it, plus many more.

- To work out the best location to place the SKU, the WMS will make decisions based on whether the SKU is slow or fast moving (for example, how accessible it should be); calculate the type of storage (carton or pallet for single picking or unit picking); the environment in which it should be stored (restricted, secure, temperature controlled, bonded, etc) and many other conditions depending on the type of product.

- Once the order is received, the WMS must be able to allocate the shipment to the right dock door for collection by the carrier.

- All this must be handled in a timely manner to prevent congestion throughout the warehouse (especially in the inbound and outbound dock areas) and ensure that deadlines/targets are being met.

e-commerce and WMS

The demands placed upon WMS are undergoing significant changes as companies incorporate e-commerce into their overall strategy. Decisions on whether to fulfil e-commerce orders from separate facilities, in-store, from existing warehouses or a combination of all three are amongst the strategic choices.

The higher volume of e-commerce orders is affecting this need for speed to fulfil, and the layout of warehouses is becoming of great importance. For some companies, the use of high-bay racking, product placement and an effective alignment of rack storage are necessary. Also, there is an increasing use of automation within such facilities with the use of robotics on the increase, as indicated by the acquisition of Kiva Systems by Amazon.

Managing the delivery process is also an increasingly difficult task as delivery locations from warehousing/fulfilment centres are no longer confined to physical stores. Now, these facilities are being used to ship either directly to the customer, a neutral site (such as a lockbox location, FedEx/UPS store or other retailer) or to the physical store for pickup. As such, technology companies such as High Jump, Red Prairie, Oracle and others have expanded their WMS, TMS and other IT solutions to meet this need for flexibility, not only for changing transportation needs, but also for order/inventory management and visibility.

CASE STUDY   Snapfulfil

Warehouse management system (WMS) provider Snapfulfil experienced a 70 per cent uplift in transactions on its system in the run-up to Christmas 2015. According to the company, for one major customer alone, Snapfulfil provided more than 100 additional licences and RF devices, and handled in excess of 150,000 transactions per day. To accommodate this increase, the company invested in extra server capacity to maintain service levels and availability to all customers during the critical peak trading period.

In 2013, the company planned for a 30 per cent uplift and in 2014 experienced a 50 per cent increase, reflecting its continued penetration in the retail sector. Snapfulfil also reported that Black Friday is driving a sharper increase in demand compared with the more gradual ramp-up previously associated with the lead-in to Christmas.

Owing to Snapfulfil's SaaS model, customers can temporarily increase the number of software licences and devices they use, for as long as they need them and revert back to their original agreement when activity levels return to normal. This provides a cost-effective and flexible warehouse management solution to support their peak trading periods.

Snapfulfil's Technical Director, Andy White, said: 'As well as allowing our customers to flex their operations in line with activity levels, Snapfulfil is also extremely user-friendly, which means that they can get temporary staff up and running on the system within minutes.' Adding: 'We also offer the highest levels of resiliency and redundancy in both infrastructure and hardware as standard and have made a significant investment in increasing server capacity to accommodate increased activity levels. This provides our customers with a robust, failsafe warehouse management solution at a time when they simply can't afford any downtime.'

Global trade management (GTM) systems

Global trade is a highly complex process that involves multiple partners as well as a diverse range of capabilities. An importer or exporter will require contact with freight forwarders, customs agencies, carriers (road, rail, air or sea), banks as well as its suppliers or customers located in foreign markets.

Not only must global trade management (GTM) applications manage the flow of goods and information between all these parties, but they must also facilitate financial transactions. At the same time, they must be flexible enough to enable regulatory compliance, including updating information on tariffs and non-tariff barriers (such as quotas).

Importing and exporting in many parts of the developing world are still bureaucratic and complicated, especially in China where regulations can vary by region and change at short notice. An automated system is essential to improve efficiency when dealing with the multiple agencies involved in the crossborder movement of goods and cut delays. It can also reduce the levels of duty being paid by utilizing free trade zones and preferential trade agreements as well as providing a robust audit trail.

A further capability that many global manufacturers are looking for is the level of visibility that will enable them to 'audit' the quality of their suppliers from an ethical and environmental perspective.

Finally, as well as regulatory compliance, GTM systems also book capacity with the range of LSPs or carriers.

In summary, GTMs include some or all of the following functions:

- **Global sourcing:** Provides information on final 'landed cost' of the product, delivery schedules and compliance implications. The information provided can inform negotiations with suppliers to ensure the most timely and cost-efficient solution. This can also include risk and quality management, ensuring that all products purchased comply with relevant safety/product testing requirements.

- **Transport management:** As with a domestic TMS, a GTM system will include contract and rate management, carrier selection and booking as well as freight cost auditing capabilities. They may also allow scenario planning, which will give shippers the ability to determine the quickest and cheapest ways of moving their goods internationally.

- **Supply chain visibility:** Due to the number of parties (and subcontracting) within an international supply chain, the location of goods and their delivery times is often uncertain. By connecting the full range of supply chain partners, GTMs have the potential to allow the tracking and monitoring of goods by creating pre-established connectivity within a global trading network.

- **Import and export management:** Covering export and import compliance checks, screening restricted parties, product classification and determining licence requirements, the GTM will interface with Customs' systems undertaking entry management, security filings and broker integration. The system will also manage duty payments, helping shippers to find least-cost options by utilizing free trade zones and free trade agreements.

International transport management systems (ITMS)

A freight forwarder will require a focus slightly different from a shipper (although many of its needs will be similar) and specific applications have been developed to meet these commercial needs.

In many respects, the freight forwarding industry has still to adopt technological developments seen in other sectors. The multiple rekeying of data is endemic, which is not only costly (in terms of labour) and slow, but is also prone to errors. The use of an ITM connected to all the supply chain partners means that one-time entry can be achieved and shipment documentation such as air waybills (AWBs), bills of lading and manifests can be generated automatically.

Similar to the transport management function of a GTM, forwarders will need links to carriers' rates in order for them to develop proposals to potential customers as quickly as possible. In the past this has required multiple phone calls to a range of carriers, and the ability of an experienced forwarder to work out the best routing. Using a set of 'rules', this whole process becomes faster and more commoditized. More proposals can be generated by fewer, less experienced staff as the software works out the best and lowest cost options, including modal choice, as well as building in margins for administrative functions such as generation of documentation.

ITMs also provide forwarders with the ability to track shipments and, by way of exception reporting, let their customers know if there have been any delays or disruptions (therefore potentially allowing for re-routing).

Other functions of ITMs include:

- consolidation of loads;
- customs clearance;
- last mile delivery/proof of delivery documentation;
- warehousing;
- invoicing;
- profit analysis.

Most smaller forwarders are using technology to manage their businesses, but usually this has happened as a result of necessity rather than as part of a strategic decision process. As technology has advanced, costs have come down as capability has increased. The general availability of solutions running in the Cloud and available on a monthly subscription basis has been a game changer. Much of the functionality now available 'on demand' is a match for the existing solutions developed internally (at great cost) by the large integrated carriers and multinational logistics companies.

The significance of this is that the operating costs of Cloud solutions are very low, their ability to scale, also 'on demand', provides tremendous flexibility. These solutions are usually developed using modern development tools and frameworks, enabling changes or adjustments to take place and be implemented very quickly. This is a significant advantage when attempting to support customer demands for flexible and adaptable supply chains. The larger forwarders have developed solutions over many years to support the business requirement of predictable, rigid operating practices capable of handling huge volumes of orders and shipments. These platforms are usually a mix of tightly integrated applications that are expensive to maintain and difficult to change. As technology continues to bring us many more sophisticated devices, especially mobile devices, the users in these large companies expect that they will be able to use these tools in concert with their corporate systems. This raises issues of security, interoperability and data ownership.

The information services functions in these companies face a daunting prospect of supporting the needs of the business, while dealing with a tsunami of different demands for access to more data, increased functionality, while managing the retirement of legacy systems and implementing new ones. Smaller forwarders using solutions in the Cloud may not yet have access to technology that is as tailored and feature-rich as a dedicated in-house solution, but if they can get a very large percentage of that at much lower cost and available within days, they will at last be able to compete – and win.

Cloud or 'on premises'?

One of the major questions facing users of supply chain execution software is whether to use a Cloud-based application or stick with the traditional practice of installing licensed software on owned servers (so-called 'on premises'). Although many companies are moving their software to the Cloud there are important factors to take into account:

▶

- How much customization is required? If your business has multiple business needs in multiple locations it may be better to install software that has been customized for these requirements rather than adopt a harmonized Cloud option. However, owing to the speed of development of these solutions, Cloud solutions will soon match or exceed the functionality of many legacy 'on-premises' solutions.

- What is the total cost of ownership? When deciding whether to use a Software-as-a-Service (SaaS) over the Cloud or on-premises option, you should factor in the replacement costs for servers and other hardware. Upgrades of SaaS may come as standard, whereas you may have to pay for them if using licensed software. This is alongside considerable cost of hardware, software and staffing. Internal system implementations will also continue over many years.

- How are user costs calculated? Details such as this are important. Will everyone who has access to the application – either Cloud or on-premises – be billed or just users?

Only by undertaking a full audit of needs and then setting these against the attributes of Cloud or on-premises can a customer be confident they are choosing the right option.

Freight exchanges

The principle of freight exchanges is very simple: to match shippers' demand for transport services with availability of supply in the market. The road freight industry is highly inefficient as demonstrated by the amount of empty trucks on the roads. This is not necessarily due to the absence of loads (although obviously in some cases it may be), but often the lack of information that would have allowed supply to be matched with demand. In other words, a shipper may not know that a road freight operator has the right vehicle going to the right destination at the right time (at the right price).

It may be surprising to many, but freight exchanges have not developed as a recent disruptive innovation. Many have been around for the best part of 20 years, for example Teleroute in the Netherlands. However, interest is growing in them not least due to the impact of innovators in other sectors, such as Uber.

Given that they have been around so long, why haven't freight exchanges already revolutionized the industry? Security is a big issue. When the shipper/freight operator relationship is commoditized through a freight exchange, one of the leading concerns is over security. The shipper may never have come across the trucking company before and is therefore reliant on the freight exchange to make sure that they are reliable, have a reputable track record and have the necessary security clearances. Many shippers are rightly concerned about the risk to their goods if these issues are not addressed fully by the freight exchange.

Freight exchanges can work in several ways. Some are what might be called 'pure' or 'neutral' exchanges where the platform matches shippers with road freight companies. Other 'exchanges' have been developed as a way for a single company – such as a freight forwarder – to let carriers know about loads that it has to move on behalf of its own customers. In effect, this is using the exchange to build a larger supplier pool of carriers. This is important for freight forwarders in order to keep their costs down, especially in times of tight capacity. The freight forwarder remains the principal in these dealings, and responsible for the quality control and security, which in many cases puts shippers off using such a tool.

One example of this is LKW Walter, the Austrian road freight forwarder. Its offering is called 'Loads Today' and is an extension of its long-standing European road freight service. Customers book their shipments through LKW Walter's Connect interface and the forwarder manages the rest of the process. Others, such as UK forwarder, Freightex, are slightly different. Their business developed from their technology rather than from a traditional forwarding background. However, both share the same concept of retaining the contact with the customer, rather than solely providing a neutral trading platform.

To overcome the problem of security and reliability of the trucking companies, some exchanges have adopted a 'closed loop' model. This means that dedicated freight exchange is set up for a major shipper, with only quality assured suppliers able to participate. In many cases these will be nominated by the shipper itself. This means that the exchange has less 'liquidity' (and so rates will be higher) but quality should not be an issue, whilst there are also benefits for the ease of transaction.

Summary

This chapter reviewed the key supply chain systems, distinguishing and explaining the difference between supply chain planning (SCP) and supply chain execution (SCE) software. It analysed the functionality of transport management systems (TMS), warehouse management systems (WMS) as well as other systems addressing the full range of logistics requirements. In addition it looked at the changing demands being placed on technology to cope with e-commerce sales and the development of freight exchanges.

Key points to consider:

- Modern supply chain environments are massively complicated. Managers require more visibility than ever to enable them to make informed decisions using 'Big Data'.

- As transport costs have grown (not least due to the surge in e-commerce shipments) transport management systems have become ever more important to maximize efficiency.

- The cost of technology has fallen, providing smaller logistics costs the opportunity to compete with larger companies on similar terms.

- 'Control Towers' have become very popular innovations. They interconnect and operate with the information systems of all of the involved parties providing the shipper with greater levels of visibility over shipment location and logistics costs.

- Global trade management (GTM) and international transport management systems (ITMS) have become essential to the crossborder movement of goods, managing the flows of goods and information between importers, exporters, Customs organizations, airlines, shipping lines and freight forwarders.

- Although freight exchanges have been around for many years, they have yet to make a major impact on the market. However, this could change in the future as more shippers become accustomed to the concept and the efficiencies they can create.

Supply chain dynamics of vertical sectors   13

CHAPTER LEARNING OBJECTIVES

This chapter will provide the reader with:

- A detailed description of the automotive, pharmaceutical, consumer goods and high-tech supply chain sectors

- Analysis of the main demand-side trends that have influenced the development of the associated logistics sectors

- An analysis of the relationships that have been developed between manufacturers and logistics service providers

- Insight into the innovations that logistics companies have developed to meet changing customer needs

- Identification of key industry sector trends and developments that will have further impact on logistics companies' corporate development strategies

Automotive manufacturing logistics

Since the 1980s, the global automotive sector has been widely regarded as the benchmark for logistics excellence. The introduction of supply chain concepts from Japan, such as Kanban and JIT, had been adopted by many European and US vehicle manufacturers. In turn, this had led to cross-fertilization across other sectors, with its focus on quality and lean supply chains.

In Europe, the onset of the Single European Market allowed vehicle manufacturers (VMs) previously rooted in high labour cost markets, such as Germany, to exploit lower cost production locations, first in southern Europe (such as Spain and Portugal) and then when the EU extended further, in Central and Eastern Europe. In North America a similar pattern has been followed with many vehicle manufacturers sourcing goods from or even locating in Mexico.

The sector hit a major roadblock in the credit-driven recession of 2008–9. Big ticket purchases, such as cars, were postponed by consumers in Europe and North America wary of the uncertain economic conditions. However, this trend was not shared in developing markets, with consumer spend in China, for instance, continuing to increase dramatically. This led to a major strategic shift in focus by the VMs.

This had implications for logistics service providers, who were now being asked to provide services to support production in Asia markets, as well as continue to serve them as export destinations.

Since then, a further layer of complexity has been added. German VMs have continued to do well, exporting to Europe and the developing world. However, other mid-market brands have suffered as the region continues its economic weakness. This has led some to dispose of assets, consider pooling logistics purchasing or change the geography of their supply chains.

In addition, the US market has seen demand recover robustly. This has resulted in substantial investment in new capacity in North America, which implies future demand for logistics services will continue to grow at respectable rates. Similarly, German VMs are also investing heavily in their German-based assembly capacity, even as others face problems making money in Europe.

VMs have become far more global in their supply chains with both finished vehicles and major components moving between continents in order to improve utilization and reduce costs. Fundamental to this has been a move to increasingly globalized vehicle platforms by many VMs. This is a globalization model driven by the need to survive rather than by choice, with the leading VMs resisting this move.

The consequences of these changes for logistics service providers are sizeable but difficult to grasp. For example, the market for automotive logistics services in China is likely to develop rapidly. However, overcoming the barriers to doing business in China will be a real problem for many automotive logistics service providers not already strongly present in the market.

Indeed, the ability to provide for VMs in emerging markets will be one of the key issues for LSPs in the near future. It is one thing to provide shipping and forwarding services to a port, another to be able to design and manage transport networks and other aspects of logistics in these markets. Yet if big Western LSPs want to access the growth available that is what they are going to have to do.

The automotive world looks like it is emerging into one dominated by a few large global VMs with operations in markets such as China, Brazil, Russia, India and elsewhere integrated into supply chains heavily rooted in North America, Western Europe and Japan. Providing the logistics systems to support this structure will be the main challenge and opportunity for automotive LSPs from now on.

The reason for the importance of logistics for the automotive sector lies in the size of capital investment in production plant and vehicle design. VMs' assembly plants can easily cost 500 million euros and there is intense pressure to utilize this investment to its maximum extent. The automotive sector is still driven by economies of scale and this means that the most successful companies are those who have the biggest plants with the highest levels of utilization. This can be characterized as 'production orientation'. To maintain high levels of utilization, raw materials and components need to be fed into the assembly plant and coordinated with the production schedule. This has been perceived as a core logistics task in the automotive supply chain and one that in the past was given to production engineers. Over the past decade, however, specific logistics management structures have been evolved to manage this process.

Production concepts in automotive logistics

In order to reconcile the imperative for economies of scale with the desire of the market for a wider choice of products, many VMs introduced 'flexible manufacturing'. VMs such as Ford, Honda or Nissan have the ability to vary the type of model being produced on a single assembly line. This means that demand can be better coordinated with supply by switching production capacity to the more popular models. This approach fits well into the 'platform strategies' that most VMs have adopted for the design of their different vehicle types. This is now fairly standard practice in the sector, although with widely varying results in terms of profitability for VMs.

The next development has been the evolution of 'build-to-order' systems within more flexible 'order-to-delivery' production environments. Systems such as BMW's KOVP and GM's 'order-to-delivery' have reduced lead times for the delivery of product and increased the ability of VMs to make the sort of product that customers wish to buy. These systems are now well established. However, the Japanese, and some German producers, have not felt the need to adopt such an approach, although even they have striven to control customer delivery lead times more aggressively. Since the recession, the predominant focus for many VMs has been to cut costs. Many have restructured huge parts of their companies and this has had enormous effects on their management systems and purchasing strategies.

This has precluded much innovation in logistics systems. Even the more healthy companies have sought to wring cost savings out of their existing systems. The result has been greater emphasis on reducing purchasing costs and increasing asset utilization.

Supply chain geography of the automotive sector

It is often said that the automotive sector is a global business. This is true only to an extent. Most of the largest VMs market vehicles on a global scale, although several of the largest produce in only one or two continents. However, vehicle production is not a 'globalized' activity in contrast with some industries such as electronics, consumer durables, clothing and furniture that source their raw materials, semi-finished goods and finished product on a global scale.

This is a trend that has been amplified through the development of China as a production location. A good example of this is a large retailer such as Wal-Mart, which has very large procurement and logistics structures located in China and feeding into its retail operations in the United States. The automotive supply chain is not like this. Most passenger vehicles are made near the market where they will be sold. Even components are manufactured near the assembly plant. The automotive sector does not have the geographically extended supply chain seen in many other sectors. Within Europe, for example, it is quite usual for 90 per cent of component suppliers to be located within 100 kilometres of the assembly plant. These distances are greater in North America, although this is simply a reflection of the larger geography of the Midwest of the United States in particular.

This supply chain geography is so pronounced that the car industry has created specific locations, known as 'supplier parks', for component suppliers next to its assembly plants. These ensure reliable communication between the component supplier and the VMs' assembly plant, easing the implementation of systems such as Just-in-Time/Just-in-Sequence production techniques.

Key to local sourcing is the need to reduce foreign exchange fluctuations. The automotive sector finds it hard to manage fluctuations in the value of finished product as it is so focused on the management of capital investment. Therefore, it prefers to locate assembly facilities in areas of the same currency as it is selling its products. As a consequence there is a constant process of adaptation to the growth of new markets. High levels of imports mark the early stages of a market, often followed by the use of 'Complete-Knock-Down', that is, components loaded into shipping containers and taken into the market to be assembled. However, the attractions of local production are so substantial that if a market grows to any significant size VMs will want to establish assembly plants in that market. The consequence of this is that the automotive sector's material flows remain predominantly local or intra-continental. Intercontinental and global material flow is likely to remain a much smaller proportion of traffic. Exceptions to this local supply geography are not frequent but are important. For example, finished vehicles are imported in noticeable quantities from Japan in particular.

Having said this, the movement of finished vehicles and components from continent to continent has been growing, as VMs respond to a larger global demand. China imports large quantities of car components as its parts suppliers cannot provide VMs (Chinese and Western) with the quality required. This again may change in the near future as large component suppliers open facilities in China.

The character of volume flows is also evolving due to the increased level of high-tech components being used within cars. This has meant that a much higher proportion of products need to be sourced from electronic manufacturers, largely based in Asia. Spend on shipping and air cargo has consequently increased significantly.

Location and size of assembly plants

Although automotive production is remaining local to large markets, there is also a contrary trend towards larger, more centralized assembly plants. The volumes going through assembly plants have increased, generally, to a point that big plants will often have production of more than 500,000 vehicles (for example, Honda at Maryville, OH, or the PSA Peugeot Citroen plants at Mulhouse and Sochoux). The reasons for this are obvious in that bigger plants mean higher economies of scale. However, the trend pulls against both the desire to produce a larger number of different model types and the need to keep production within a currency area. Other industries solve this problem by moving to global production centres; however, the automotive sector uses flexible production techniques (see above) to attempt to deal with this apparent contradiction.

The impact of new production trends on transport demand

All of these developments – flexible production lines, build-to-order systems, leaner production – in automotive logistics over the past 20 years have one thing in common. They increase the demand for transport. The realization of the cost of inventory, flexible scheduling of production assets, shorter lead times that are characteristic of contemporary logistics operations on the automotive supply side, imply a trade-off between inventory and capital costs against transport costs. Although the dynamics of this trade-off are well known, VMs are reluctant to admit to it. Most will attempt to limit the increase in transport utilization through new management organizations or new methods of purchasing.

Despite this, the improvements in productivity resulting from management concepts such as JIT rely on the power of cheap transport. Potentially one of the most important developments in the future is the relocation of production to low-cost regions such as Central Europe or even China. If this happens it will not only depend on the availability of transport resources, but particularly in the case of China, availability of transport will also drive choices of location. Therefore, although transport is perceived to be a relatively unimportant resource within the automotive industry, it is in fact one of growing influence that is increasingly affecting the nature of production in the sector.

Dealerships, retailing and logistics around the world

Despite attempts to reform automotive retailing and 'after sales' service sectors in both Europe and the United States, the sector remains an anachronism. In most other sectors, any analysis of logistics would start at retailing. However, the traditional 'production focus' of the automotive sector has had a big impact on its retailing structures.

Almost all contact with the customer is through the franchises that purchase the right to sell vehicles on behalf of one particular VM or brand. VMs have in the past valued control of their assembly facilities higher than contact with their customers. Not that they have been willing to accept a free market in retailing their products. Dealerships are very much client companies of the VMs, who are controlled by the VMs' ability to withdraw the franchise.

That this structure is the product of the wider imperatives of the automotive sector is illustrated by the replication of similar retailing structures across the developed world. In no major market are there large independent retailers with autonomous purchasing and marketing strategies and independent logistics systems. In the United States, whilst the approach to automotive retailing is different from that in Europe, retailers are still franchises dependent on the instructions of the VMs. In the United States and the rest of the Americas automotive retailers have traditionally been holders of stock. Larger operations, although dedicated to one brand, will hold several months' worth of stock-turn.

The reason for this is that the US consumer is more orientated to 'impulse purchases' than in Europe or Japan. The length of ownership in the United States also tends to be shorter. This difference in approach to retailing has its effects both on the nature of the product that is traditionally of a lower quality than, for example, in Europe, and to approaches to production. Production batches in the United States are usually much larger and vehicles produced with higher equipment levels than in Europe.

Vehicles are then sent out to dealerships where customers expect to drive away a vehicle on either their first or second visit. In Europe it is very different. Although countries vary, the largest single market, Germany, has a strong orientation to 'build-to-order'. Customers put in an order for a new car many months in advance, expecting to keep the car for many years.

The ability of the VMs to control retailing activity is of increasing importance owing to the spread of 'build-to-order' production systems. In most systems of this type the specification of the car is set within the dealership, with the dealership staff inputting data into the VMs' order capture IT systems. If the market were to revert to a free market these complex systems would have to be redesigned. The above types of build-to-order systems are distinctively European and specifically German in approach.

Although GM and Ford have different production/supply chain management/retail systems in the United States, they have moved appreciably towards the German BTO model, not least due to the cost benefits it offers. On this basis it is reasonable to assume that this trend will continue and the model of dealerships holding large quantities of stock will be phased out. The exceptions to this approach are Toyota, Honda and the other Japanese VMs (with the exception of Nissan, which is influenced heavily by Renault). The Toyota Production System (TPS) does have similarities to the increasingly influential KOVP at BMW; both are designed to optimize capacity on the production line.

Different types of inbound logistics operations

The nature of inbound logistics operations does vary to a degree. Whilst all need transport and consolidation services, the manner in which this is delivered does change. For example, suppliers feeding into German VMs in Germany tend to have a requirement for consolidation centres near the VM assembly plant.

This is very much the case with Mercedes-Benz (MB) Passenger Car plants where suppliers usually opt to hold inventory in a consolidation centre near the plant to facilitate immediate availability of stock (Figure 13.1). This is further complicated by some major suppliers having assembly facilities within the MB plant. In contrast, in Toyota plants this is not the case.

Here Toyota's LSPs will collect from suppliers and consolidate components at a dedicated facility at the plant. Toyota will require the supplier to set aside part of his loading bay for Toyota-destined supplies, but the supplier should be operating under the kanban system and therefore should not need any further inventory management systems (Figure 13.2).

Component suppliers are also faced with contradictory demands from vehicle manufacturers. On the one hand VMs want suppliers to invest in logistics or assembly facilities near assembly plants. For example, Mercedes-Benz Passenger Cars/Smart wants suppliers to have on-site assembly

Figure 13.1 Mercedes-Benz Passenger Cars component feed

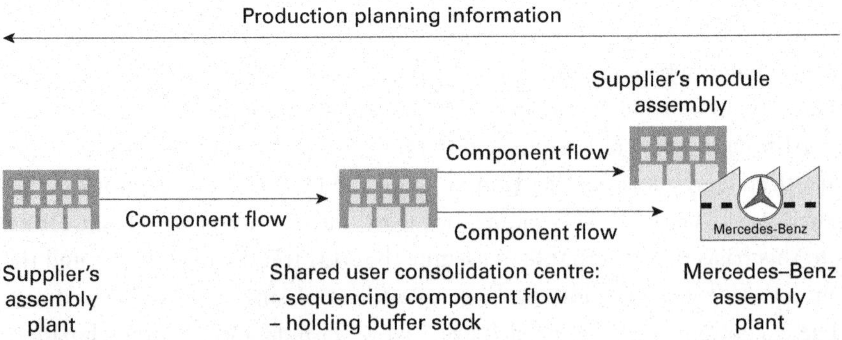

Production planning information

Supplier's module assembly

Component flow

Component flow

Supplier's assembly plant

Shared user consolidation centre:
– sequencing component flow
– holding buffer stock

Mercedes–Benz assembly plant

Component flow

Mercedes-Benz

SOURCE: Transport Intelligence (2014)

Figure 13.2 Dynamics of Toyota component feed

Kanban & Containers
back to suppliers

Inbound Component Flow

TOYOTA

Supplier's assembly plant

Inventory placed in loading bay

Inventory delivered to consolidation centre at plant

Toyota assembly plant

SOURCE: Transport Intelligence (2014)

capabilities. This of course requires investment by suppliers; however, VMs are unwilling to commit themselves to suppliers for long enough to ensure that the investment is covered.

The reasons for this are:

- the increasing trend for VMs to have several different types of vehicle produced at one assembly plant;

- continuing variability in sourcing of similar components leading to variability in the volume of component feed to an assembly plant over the medium term;

- frequent changes in vehicle model/design affecting the volume of component feed.

Consequently, there is a danger that suppliers will be left with facilities at or near the VM's assembly plant, which are redundant or underused. Many LSPs view this as an opportunity for out-sourcing, with several suppliers sharing facilities owned and run by the LSP. This appears logical; however, it conflicts with the unwillingness of many suppliers to out-source assembly operations that they regard as core-competencies. Logistics is usually one of the core functions of such 'near-plant' facilities.

For example, the main function of 'Sequencing Centres In-line', usually referred to as 'SILS' or 'Regional Assembly Plants', is to break-bulk, and feed components into the VM's assembly plant in sequence dictated by the production schedule. This would suggest that LSPs are well positioned to offer such services within shared-user facilities. This is certainly the case in many plants. However, many larger suppliers are very aware of the importance of logistics as a core-competence and are unwilling to relinquish it to LSPs on a large scale. As a consequence the market for such centres may appear more promising for LSPs than in reality.

Pharmaceutical logistics

An industry in transformation

Economic and globalization trends are having a major impact on the pharmaceutical drug manufacturing sector and hence on the associated logistics industry. Whilst multinational drug manufacturers struggle with rising costs, expiration of blockbuster drug patents and changes in government legislation within their largest markets, Europe and the United States, opportunities are increasing within Asia and South America. These trends have resulted in manufacturers re-engineering their supply chain strategies.

In the past, little attention was paid to supply chains as manufacturers were focused on drug sales and development. In particular, the changing government role within the pharmaceutical drug industry, especially in the Europe and United States markets, has meant that manufacturers are now faced with supply chains that are not effective in a sector that is in transformation.

With the globalization of the drug manufacturing sector, companies are targeting emerging markets such as China and Brazil as locations not only to sell to but also as locations for out-sourcing such operations as manufacturing, research and development and clinical trials. However, an array of issues such as security, intellectual property and knowledge of government legislation within these emerging markets has resulted in manufacturers turning to logistics providers for assistance.

The global pharmaceutical logistics market is growing quickly with the largest increases noted in Asia and South America. Logistics providers are expanding their service offerings and their geographic reach to meet the needs of the sector. To prove successful, however, logistics providers will need to demonstrate an understanding of the special needs of the pharmaceutical industry. Many manufacturers within the industry have shied away from using logistics providers in the past due to their lack of industry knowledge. To counter this, market leaders including FedEx, DHL and UPS have sought to demonstrate their knowledge and understanding of the pharmaceutical drug manufacturing industry by introducing specific solutions. For example, the growing demand for biopharmaceuticals has resulted in the need for temperature-regulated transportation. Logistics providers have introduced special temperature-controlled containers and monitoring systems to ensure temperatures remain constant. Also, the need for temperature-regulated warehousing is developing.

Along with the introduction of temperature-regulated solutions, logistics providers are also providing consulting services to assist manufacturers with such issues as trade and compliance concerns as manufacturers expand into the fast-growing emerging markets of Asia and South America. Also, management of clinical trials, samples, returns and recall management and management of marketing materials are some of the additional services logistics providers are offering to the drug manufacturers.

The global pharmaceutical logistics market

The global pharmaceutical logistics market is in a state of change. In the past, supply chains were neither flexible nor cost effective as many pharmaceutical manufacturers appeared to be little concerned about the efficiency of their supply chains. However, as many blockbuster drugs' patents expire and facing mounting government regulations and increasing competition, supply chains now have to be assessed in order to remain competitive.

In the blockbuster drug model, oral solid-dose pills were shipped to a small number of wholesalers who then moved them on to retailers. However, as the market shifts towards personalized healthcare, an increasing focus is on a narrower group of individuals. Many of these newer drugs require more complex manufacturing and distribution processes than shelf-stable pills. Also, the push for safety in the supply chain is a factor in requiring backward visibility to manufacturers' suppliers and suppliers' suppliers in a robust and real-time way.

Fluctuation in demand for branded and generic products, and changes in distribution channels are also driving the continued evolution of supply chain models. For example, the loss of patent protection is impacting the supply chains of both manufacturers and large retailers. The majority of generic drugs are now delivered direct to retailers in the United States and many large retailers work directly with manufacturers to integrate products into their own distribution network for less complexity and cost. New direct-to-patient, high-cost speciality therapies are also causing manufacturers to reconsider how they take products to market in order to better respond to consumer demand.

The growth in emerging markets adds another level of complexity. Global pharmaceutical out-sourcing has become increasingly prevalent, but is creating a complex and risky supply chain environment. This global expansion is making it more difficult for pharmaceutical manufacturers to manage their supply chain. The need for a flexible supply chain is great as the industry undergoes changes in product mix, manufacturing routes and distribution channels for different kinds of products.

Many manufacturers have grappled with these changing supply chain needs and are beginning to realize the benefits of out-sourced logistics partners. Companies see the benefit of shifting responsibility to a global LSP that is likely to have access to more facilities and resources, and consequently, a greater capability to respond quickly to changing business needs.

Pain points in the pharmaceutical supply chain

As the pharmaceutical manufacturing industry adapts to its changing environment, its supply chain will need to become more flexible in order to respond more quickly to these changes. Based on surveys conducted by logistics providers and the pharmaceutical industry, some of the identified pain points include information technology, legislation, regulation and security of products (UPS, 2014).

To address the issue of various government regulations and security issues, the pharmaceutical manufacturer must have near-complete visibility of its supply chain. However, as the manufacturer expands its operations throughout the world it becomes difficult to connect to not only its primary suppliers but also to its suppliers' suppliers. According to some manufacturers, the primary method used to gain visibility into suppliers' practices is a periodic audit. Many still manually aggregate the data.

Many industry executives are also concerned about the willingness of suppliers and distributors to provide information to address regulatory requirements. Hurdles exist in implementing the necessary technology including cost, the difficulty of implementation, lack of industry standards and lack of regulatory requirements and guidance.

Progress is being made as a variety of industry consortia have been established to address these issues. Many logistics providers offer visibility solutions that could benefit manufacturers. They also have introduced specific industry solutions to address visibility of products whilst in transit, particularly for those products that require temperature monitoring. For example, Schenker offers an RFID solution to monitor products' temperature as well as to track the cargo from origin to destination.

Logistics and transportation service offerings

Cold chain

Growing global demand for complex drugs is increasing demand for cold chain solutions. Healthcare products that are temperature-sensitive require refrigeration during transportation and storage. Further, these products may also have a short window of viability, which makes rapid transport essential.

Airlines have increasingly developed products to make the transit of pharmaceutical products more reliable. For example, British Airways World Cargo's offering, 'Constant Climate', launched an SMS customer update service and broadened the scope of its service to include passive temperature-controlled packages and shipments. Its SMS offering updates customers by text message or e-mail at key milestones through the airfreight journey.

Ocean carriers are also announcing cold chain solutions for the pharmaceutical industry. For example, APL introduced a system for monitoring onboard refrigerated containers via satellite communications.

Innovations in packaging design

Packaging technology is also continually evolving. CryoPort Systems Inc and FedEx Express announced the signing of an agreement to provide an 'innovative and breakthrough' frozen shipment solution for the life science industry. The solution allows for products to remain frozen at temperatures below −150°C for up to 10 days, unlike dry ice shipping, which often requires re-icing during transit.

In 2011, UPS introduced a new airfreight container for healthcare products. The PharmaPort 360 addressed a key industry issue of safeguarding healthcare shipments in the supply chain by enabling near real-time monitoring and maintaining product temperatures in extreme outside conditions. The PharmaPort 360 container, manufactured by Cool Containers for UPS, maintains strict temperatures by utilizing both heating and cooling storage technology, allowing it to tolerate a significantly wider range of extreme ambient temperature changes. The container more effectively maintained temperatures critical for protecting medicines that need to stay within the required 2–8°C to prevent spoilage. The PharmaPort 360 also sustained its protective temperature range for more than 100 hours, which was an important factor as more supply chains

▶

extend globally and healthcare products needed to travel farther to reach markets.

Envirotainer is a provider of air cargo cold-chain transportation solutions. The company works with both pharmaceutical manufacturers and logistics companies to provide a variety of packaging, container and other cold-chain solutions. The company also developed an industry accreditation and certification programme to acknowledge those service providers are capable of properly managing cold-chain shipments. Accredited airfreight forwarders are Agility, Cargo-Partner, DB Schenker, DHL, FedEx, Kuehne + Nagel, Panalpina, Uti, World Courier and Panther. Accredited airlines include Air France/KLM, American Airlines, British Airways, Korean Air and Emirates.

Distribution services

Distribution and warehousing services within the pharmaceutical logistics market can be complex due to government regulations, security and safety of the products. As such, inventory management is more than just ensuring adequate inventory levels to meet demand. For example, if a temperature-sensitive drug arrives at a distribution facility prior to receiving government approvals to market the drug to the public, the inventory must be isolated. Data is then collected from temperature loggers within the shipment and communicated back to the manufacturing plant. The product cannot move from the quarantine area to a primary storage location until the plant indicates that temperature readings were satisfactory to ensure product safety and compliance and government authorities have approved the product for sale. Also, packaging and labelling is regulated and often differs from one market to the next.

Reverse logistics

The proper management of recalls is very important. The ability to implement reverse logistics, including recalls, in an organized manner is critical to containing the potential damage from an incident. Products not properly reclaimed and destroyed may end up being resold illegally. The Healthcare Distribution Management Association (HDMA) estimates 3–4 per cent of products that leave pharmaceutical warehouses ultimately are returned. Of the estimated 3–4 per cent of products returned, it is also estimated that about 1.5–2 per cent of pharmaceuticals manufactured will be destroyed.

The majority of major logistics providers offer reverse logistics services; however, there are niche players such as Genco that provide returns and recall management solutions specifically targeted to the pharmaceutical drug industry.

Consumer goods and retail logistics

The consumer and retail industries are hugely important for the global logistics industry. In the contract logistics industry, they account for more than half of all revenues. Although most movements of consumer goods (which include food and drink) take place at either the local or national level, an important and growing segment occurs on an international basis.

Consumer packaged goods (CPG) manufacturers have complex supply chains. Not only do these companies produce a range of foodstuffs, beverages, cleaning products and beauty goods (a number of which may be classified as hazardous), they also operate in a range of temperatures (from ambient, through various levels of chilled, to frozen). Add in a mix of national production and overseas production and the logistical requirements are vast.

In Europe, the consumer goods industry was transformed by the advent of the Single European Market. This allowed manufacturers to exploit the lower labour costs of the peripheral members of the EU (such as Spain and Portugal) whilst being able to export unfettered to the rest of the region. Improving infrastructure meant that transport costs were comparatively low, which allowed manufacturers to centralize their distribution.

Meanwhile, the migration of consumer durables manufacturing to Asia Pacific meant that sea and air gateways to Europe evolved into important logistics nodes for the distribution of imported goods.

At the same time as this, the manufacturers' relationship with retailers changed, as retailing became much more centralized. There was a shift in the balance of power in the supply chain which, as we will see, resulted in the imposition of several logistics initiatives, not least factory gate pricing (FGP).

General food and drink production and distribution still largely takes place on a local or national level. It is undertaken by a range of contract logistics or local hauliers, with high levels of competition in a largely fragmented market.

However, at the CPG level (dominated by manufacturers such as Procter & Gamble and Unilever) supply chains are far more regionalized. Production locations have been centralized with a focus on economies of scale. Whereas many food types are produced for local tastes, consumer packaged goods (such as razors or toiletries) have across-the-board appeal.

Global supply chains exist where the production emphasis is on cheap labour. Goods falling into this category include toys and other durable goods (including consumer electronics). Freight forwarders and shipping lines have a much bigger role in these intercontinental movements of goods. However, global 3PLs can also play a part in providing value adding services, for instance in consolidation centres (see below). Goods often come through major gateways (such as Rotterdam or Antwerp in Europe) and are then stored and distributed from European Distribution Centres (EDCs) often based in Belgium or the Netherlands. Others are moved from the gateway ports directly to national distribution centres (potentially owned and managed by the major retailers).

It is impossible to look at the consumer sector in isolation from developments and trends in retailing. Supply chain strategies of the major manufacturers have necessarily been influenced by the growing power and leverage of international retailers such as Walmart or Tesco. Retailing is now being transformed by e-commerce and this is described in more detail below.

Consumer packaged goods (CPG) sector

The CPG market is highly fragmented, comprising many different product lines requiring different distribution chains. The products falling within this sector include food (ambient, chilled and frozen), dairy products, beverages (dry and wet), healthcare (soaps, deodorants, etc), household products (cleaning products often hazardous) and cosmetics.

The market for consumer packaged goods has changed hugely over the past 10 to 15 years. Once, it was dominated by national 'champions' who also had a global presence. It is now dominated by global brands and is one of the most influential in the world.

The sector has experienced a series of challenges, including the economic downturn, increased competition, food scares and new consumer trends. Whilst these challenges pose a threat to some companies they can be an expansion opportunity for others. In response to these new challenges, CPG companies are improving competitiveness by restructuring and intensifying the fight for market share through product differentiation and/or the development of new food products.

Amongst the traditional leaders in the sector – Procter & Gamble and Unilever – there has been a clear shift towards products with greater complexity and added value. Both companies have seen a transformation in their product line: Unilever has sold many of its key frozen food brands; P&G has bought Gillette and both have increased their involvement in health and beauty products. This illustrates that there has been a shift away from:

- products dependent on access to basic raw materials, such as fats;
- products very dependent on the low-cost/high-volume production;
- products wholly dependent on access to large distribution capabilities.

And a move to:

- high-value added products with an aspect that strengthens the brand – for example, beauty products;
- complex products such as 'over-the-counter' pharmaceuticals or razors.

The supply chain of the consumer product sector and its associated production activities has traditionally been affected by the high volume and commoditized nature of the products being sold and the need to source raw materials/ingredients.

The big CPG companies used to be highly orientated towards basic household items such as soap. These were delivered in different forms but they were consumed rapidly and in large quantities. Consequently, it made sense for production not to be too far removed from the area of consumption. The result was a strong orientation towards national based companies. Whilst the sector did not suffer from the 'national champions' syndrome seen, for example, in the car industry, most consumer products consumed in a country were produced in that country. Therefore, up until very recently CPG companies were organized on a national basis.

This is changing remarkably slowly. Indeed, for many product categories within the consumer goods sector it remains the case that product is manufactured near to the market.

However, CPG companies are now beginning to change:

- Their relationship with the customer has changed as the sophistication and power of retailers has increased.
- Their products have changed, especially their dependence on fat-based staple food and cleaning products.

Therefore, whilst there is still a substantial volume of 'in market' production of goods such as soap powders and highly commoditized food products such as spreads, manufacture of stronger food brands is more concentrated on a regional or continental scale. Health and beauty products also have a more regionalized production approach.

A further qualification about the supply chain dynamic is the issue of inbound raw material. The traditional 'staple' products were heavy users of agricultural commodities, in particular various types of fats. These were sourced globally with tropical agricultural products being sourced on international markets and shipped to production locations usually located in major seaports. Again, whilst this model still applies to multiple product lines, many of the new product categories are quite different and do not use these raw materials.

A further observation should be made about the coherence of CPG supply chains. A key imperative is to 'get closer to the customer'. This means organizing marketing activities at a national level, as most market idiosyncrasies are expressed nationally. These activities are generally concentrated around advertising and marketing issues related to product design. In addition, the question of relations with retailers is usually handled at the national level.

Regionalization of supply chain geographies

Originally, the supply chains of CPG companies were dominated by the need to obtain raw materials for their products. Consequently, manufacturing facilities were often located near ports. This is now changing. Inbound logistics is less important; 'outbound' logistics, that is the management of finished product, is now the dominant concern. That said, the utilization of production capital assets has also become a more important cost driver, leading to important redesign of the supply chain.

However, the dominant feature of the CPG supply chain is the focus on retailing. This combined with the high volume, low value nature of most products sold, means that production and inventory management locations cannot be too far from the consumer.

There is a clear trend amongst all of the major producers to improve the cost base of their supply chain by consolidating production facilities. This trend is also reflected to some extent by a centralization of inventory. This should not be exaggerated as most products need highly distributed inventory near retail locations (although this is complicated by the varying role of the retailer in managing stock). None the less, the major companies are creating larger warehousing complexes serving national markets. Crucially these are served by more intensive road freight services.

Durable goods

Whilst CPG companies largely utilize regional supply chains, durable goods are mainly manufactured in the Far East and moved by ship to consumer markets in Western Europe and North America. The phenomenon of globalization has been examined in much depth elsewhere in the book, but consumer goods have been the major beneficiary.

The bulk of consumer goods are bought for sale by the major retailers. Traditionally, they have worked through purchasing companies and of these Li & Fung is the largest. It sources goods for companies such as Walmart, Target and many others.

However, one of its largest customers, Walmart, appears to be making several changes to its purchasing strategy. In January 2013, the company announced plans to 'significantly' boost its sourcing by US $50 billion from domestic suppliers over the next decade. According to data from Walmart's suppliers, items that are made, sourced or grown in the United States account for about two-thirds of the company's spending on products for its US business.

Walmart's international sourcing may also change. Last year, Li & Fung announced that Walmart would not be executing its option to buy a global sourcing business, Direct Sourcing Group, set up by Li & Fung in 2010 to solely support Walmart's international retail sourcing operations. That led many to say Walmart was planning to cut out the sourcing intermediary.

Not only is Walmart looking to cut costs by removing or reducing the use of companies such as Li & Fung, but it also has the desire to gain more visibility and knowledge of its vast supplier network. In 2012, Walmart was the recipient of intense negative publicity owing to a fire in a Bangladesh manufacturing facility used by a supplier. As a result of this, Walmart has adopted a 'zero tolerance policy' for violations of its global sourcing standards, and plans to sever ties with anyone who subcontracts work to factories without the retailer's knowledge.

Other companies such as Apple and Nike have also received negative press due to manufacturing practices and as such are working towards corrective measures. Improvements in visibility and collaboration are needed and are increasingly being adopted by retailers.

For many, the re-shoring trend has been beneficial as these companies are perhaps more adept at managing domestic suppliers. Still, a good deal of retail manufacturing will continue in Asia and companies such as Li & Fung provide valuable knowledge and assistance for companies that are in need of such services.

Consolidation services

One of the best ways in which retailers and manufacturers can save money on shipping costs is to consolidate less-than-container loads from multiple suppliers to make up full container loads. These are then shipped to distribution centres in Western Europe or North America. Consolidating shipments into a single unitized load reduces the overall transportation cost per unit as well as increasing efficiency.

The point of consolidation is usually at the port of origin. Ports in southern China are particularly important, owing to their close proximity to Chinese exporters, although some shippers use major trans-shipment hubs such as Hong Kong or Singapore. In these cases bringing together shipments from multiple countries of origin considerably increases the levels of complexity, as containers can be held up due to inbound shipment delays or customs issues.

Although consolidation has been around since the 1970s, it is becoming an increasingly important strategy, not least because of the proliferation of products that retailers are importing. This has led to smaller order levels that would ordinarily increase the per unit transportation costs. The economic downturn has also reduced retailers' order sizes, which has had the same effect. Rather than wait for sufficient demand to fill a container, consolidation services can ensure that containers are shipped in a timely fashion, thus reducing inventory holding costs as well.

Some importers have also implemented so-called distribution centre (DC) by-pass programmes, which avoid the use of a DC in the end-user market. By sorting and consolidating at the point of origin and shipping direct to the customer, distribution costs and transit time can be reduced. Using local labour, consolidation centre services can be undertaken more cheaply than in a developed market. There is also the opportunity to carry out quality control closer to the vendor rather than when it arrives in the end-user market when it is too late to rectify a problem with the order.

This element of control that consolidating at origin provides shippers is also useful in balancing supply with demand. With the rise of the Asian consumer markets in particular, shippers are often supplying markets not only in Europe and North America but also throughout the Far East. Using an upstream consolidation centre gives them the ability to allocate inventory at the latest possible moment and avoids accumulation of stock in national/regional warehouses.

Hong Kong is probably the best known location for consolidation services. As a deepwater port it originally attracted shipments from the Pearl

River Delta special economic zones as the local ports were not able to accommodate large container vessels. Although this included the transshipment of containers, it is estimated that 75 per cent of goods transiting Hong Kong were consolidated. As its competitive advantage has dwindled over the years with the development of deepwater ports throughout China, Hong Kong has sought to position itself as a key location for value adding logistics services.

Challenges in developing countries

Downstream CPG supply chains are expanding rapidly into developing markets, and this is providing manufacturers with considerable challenges, as well as the evident opportunities.

One of these challenges relates to the different levels of development in retailing structures. Although in China and India major grocery retailers are growing fast, in many areas of the Indian subcontinent in particular 90 per cent of sales are through very small general retailers.

In parts of Asia, poor road infrastructure has resulted in a high degree of supply chain uncertainty and this has had a big impact on CPG manufacturers' cost structure. It has created an environment in which transport spending is a much higher proportion of overall logistics costs than in the West, driven in part by the fragmentation of the transport supplier base as well as the weakness of the transport infrastructure. In contrast, lower labour costs have resulted in cheap warehousing, although this is often not effectively used to reduce transport costs.

That situation is quite distinct from the one facing companies in Europe and North America, where many are rethinking their supply chain's intensity of transportation use, driven not least by the need to reduce costs and carbon emissions.

Retail trends

The consolidation of the retailing sector has had a fundamental influence on the development of the associated consumer goods industry, which has become more regionalized/globalized as a result. In most cases, manufacturers have been able to rationalize the number of distribution centres they operate as they no longer need to make multiple deliveries over large geographic areas. This has had significant consequences for the logistics industry.

National retail markets have been transformed in many developed countries over the past 30 years. The large grocery multiples – such as Tesco, Carrefour or Walmart – have driven consolidation in the market through highly efficient distribution channels. Prior to this the retail sector was characterized by a three-tier model – manufacturers, wholesalers and retailers. These days in many markets the wholesaler has largely been driven out and this has had major implications for supply chains and logistics providers.

In 1982 the Institute of Grocery Distribution in the UK estimated that retailers were responsible for about 32 per cent of final deliveries to stores. After decades of restructuring relationships with their suppliers, and cutting out the role of the wholesaler, almost 100 per cent of deliveries are made to stores through retailers' own distribution centres. This has resulted in a step change of cost reduction – for both manufacturers and retailers. One UK consultancy, Logistics Consulting Partners, estimates that logistics costs fell in real terms by 70 per cent over a 25-year period. This increased the grocery multiples' competitive advantage, placing even more pressure on high street retailers.

Another key dynamic driving change has been a focus on retailing space. Adopting supply chain concepts that were being employed by other sectors such as Just-in-Time, allowed retailers to eliminate in-store stock holding, maximizing display space and reducing inventory. This obviously relied upon fast and efficient replenishment and the sophisticated logistics required to facilitate it.

Although the major changes to retail distribution channels occurred mostly in the 1980s and 90s, more recently supermarkets introduced factory gate pricing (FGP), which had been pioneered in the fashion and automotive industries. Under FGP, products are no longer delivered at the retailer distribution centre, but collected by the retailer at the 'factory gates' of the suppliers. Owing to both the asymmetry in the distribution networks (the supplier sites greatly outnumber the retailer distribution centres) and the better inventory and transport coordination mechanisms, this results in major cost savings for the retailer.

The major grocery multiples found that the move to FGP was able to:

- reduce product cost and inventory;
- achieve supply chain visibility and control in vehicle planning, scheduling and utilization through enterprise compatible systems throughout the product supply chain;
- reduce waiting time at supply and delivery locations;

- decrease empty running through backhaul capacity – it is estimated that up to 35 per cent of all truck miles are run empty and that truck utilization could be increased by FGP on average by 15 per cent;
- improve vehicle performance in time, load and distance;
- increase product visibility through the supply chain;
- utilize buying power and supply chain knowledge in 'partnership' negotiation;
- reduce carbon emissions.

In some respects the implementation of FGP is the logical conclusion of the centralization of distribution strategies employed by retailers in the 1990s. By absorbing the costs of establishing these new supply chain structures, including the increased transportation element, they had unwittingly reduced the logistics costs of their suppliers as well. The implementation of FGP allowed the retailers to un-bundle product and logistics costs, reducing suppliers' margins and finally obtaining a contribution towards the cost of distribution.

Diversification of retailer product offering

Growth in the supermarket sector across Europe is being driven not by sales of food but rather by the ever-widening range of non-food goods being made available by retailers. Specialist stores are coming under severe pressure from the multiples, right across Europe as retailers look to tap into general merchandise as a way of increasing new sales growth on top of a more mature food market.

The growth of non-food sales has been driven by a number of developments, including:

- the growth of the hypermarket format;
- the drive to make space in supermarkets work harder;
- the development of non-food dedicated store formats (that is, Asda Living and Tesco Direct).

Healthcare, toiletries and household products are as important to a supermarket's core offer as food, and therefore, it is important that the range and pricing meet shoppers' expectations.

The expansion of the range of products being offered by the major supermarket chains has created opportunities for logistics service providers to bid for major new contracts with existing clients. The larger players generally benefit from consolidation within the retail sector, with the supermarkets taking market share from the more fragmented high street stores. The latter offer few opportunities for the major LSPs in terms of contract size or complexity.

High-tech manufacturing

The global high-tech market is undergoing a vast change. Globalization has given rise to increases in competition and new products, both of which have had profound effects upon the high-tech supply chain. Companies within this market compete on tight margins resulting in many turning to their supply chains for a competitive edge.

As cost management and operational efficiency are top priorities for high-tech companies, the ability to operate the leanest, most cost-effective and adaptable supply chain usually results in success. Apple has proven this over the past few years and its supply chain is considered an example for many companies to strive towards.

As a result of the industry's quest for cost management and operational efficiency, manufacturing has moved away from the mature markets such as the United States and Europe and into Asia. However, as costs such as raw materials and labour rise, Asian companies are now looking for alternative sourcing locations. A major shift of supply sourcing is now occurring within the region and this is expected to increase, resulting in the growth of intra-Asia tradelanes.

Although Eastern and Western China are expected to remain the top sourcing locations for many high-tech manufacturers and solutions providers over the next five years, Taiwan, Thailand, Japan and South Korea are likely to see increases as well.

Innovation in high-tech supply chains

The global high-tech industry is best described as one of constant innovation and change. Those companies that are the quickest to adapt and innovate are the ones to achieve market leadership in this highly competitive industry. As a result, consolidation persists as companies turn towards mergers and acquisitions as a means to acquire the latest technology or expand into a new service offering.

Not only has consolidation increased but the effect that Apple has had on the industry has been truly remarkable. The introduction of the iPhone and the iPad have changed both the PC and cellular mobile phone industries and have created a blurring of these two high-tech sub-segments.

As a result, the entire supply chain has undergone great changes – from the original equipment manufacturer (OEM) to the contract manufacturer, distributor, retailer and finally to the end customer. These changes have resulted in shifts in manufacturing locations and transportation modes as well as shifts in business strategies. For many OEMs there has been greater emphasis towards software as opposed to hardware.

Logistics providers have responded to these changes by introducing specialized solutions to meet the industry needs. Niche logistics providers have also emerged – those providers that work mostly with high-tech companies. For example, owing to the ever-shortening lifecycle of high-tech devices and increasing regulations that manage the disposal of these products, logistics providers and other partners within the high-tech supply chain have introduced specialist reverse logistics operations as well as other aftermarket solutions.

Logistics providers have also launched targeted services particularly as shippers opt for less expensive means of transportation such as ocean and, in some cases, even rail services. For many air cargo providers, particularly those that operate along the Asia tradelane, there has been an overdependence on high-tech product launches over the years and due to the rise of oil prices, the shift towards ocean freight and slowing demand, over-capacity issues have occurred.

High-tech supply chains

The typical high-tech supply chain is highly complex, characterized by fragmented distribution channels and remote manufacturing locations. The number of companies involved in different aspects of getting a product to market can lead to high degrees of inefficiency in the supply chain, resulting in either too much or too little inventory being stored at different locations.

As an example, an original equipment manufacturer (OEM), such as Hewlett-Packard or Acer, is likely to out-source production to an electronic contract manufacturer (ECM), which may well be located in a remote, low labour-cost market (such as China) and will have its own supply chain. The OEM will then deal with a distributor who will, in turn, deal with a reseller. Other parties supplying goods such as peripherals or software will also be involved.

Given the short product lifecycles that are typical in the market (new releases and developments come out continuously throughout the year), it is critical that for a supply chain to remain competitive, information and product must flow as seamlessly as possible. OEMs have a short window of opportunity to make significant margins on a product before competition catches up. However, there is a trade-off between being able to take advantage of the initial demand and the risk of overproduction. In the 1980s, many companies were guilty of overproduction, which left them with high levels of redundant product. Since then the industry has attempted to work with very low levels of inventory, whilst keeping stock-outs to a minimum. Best practice will involve collaboration between supply chain partners in terms of data-sharing, with some companies providing visibility to real-time information.

Transport of high-tech goods

Airfreight has tended to be the transportation mode of choice for manufacturers to ship high-value, high-demand goods. However, when Steve Jobs returned to Apple in the late 1990s, planning for airfreight took on a strategic and competitive edge for shippers – one that has benefited airfreight providers and freight forwarders alike since. Jobs booked all available airfreight space to ensure that the company's iMacs would be available in time for the holiday season, thus handicapping rivals who later faced a shortage of capacity.

However, as a result of the high costs associated with airfreight, companies such as Acer and HP are turning more towards ocean freight. Lower value computer components such as keyboards and mouse devices have moved by ocean for a long time. Intermediate value components such as monitors have been migrating to ocean, though high-value components such as computer chips will more than likely be always shipped by air.

According to some industry estimates, based on value, 60 per cent of computers and related components are flown by air, and 40 per cent move by ocean. But on a weight basis, only 15 per cent move by air, compared with 85 per cent by ocean.

Whilst the obvious advantage of ocean freight is the much lower cost of transportation, it also has disadvantages, in particular longer transit times. Computers shipped by ocean must be built four to six weeks earlier than if shipped by air. That creates the risk of a substantial decline in a product's value during the shipment period.

There is also the risk that an order might be cancelled whilst the goods are on the water, and there is a greater risk of damage. There are also higher inventory costs. Unexpected delays, such as the backlogs at ports can tip the balance of any cost-benefit equation.

In 2010, Dell, the global computer manufacturer, started an overhaul of its supply chain by increasing the volume of Notebooks that it shipped by sea from 20 per cent (an increase from 5 per cent the previous year) to around 70 per cent.

According to a senior director of Dell, shipping via ocean freight had already created a '$35 million benefit' as the company 'penetrated this opportunity', as he put it. The core of Dell's strategy, of course, was cost management – recession-related losses and fierce competition in the PC market had put an emphasis on cost-cutting.

This is a classic response to a market maturing and the effects of global price deflation in the technology sector. Dell realigned landed costs with the selling price in the market by shifting modes.

The decline in the price of laptops illustrates the cost challenges computer makers face. When they first became popular, they typically cost US $3,000. Now they can cost as little as US $400. But there has been little movement in the cost of airfreight, meaning the cost of transportation as a percentage of the total selling price has surged. So a shift to ocean transportation, which typically costs one-tenth the price of airfreight, is a logical way to cut costs.

Companies successfully utilizing an ocean shipment strategy have had a different supply chain structure. According to some within the industry, companies such as HP handled the longer lead times by building to a forecast, maintaining a finished goods inventory, having a large distribution network, and by offering very little customization. This is very different from Dell's traditional build-to-order strategy, extremely low inventories of finished goods, direct sales to customers and extensive configuration options.

Hewlett-Packard (HP) launched a rail-sea link to move product by rail, on a relatively expedited basis, to the port in Shenzhen and then by sea to the ports of Long Beach, Rotterdam, etc. According to HP, it takes 20 days transit time by ocean, port to port for a Notebook made in China to reach the port at Long Beach. It takes 39 to 40 days to reach Rotterdam.

The increasing need to cut costs but also to get products to its markets as quickly as possible, also resulted in PC manufacturer Acer testing a new transportation method – shipping computers by rail via Chongqing in China through Kazakhstan, Russia, Belarus, Poland and into Germany. This takes 18 to 20 days, undercutting sea freight by about one week to 10 days and though it costs more, it is still cheaper than shipping by air.

High-tech logistics services

Besides the traditional warehousing/distribution services offered such as kitting, labelling and repackaging, a growing number of logistics providers are expanding their capabilities into aftermarket services for high-tech companies.

Aftermarket

Long known as a way to promote a positive customer experience, aftermarket services also provide revenue streams for OEMs and logistics providers. 'After sales' is also known by a variety of other terms such as 'reverse logistics' and 'returns/services management'. The processes involve the receipt of previously consumed products for the purpose of repairing or ensuring proper disposal. A host of components play into this service including returns, repairs, recycle, disposition, all of which are increasingly dependent on growing regulatory compliance. In its simplistic format, the after sales supply chain may be demonstrated by Figure 13.3.

Figure 13.3 High-tech aftermarket sales supply chain

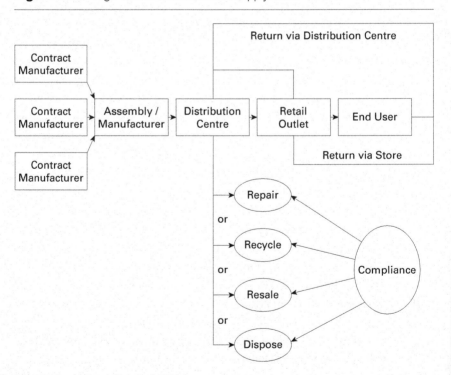

SOURCE: Transport Intelligence (2012b)

- An end user returns a product such as a mobile phone or tablet via instructions usually from the store or e-retailer in which it was purchased.

- The product can be returned via the store or directly mailed to a service centre. In many cases, service centres are part of a distribution centre. If the product is mailed, usually a printable prepaid label is provided for the end user – another measure to ensure proper customer service.

- Once received by the service centre, the product is evaluated based on the end-user's description of issue and may include the following:

  1 return for replacement;

  2 repair and return to end user;

  3 repair but provide end user with alternative product;

  4 resale;

  5 dispose of product, which may involve recycling and/or disassembling products and reselling components and lastly dispose of goods per government regulations.

Returns/repairs

As a whole, the electronics industry spends more than US $19 billion on returns every year. Warranty claims and repairs are a major part of the reverse logistics process, requiring varying methods for receiving, tracking, processing, repairing, and ultimately redelivering the product to the consumer. Over the years, the level of high-tech returns has become increasingly apparent, resulting in a sub-industry dedicated to electronic repairs.

In the electronics industry, the average return rate on sales is 8 per cent but the return rate within subcategories can range from 4 per cent to 15 per cent. Perversely, many of the returns are not even defective. It is estimated that the non-defective rate for consumer electronics hovers around 65 per cent of total goods returned, meaning only 35 per cent of the returns are actually defective. The non-defective product may be in perfect working order or slightly damaged by the customer but still repairable.

Logistics providers such as DHL, Kuehne + Nagel, New Breed Logistics and UPS provide repair services as well as specialized companies such as Brightpoint and contract manufacturers such as Celestica and Flextronics. All of these companies screen the products and analyse the status of returned products to determine the next processing step, whether it is to scrap the product or repair it.

Field service/spare parts logistics

A challenge for companies is that of stocking enough spare parts at all times. For those companies that need to service customers in the field, this is especially a concern particularly as contracts often dictate short lead times to dispatch a technician and/or required part for replacement. As a result, warehousing not only involves storage and handling in central or regional facilities but it also involves storage and time-critical handling in strategic stock locations in order to get the part to its final destination in as short an amount of time as possible.

Logistics providers such as UPS, FedEx, DHL and CEVA all offer solutions for this market. Typically, they will manage a network of strategic stocking locations that manage the delivery of 'mission critical' and scheduled parts to customers, field engineers or Pick Up Drop Off (PUDO) points.

Summary

Each individual industry 'vertical' sector has its own unique set of supply chain and product attributes. This has meant that over the years the logistics industry associated with each of these sectors has developed very differently to meet these varying requirements. This chapter looked in depth at four of the key verticals: automotive, pharmaceutical, consumer goods and retail, and high-tech. It outlined the most important demand-side trends – from lean production techniques to after sales strategies – and highlighted the impact these have had upon the logistics sector and the services and capabilities that have been developed to meet customer needs.

Key points to consider:

- Major opportunities exist for logistics providers in the automotive sector in developing markets such as China, Brazil, Russia and India, as vehicle manufacturers invest in these fast-growing regions.

- Whereas the automotive sector was once dominated by European or US-centric flows of materials, auto logistics networks must now encompass markets in Latin America and Africa, as well as throughout Asia.

- The pharmaceutical market is globalizing as manufacturers target growing middle-class populations in the developing world. This will create opportunities for the global logistics companies in these more challenging markets.

- The nature of drugs is also changing. Biopharma drugs are much more important to the industry, but require specialist handling and temperature-controlled conditions. This will be a key challenge for the logistics sector.

- Regional and global consumer packaged goods supply chains, predicated on the cheap cost of transport, will need to be reviewed should the price of fuel increase substantially.

- Retailers are looking carefully at their sourcing strategies not only from a cost perspective but also ethical. This may lead to increased manufacturing in near-sourcing locations and result in the reduction of global flows of goods.

- High-tech manufacturers are flexing their supply chains to allow them to utilize lower-cost sea freight strategies, rather than to rely on air cargo. This will reduce transport costs, but increase inventory risk.

Risks in global supply chains

Rebalancing 'external' and 'internal' risks

External threats to supply chains have received considerable attention following the well-publicized natural disasters in Japan and Thailand in 2011. However, understanding of these risks is at a very early stage. One survey, undertaken for the World Economic Forum, found that 30 per cent of respondents estimated losses of 5 per cent of annual revenue from supply chain disruption. However, more than a quarter of respondents were not able to place a figure on the financial impact of a disruption (WEF, 2013).

It is not that the risks themselves have become more acute. After all, there have always been wars and natural disasters. Rather it is the evolving supply chain and production strategies of the major global manufacturers that have changed, leading to a rebalancing of the risks inherent within various parts of the supply chain.

One distinction that can be made is between 'internal' and 'external' risks. For example, in the 1980s the personal computer sector adopted traditional manufacturing practices involving the outlay of huge amounts of capital.

The risks were clear as many of these companies quickly went out of business when their forecasts proved hopelessly wrong. From this period new business models were developed, which allowed manufacturers to focus on design and marketing and let their supplier bear the risk of production.

This process has been referred to as 'un-bundling' of production. In other words, in this example, 'internal' risks were out-sourced to contract electronic manufacturers. This, however, did not leave the OEMs risk free – rather the 'internal' risks were transformed into 'external', that is those that are inherent in extended supply chains. The risks have changed but are still there and are just as business critical.

The 'un-bundling' of various production processes has led many OEMs to evolve into what are, in effect, managers of integrated and complex networks of remote but interlinked suppliers. In some cases this has produced greater levels of risk, and in others it has had the opposite effect. There is no doubt that extended supply chains are more vulnerable to external threats, but on the other hand, such networks have also dispersed risks to a number of markets by reducing centralization.

A small supply chain, for instance, with a single production facility is highly vulnerable to external events, whereas a large, complex supply chain with multiple supplier options has the potential to be much more robust through a greater number of sourcing options. Each option may have higher supply chain risk attached, although the probability of overall network disruption is less than in a small supply chain (see Figure 14.1).

The move towards more complex supply chains has its own risks, related to a reduction of visibility and the development of suboptimal networks. With Asia transforming from a production market to a consumer-led economy, this will only add extra layers of complexity into sourcing and out-sourcing decisions for Western manufacturers. Timeliness, reliability, information sharing, quality and design, along with wider benefits resulting from shared labour skills and knowledge all need to be weighed along with levels of visibility, management control and, of course, external risk.

Figure 14.1 Global supply chain risk – probability of disruption

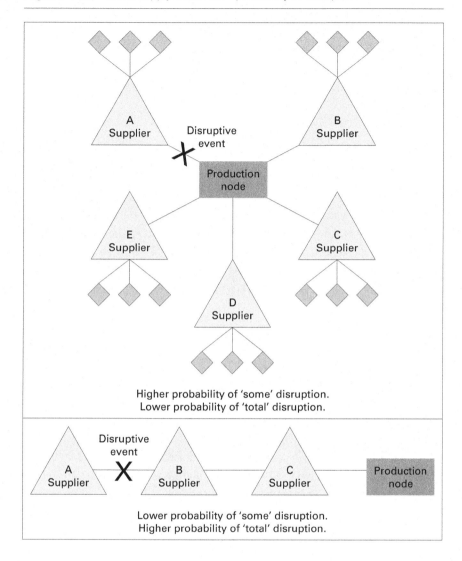

Higher probability of 'some' disruption.
Lower probability of 'total' disruption.

Lower probability of 'some' disruption.
Higher probability of 'total' disruption.

Globalization has also brought risks. Extended supply chains mean longer lead times (and less agile response to market conditions); more handoffs between parties; more challenging quality control as well as exposure to currency fluctuations, labour disputes, shipping costs, corruption, theft and natural/geopolitical instability. An understanding of this has led to many manufacturers adopting a hybrid strategy of remote production combined with near-sourcing.

The cost of transport (on which globalization is predicated) is also overlooked as a major risk. This not only includes shipping rates, which have been volatile over the past few years (in early 2012 shipping rates per TEU rose by US $1,000 overnight on Asia–Europe tradelanes) but also cost of fuel.

CASE STUDY   ASOS warehouse disaster shows hidden costs of supply chain risk

A fire that occurred in June 2014 at the global distribution centre of online retailer, ASOS, highlighted many of the risks to which modern supply chains are exposed. The global retailer kept 70 per cent of its stock at its distribution centre in Barnsley, UK, and it is believed that the fire affected more than £30 million (US $50 million) of inventory. The facility was more than 600,000 square feet (60,000 square metres) and the fire spread to four floors.

ASOS's operation was disrupted for a weekend with the retailer suspending orders over its website, although these recommenced early the next week. The retailer's share price fell by 2 per cent.

One of the problems of operating global distribution centres is the concentration of risk in one location. Centralization of logistics operations makes sense on an operational basis in terms of keeping stock levels low and reducing redundancy. However, if external risks such as fires, floods and security issues are costed in, then suddenly this approach can appear flawed. Although ASOS had insurance and the disaster could have been a lot worse, there were still implications for the retailer in terms of customer service and reputation.

To get back up and running so quickly, ASOS obviously had good contingency plans in place, no doubt helped by an earlier experience when its previous distribution centre in the UK was badly damaged by an oil depot blast. However, this further disaster demonstrates the systemic fragility of many global supply chains and perhaps suggests that it would be sensible to spread risk over a number of locations, despite an increase in internal supply chain costs.

Quantifying supply chain risk

Manufacturers usually adopt one of three strategies when dealing with risk:

1 Inventory management – build up buffer stock.

2 Sourcing – developing contingency strategies for specific suppliers or supply chain links.

3 'Acceptance' – doing nothing as costs of mitigation outweigh benefits.

Deciding on which strategy to adopt relies on understanding the cost implications of each approach.

One pharmaceutical company undertook a cost-benefit approach to working out how it should mitigate supply chain risk. They used insurance and industry data to estimate the frequency and duration of disruptions, and using scenario planning software they worked out how many weeks a year their production would potentially be affected. They were then able to set inventory holdings at a level that would minimize disruption. Of course, the weakness of this approach was that, although it minimized disruption, the strategy imposed huge additional costs on the organization, not only from the financing of the additional inventory, but also from the risks of redundancy of stock.

Modelling exercises also need to take into account the length of disruption as well as the probability. There are other variables: for example, the length of time it takes for alternative suppliers to ramp up production. One other interesting factor that impacts significantly on the extent of disruption is the location of the event within the supply chain. The further upstream it occurs, the longer the disruption to supply. The reason for this is that downstream processing locations act as bottlenecks and take time to fulfil back-orders once upstream supply is switched back on.

In many respects, effective supply chain management is all about the trade-off of one set of risks against another. Keeping higher amounts of stock in various locations is not necessarily a good response to the threat of disruption as this is not only costly, but in high-tech sectors, for example, where product lifecycles are low, would be business critical.

Lean supply chains are also a double-edged sword. Whilst they are working efficiently they have the potential to reduce inventory levels at the same time as maintaining/improving customer service. However, there is no doubt that they are less resilient to external shocks, as they do not provide a safety net when supply chains break down.

In effect, what has happened in the past is that inventory levels have been used as 'insurance' against risk. If there have been disruptions to supply or to transportation, 'buffer' stock has allowed production or sales to continue unaffected. Insurance companies that are now entering the supply chain risk market are allowing manufacturers to out-source this risk, whilst keeping inventory levels to a minimum. Quantifying the risk for insurance companies (as well as manufacturers) is a major challenge.

Types of supply chain threat

When people talk about supply chain risk, they usually mean 'external' threats. As we have discussed, though, the relationship between external and internal risk is very close. For example, increasing inventory levels increases 'internal' risks (redundancy, wastage, financing, etc) but mitigates external risks (the impact of a disruptive event on supply).

The reverse is also true; reducing 'internal' risks can increase 'external' risks. For example, the problems that Toyota faced in the United States relating to a malfunctioning brake pedal design were blamed on a supplier. One estimate put the total costs of this supply chain catastrophe to Toyota at US $2 billion, not including lost consumer confidence. With 60–70 per cent of a vehicle manufacturer's inventory managed by the supply chain, quality control is obviously a huge issue.

Table 14.1 Global supply chain risk – Supply chain internal and external characteristics

Supply chain characteristic	Internal risk	External risk
High stock levels	High	Low
Lean supply chains	Low	High
'Bundled' in-house production	High	Low
'Un-bundled' out-sourced production	Low	High
Globalized sourcing	Low	High

This perhaps can be seen as the inevitable consequence of a trade-off between these different types of risk. However, one piece of research suggests that when out-sourcing production (and risk), only 10 per cent of manufacturers undertake any sort of risk assessment.

Where external events have had most impact, this has been due to insufficient risk assessment. One such example was the floods in Thailand. Here the risk of centralization (which can occur in any geography) was transplanted to a remote region where risk was not fully understood. The high-tech manufacturing cluster that developed in Thailand had comparative advantage in terms of leveraging a local production ecosystem whilst offering low-cost labour. The fact that this cluster developed in a region of South East Asia was not the problem; rather that a consolidation of specific competences had been allowed to develop in an exposed, flood-prone location.

External threats to supply chains can be divided into four main categories:

Environmental

These include a wide range of events including extreme weather, earthquakes, tsunamis, floods and even volcanic eruptions. The economic cost of natural disasters was estimated by insurance company Swiss Re at US $194 billion in 2010. The supply chain consequences are derived from not only the disruption of production but also the impact on transportation services and infrastructure. A WEF/Accenture study found that following the Japanese tsunami/earthquake the operating profits of 15 leading multinationals fell by 33 per cent in the subsequent financial quarter directly as a result of supply chain disruption.

Geopolitical

Tensions in the Middle East are a considerable source of risk for supply chains, especially affecting transit routes such as the Straits of Hormuz and the Suez Canal.

Terrorism also falls into this category, the most obvious example being the events of 11 September 2001 in New York. A more recent example, described below, relates to the bombs placed in packages originating from Yemen. It should be noted that as regulators seek to limit the impact of a terrorist event, they risk increasing supply chain costs by high levels of security-driven regulations and procedures.

Piracy has also been a major issue for some supply chains. Millions of dollars have been paid to pirates off the Somali coast and shipping lines have been forced to divert to longer routes to avoid the problem areas. Other costs include increased insurance; security and guards; increased steaming speeds; higher wages for seamen (danger money) not to mention indirect payments for military operations.

Economic

One of the most pressing supply chain risks from an economic perspective is what can be termed 'demand shocks'. An example of this is the disruption caused by the company failure of suppliers following the 2008 recession. This was particularly relevant to the high-tech and automotive sectors where supplier bankruptcy was prevalent. Many of the problems were caused by manufacturers 'switching off' supply from remote suppliers, and although this had a short-term positive effect on inventories and balances, it meant that when demand picked up strongly in 2010, manufacturers were unable to meet demand.

'Supply shocks' are less obvious, but a material threat all the same. The volatile nature of shipping rates could fall into this category. In early 2012, shipping rates on Asia–Europe routes increased by about US $1,000 per TEU (from about $650 to $1,650) – a situation that most shippers would find difficult if not impossible to predict.

Manufacturers are ever more exposed to currency risks given the globalized nature of their suppliers and customers. Given the eurozone debt-crisis and the impact this has had on the strength of the euro against the dollar, this risk is likely to have significant financial impact in the coming years.

Technological

Technology failure/outage is a major concern to shippers, although as yet there have been few significant incidents. A lot of money has been spent by agencies, such as the Pentagon, in assessing and planning for a 'cyber terrorist' attack, although minor disruption to date has come from power failures or accidents. More reliance in the future will be placed on information and communications networks as the supply chain industry becomes increasingly paperless and this will only heighten the risks. However, actually measuring the true nature of the threat and robustness of information systems is difficult.

Even localized events can have a major impact on global supply chains (see Figure 14.2). For example, an earthquake such as the one in Japan in 2011 may be very localized in geographic terms, but has worldwide implications for supply chains that depend on a large number of suppliers clustered in the affected area.

Shipping rates, in contrast, are a global phenomenon. They affect all supply chains, but although serious, have less of a catastrophic impact.

Figure 14.2 Global supply chain risk – external event impact on supply chain (illustrative matrix)

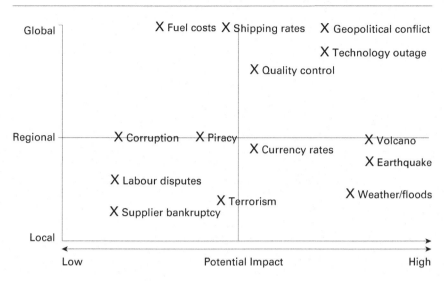

A geopolitical conflict, depending on where it takes place, could have a very serious, disruptive impact at a global level. A supplier bankruptcy, on the other hand, may be a local problem, and if contingency plans are in place, may not be serious.

Of course, the seriousness of each of these threats is very specific to each supply chain as well as the level of disruptiveness of the event in question.

Unknown unknowns...

The most disruptive supply chain events are those which have not or cannot be planned for. Therefore, it is perhaps more useful, rather than look at past events in order to gain some insight into the future, to identify weaknesses in supply chains instead. Addressing vulnerability is the best way to mitigate the impact of a disruption, although there still remains the issue of how much time and money should be invested on each perceived weakness.

The World Economic Forum's Supply Chain and Transport Risk Survey 2011 identified the least effectively managed supply chain components as rated by respondents. The top five are:

1 Reliance on oil

2 Shared information

3 Fragmentation along the value chain

4 Extensive subcontracting

5 Supplier visibility

As the survey analysis points out, three of these components relate to visibility and control. Improvements in technology can mitigate this type of risk. For example:

- Development of supplier/buyer communities and the use of social media technologies within supply chain communities could be one way in which risks can be reduced.

- 'Sense and respond' technologies allow for greater awareness of the location of products in the supply chain, and hence enabling better decision making/rerouting.

The development of information technologies will play an important role in the mitigation of supply chain threats. There is little prospect that these risks will diminish – some may even increase. Therefore, the ability to react to events will become the key competitive differentiator, and technologies that enable an enhanced level of supply chain agility will become highly sought after.

However, the adoption of more technology will also play a role in increasing risks. Increasing reliance on technology will leave supply chains open to 'cyber attacks' or even accidental outages. Whilst technology will lead to greater levels of efficiency, it will also mean that maintaining robust networks will be ever more critical.

Despite this it is the industry's reliance on oil that is of primary concern. Given the relationship between geopolitical tension, the global economy and the price of oil and the extreme volatility that this causes, it is clear that alternative strategies must be developed. This could entail a rebalancing of the inventory/transportation equation as shippers position stock in closer proximity to end users. This will increase stock levels, but reduce transport costs. Of course, as mentioned above, this has risks in its own right and these need to be taken into account in a holistic supply chain management strategy. It could also entail a move from global supply chains to near-sourcing of products, especially utilizing less fuel-intensive modes of transport.

Sector resilience to threats

The characteristics of some supply chains make them more vulnerable to supply chain threats than others. Figure 14.3 illustrates this point. The high-tech sector, for example, relies heavily on global supply chains that are typically high value, lean and un-bundled/out-sourced. The pharmaceutical supply chain is much less globalized (although becoming more so), and although there are intrinsic risks for the products themselves, the high level of in-house production/distribution mitigates many of these risks. With greater levels of out-sourcing in this sector, the external risks are set to rise. Food supply chains tend to be local, characterized by low product value and, in most cases, have low levels of risks attached. However, the horse-meat scandal in Europe in 2013 showed very clearly, for processed foods at least, that the sector was not immune to corruption and criminality involving wide-scale substitution. Food supply chains were shown to be complex and lacking in transparency, which ultimately created issues of security and process integrity.

Figure 14.3 Global supply chain risk – sector threat resilience

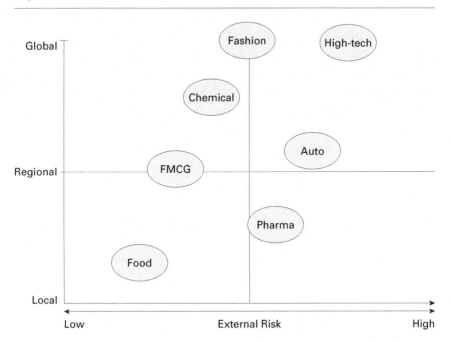

Case studies: Supply chain disruption

Natural disasters

Japanese tsunami

The impact of Japan's 2011 earthquake and tsunami on global supply chains was dramatic with production across a whole range of sectors badly affected.

The Japanese electronics sector was amongst the hardest hit. Output of NAND flash memory, on which new consumer electronic equipment depends, was disrupted, albeit on a temporary basis. Many wafer fabrication plants, supplying the semiconductor industry, remained closed whilst aftershocks continued to take place.

More surprising was the effects on other industries. The Japanese automotive sector traditionally has a highly localized supply chain with mechanical component manufacturers located next to major assembly plants. Although these supplier parks were not affected, production was halted all the same.

One reason why these automotive plants were hit is the increasing number of electronic components in new motor vehicles. Already a huge part of the value of new cars, electronic component sourcing differs from that of mechanical parts. Increasingly the more complex assemblies are sourced globally, with physically small yet important and expensive products often moved by airfreight from distant production locations. This illustrates an emerging trend in the automotive supply chain.

Plants beyond Japan suffered as well. For example, Toyota's plant in the UK shut down production due to uncertainties over component supply. Renault's Samsung plant in South Korea also slowed output due to problems accessing its supply chain, part of which it shares with Nissan.

In fact, supply chains in the electronics sector, heavily dependent on Japanese production, were affected right across Asia. There were reports of key electronic components being in short supply as leading electronic manufacturers such as Sony, Sharp and Panasonic shut plants.

Japan has a large chemical sector much of which is located on the coast. Many of these facilities were damaged, with Dow Chemical reporting one of its facilities flooded.

However, things could have been worse. More widespread disruption was prevented by global supplies of flash memory on hand having built up over the previous two months. Manufacturers were also able to shift production from Japan to facilities outside the country.

It is believed as a result of the tsunami that manufacturers increased orders to buffer against future supply chain disruptions. Higher inventory could become the 'new normal' in the future, a calculated measure deployed to mitigate the disrupting effects of natural disasters.

Thailand floods

In 2011, Thailand suffered one of the worst floods in five decades. The floods began in July, but steadily worsened throughout October, and were mainly limited to northern and eastern areas around Bangkok. However, these affected areas were home to hundreds of manufacturing facilities that were completely flooded. The automotive and hard disk drive manufacturing industries were amongst the hardest affected.

Japanese car makers that had just started to recover from the earthquake and tsunami now faced shortages of key parts made in Thailand. Toyota and Honda both had to halt production at facilities even in North America because their Thai suppliers were flooded.

The hard disk drive manufacturing sector was particularly affected. Thailand is the second largest country for production of hard disk drives after China. Toshiba, the fourth largest producer of hard disk drives halted all of its production in Thailand; however, Seagate, the second largest producer of hard disk drives, did not have to stop production because its factories were in the north-east where flooding was less severe. Shortages of supplies lasted into the first quarter of 2012. Prices increased 20–40 per cent.

Subsequently, semiconductor chip manufacturer, Intel, warned that its revenues and profits would be lower than expected due to shortages of hard disk drives in the industry. Owing to the closures, Intel's customers were not able to source sufficient volumes of hard disk drives to meet demand, and cut down on their microprocessor inventories. Intel warned that the shortages would continue into the first quarter of 2012.

Intel was not the only manufacturer struggling. Dell also missed sales targets in its quarterly results due, in part, to shortages of hard disk drives. However, management said that it had made strategic purchases of inventory elsewhere in an attempt to overcome this problem. This inevitably came at a cost.

Thailand supplies about 40 per cent of the world's market of hard disk drives. The supply chain problems that high-tech manufacturers were facing reopened the debate over the wisdom of sourcing from suppliers clustered in such a vulnerable area.

Icelandic volcanos

The eruption on 14 April 2010 of Iceland's Eyjafjallajokull volcano (the second eruption in a month) caused havoc throughout Europe and beyond. The impact of this first eruption in 190 years continued even after airspace restrictions were lifted.

The regulators' decision to shut down airspace in Britain, Norway, the Netherlands, Germany, Austria, Belgium, Denmark, Finland, France, Germany, Latvia, Luxembourg, Poland, Slovakia, the Czech Republic, Bulgaria, Sweden and Switzerland cost airlines some US $200 million per day from cancelled flights and caused the European economy to suffer massive losses in lost business.

The obvious reaction by logistics planners was to use other modes of transport for intra-European movements. The main problem was handling intercontinental traffic. As a contingency, freight forwarders and airlines set up hub activities in airports in southern Europe. For example UPS flew some freight to Istanbul and moved it into Europe by road. Other providers used North African or even Middle Eastern airports.

The supply chain consequences were felt further afield than in Europe, and no more acutely than in East African markets. Here perishable air cargo, such as fresh fruit and flowers, backed up at airports and, given the lack of appropriate temperature-controlled storage facilities, much of it was ruined. This caused considerable hardship to exporters and their employees.

Conflict and political unrest

The Middle East

The security situation in the Middle East has huge implications for the rest of the world both politically and economically. Nowhere is this more evident than in Egypt, which is transited by the Suez Canal, a route of strategic importance for goods moving between Asia and Europe. The canal handles about 8–10 per cent of the world's trade and it is transited by more than 17,000 ships a year.

The volatile political situation in Egypt, first with the overthrow of President Mubarak and then President Morsi, has therefore been of immense concern to the shipping industry. Not least because, after the Straits of Hormuz (also threatened earlier this decade by a breakdown of relations with Iran), the canal is the second most important pinch point for oil and liquefied gas heading from the Middle East to Europe and North America.

Any geopolitical or security event that resulted in the closure of the Suez Canal would have major implications for shipping and world trade. It would force ships bound to and from Asia to use the Cape of Good Hope in South Africa instead, adding several days to the transit time. Whereas ships using the Suez Canal only travel 12,000 kilometres from the Arabian Gulf to London, those choosing the Cape of Good Hope would travel 20,900 kilometres. In terms of days, such a transit would be 14 days compared with 24 days.

Going via the Cape would increase not only operational costs such as fuel, chartering, crewing (impacting on rates charged to shippers), but also add significantly to inventory costs as shippers would have to bear an additional 10 days of capital.

Threats to the Suez Canal come from a number of sources:

- civil war in Egypt;
- local Islamic extremists;
- international terrorist organizations such as so-called Islamic State;
- a wider Middle Eastern conflict.

Each of these threats has a varying level of probability. The present poor security situation in Egypt is perhaps the most pressing as the Suez Canal would become a valuable strategic asset to both sides in a civil war. At present the Egyptian military has provided sufficient security, ensuring that operations were not affected even during the uprising against Mubarak. However, the latest conflict between the Muslim Brotherhood and the Egyptian army risks becoming far more serious to the long-term stability of the country. Providing US $5.1 billion in revenue from tolls, there is an obvious interest to all sides to keep the canal open. However, it could also be used as a bargaining chip in any political manoeuvring that may occur.

In September 2013, three men launched an attack with guns and a rocket-propelled grenade on a Chinese vessel transiting the canal, the COSCO *Asia*. Although the three men were quickly apprehended and little damage was inflicted, the proximity of land to the ships makes them easy targets, and highlights the need for strong security on either side of the canal.

Economic/demand shocks

Cisco's troubles typify supply chain challenges

In June 2010, the Council of Supply Chain Management Professionals (CSCMP) asserted that the sharp destocking experienced during the recession had disrupted supply chains and that many organizations had to resort to emergency measures to cope when demand picked up. This, according to the Council, was behind much of the boom in airfreight seen in the previous few quarters as manufacturers desperately sought to source components and support increased production. What emerged were some examples of such supply chain stress.

Take Cisco, a huge company built on the design of the hardware that makes up the infrastructure of the internet. For much of 2010 Cisco was in crisis due to the malfunctioning of its supply chain. Its customers complained that the company could not deliver its products on time or, in some cases, even deliver them at all. Engineers maintaining infrastructure such as data centres were facing a wait of up to 12 weeks for basic switching components.

The origin of the problem clearly lay with Cisco's suppliers, many of them based in China. According to a statement from Cisco itself, the issues were, 'Attributable in part to increasing demand driven by the improvement in our overall markets... the longer than normal lead time extensions also stemmed from supplier constraints based upon their labour and other actions taken during the global economic downturn'. In other words, component suppliers laid off workers during the recession and reduced capacity. Consequently, there was not enough production capacity to fulfil demand.

It was also very interesting to see the reaction of customers to the worsening supply situation. According to Cisco, this led customers, '... to place the same order multiple times within our various sales channels and to cancel the duplicative orders upon receipt of the product, or to place orders with other vendors with shorter manufacturing lead times'.

In its statement Cisco said that, 'Our efforts to improve manufacturing lead-time performance may result in corresponding reductions in order backlog. A decline in backlog levels could result in more variability and less predictability in our quarter-to-quarter net sales and operating results'. This might be taken as typical 'squirreling' behaviour where customers increase inventory levels in an environment of uncertainty. The result is 'lumpy' demand, with wild swings between shortage and over-stocking.

The economic stress being visited upon supply chains led in turn to a failure to manage inventory properly. This in turn affected the management of transport. Or in the words of Cisco, 'We have experienced periods of time during which shipments have exceeded net bookings or manufacturing issues have delayed shipments, leading to nonlinearity in shipping patterns. In addition to making it difficult to predict revenue for a particular period, nonlinearity in shipping can increase costs, because irregular shipment patterns result in periods of underutilized capacity and periods in which overtime expenses may be incurred, as well as in potential additional inventory management-related costs.'

In other words, this statement meant Cisco, an erstwhile poster child of supply chain excellence, faced immense challenges in its logistics.

Terrorism

Yemen-originated terrorism

The placing of a parcel bomb on a Qatar Airways plane between Sana'a, Yemen, and Dubai as belly-hold freight amplified the issue of security for the airfreight sector. Whilst it was disturbing that terrorists were able to penetrate the networks of FedEx and UPS, the Qatar Airways incident demonstrated that the whole of the airfreight industry is affected by the problem.

Although freight industry organizations cautioned against an excessive security clamp-down, politicians in Britain and the United States committed to security reviews. This reaction by the authorities is likely to take the form of more inspection and scanning, possibly leading to the wider use of 'explosive detection systems'. These are complex pieces of engineering that are both slow and very expensive, but they do offer better performance against nitrate-based explosive than x-ray systems.

In the latest cases the core problem is that the primary systems put in place to prevent the loading of explosive devices failed. Both the surveillance technology being used at present and the 'Known Consignor' system were either deceived or by-passed. It is worth observing that it was the Express providers who were targeted as these systems are possibly more open to the general public and therefore may offer greater opportunity to hide the identity of the person placing the package in the system.

The lesson that the incidents appear to give is that the nature of the threat is dynamic rather than static. The individuals placing the bombs into the freight systems designed the devices to deliberately evade the security systems. This displayed both a knowledge of the security systems used and the ability to design a device capable of evading these systems. Therefore any effective new security systems put in place by the air cargo sector is going to have to be both proactive and continually adaptive.

In truth there is nothing particularly original about the approach taken in the most recent devices. The bomb on Pam Am 103, which blew up over Scotland in 1988, had strong similarities in design. However, the innovation of disguising explosive as printer-toner illustrates an evolution in the nature of the problem. The airfreight business systems must in turn evolve to anticipate such developments. It must achieve this whilst not crippling the operations of the business either in terms of time to scan each consignment or cost. Either way the cost penalty of developing such a response quickly and across the whole air cargo system is likely to be substantial.

The question is whether to approach the security with a risk-based strategy that relies on characteristics of a shipment to identify packages for increased scrutiny or one in which all shipments are subject to some form of physical inspection.

Proponents of comprehensive physical screening argue that it is the only way to ensure adequate security, whilst advocates of risk-based approaches argue that comprehensive screening is too costly and too time consuming. Costs of implementing 100 per cent screening is estimated to be more than US $3.5 billion over a six-year period. Not only is this an expensive approach but probably an inefficient one as shipping delays are likely to occur with this method.

Under the current air cargo security system, a number of risk-based strategies are being implemented and expanded to evaluate the security risk of air cargo shipments. Existing programmes such as the Known Shipper Program and the Certified Cargo Screening Program, both of which have been in place for several years, are being studied for potential enhancements and expansions.

Another measure that must be taken on is technology. The US Transportation Security Administration (TSA) has approved a number of x-ray, bulk explosives detection systems and explosives trace detection machines for screening air cargo. However, these are variations of technologies used for screening checked baggage and carry-on items. Unfortunately, none of these devices are capable of effectively screening palletized or containerized cargo, which makes up 75 per cent of all cargo carried on passenger planes. Instead, screening must be done on individual cargo items. As a result, the TSA is studying various new technologies.

The US Department of Homeland Security and the TSA will also need to monitor and provide a solution for international air cargo entering the United States. Most of the focus has been on air cargo screening of out-bound domestic US cargo. Although the TSA lacks the direct authority to dictate screening requirements at foreign airports for US-bound cargo, it could potentially impose regulations on foreign carriers, as well as US carriers. However, enforcement overseas would be up to authorities in other countries. If they do not concur with the US approach, disagreement over security standards could complicate US foreign relations and could potentially impact foreign trade.

Conclusion

Although global supply chains have created mutual benefits for developed and emerging markets alike, these same supply chains have increased risk to the global economy. Reliance on production in markets such as China and the rest of Asia Pacific has put Western economies at the mercy of a series of internal and external threats to its extended supply chains.

Production in remote locations has brought with it increased exposure to environmental threats such as the tsunami in Japan and the floods in Thailand, both of which have been important in raising the issue of supply chain vulnerability. These events brought massive disruption to automotive and high-tech supply chains, but both could have been much worse. The first step for many manufacturers will be to accept that global supply chains bring with them risk. However, once the threats have been identified, quantifying them will be harder still.

Summary

Over the past three decades and more, manufacturers have sought to take advantage of low-cost labour in developing countries and, at the same time, reduce inventory levels. These strategies have been called into question by catastrophic events such as the Japanese tsunami, which resulted in major supply chain disruption. This chapter looked at these risks in more detail and how many manufacturers have ignored them in their rush to drive down costs. It reviewed the type of threats, ranging from geopolitical to economic, and detailed some of the major disasters that have occurred and their implications for supply chains.

Key points to consider:

- When developing their supply chain strategies, manufacturers need to take a holistic approach to costs – not just focused on inventory or labour, but measuring the impact of disruption.

- Many companies have adopted a 'virtual manufacturing network' approach – out-sourcing component supply to multiple and remotely located suppliers. This has extended and complicated supply chains, making them more vulnerable.

- Transport bottlenecks – a 'gateway' port such as Rotterdam or the Suez Canal, for instance – are at risk from terrorist attack or even just a collision. The concentration of shipping at these points and the growth in the size of container vessels is increasing these risks significantly.

- Many manufacturers have very little visibility below Tier 1 or Tier 2 suppliers. This is a major problem if a supplier of a unique product is disrupted.

- Technology dependence means that manufacturers, retailers and logistics providers are considerably at risk from cyber-attack or outage of some sort. However, the supply chain visibility that technology can provide, can also be used to mitigate the impact of disruption by improving decision making.

The
e-commerce
logistics
phenomenon

15

CHAPTER LEARNING OBJECTIVES

This chapter will provide the reader with:

- A description of e-commerce and the impact of e-retailing upon the logistics sector

- An analysis of logistics segments related to e-commerce and how they have developed to meet the evolving needs of customers and parcel recipients

- Innovations in alternative delivery locations such as lockers, click and collect and parcels shop networks

- An overview of the growth of two of the world's fastest-growing e-retailers, Amazon and Alibaba

One of the biggest trends to impact on the global logistics industry over the past 10 years has been the emergence of e-commerce. Whilst the retail sector in the developed world has stagnated due to the economic situation, e-retailers have seen volumes grow significantly. The changing business model has meant that whilst logistics and transport companies tied to traditional retailers have struggled, those which have been able to embrace the new distribution channels with a host of new services have prospered. Not least amongst these have been the parcels companies responsible for last mile 'B2C' deliveries. The phenomenon has also created a welcome new revenue stream for the post offices.

Not all retailers have been quick to adapt to this phenomenon. Long-time UK retailers such as HMV, Jessops and Comet have faced restructuring or even bankruptcy. Their inability to adapt to the rise in online retailing played a major role in their problems. e-retailers such as Amazon.com and eBay have brought a new business model to the retailing industry – stores open 24/7 via a consumer's laptop or mobile device, the ability to compare products and prices, and delivery to the consumer's door.

Being able to adapt to a changing retail industry and respond to these changes with a flexible, agile supply chain is now a necessity for retailers to survive. As an increasing number of 'brick-and-mortar' retailers embrace e-commerce they will need to bolster their supply chain to provide a successful multi-channel experience for the consumer.

International retailers such as Tesco and Walmart have been able to make the leap as have several traditional catalogue companies such as Germany's The Otto Group and the Netherlands' Wehkamp. Pure-plays are also making headway. ASOS, an apparel and accessories online retailer has achieved success in not only its home market of the UK but it is now expanding into Europe, the United States and also has expansion plans for Asia. US-based retailers and pure-plays are expanding into the European market as well. In fact, Amazon is the largest European online retailer and eBay is right behind it in many European countries.

Logistics providers and postal services have responded to some extent to the needs of retailers, pure-play and brick-and-mortar alike, to compete effectively in the market. Many have tailored solutions for transport, fulfilment and returns and also additional value added services. Logistics providers are also playing a role in many retailers' strategies as they expand services into new international markets.

However, although mail, express and logistics companies are benefiting from the growth of e-commerce, a large proportion of logistics functions are still not out-sourced, as retailers believe that they are better positioned to undertake these operations themselves. Likewise, the product range provided by carriers is very patchy – as is service quality.

What is e-commerce?

The term e-commerce can have a very broad meaning overall and refer to many different aspects of business, including selling online directly to customers using a virtual storefront.

Some of these models include:

- Business-to-business or B2B – B2B e-commerce involves the buying and selling of physical goods between businesses.

- Business-to-consumer or B2C – The most common type of e-commerce; many large electronic retailers or 'e-tailers' fit this model, including Amazon.com.

- Consumer-to-consumer or C2C – In this model, the online platform serves as a connection between two individual consumers who wish to make an exchange. Amazon.com can sometimes fit this model as they allow individual sellers to resell items (regardless of whether they were purchased on Amazon) to other individuals. Currently, the leader in C2C commerce is online auction site eBay.com.

UK retailers were early adopters of multi-channel strategies but German retailer Saturn led the way in mainland Europe by launching a click and collect service bridging their online website with the offline in-store. As a result, the brand is experiencing much stronger customer engagement.

The ability to not only adapt to a changing retail industry but also to respond to these changes with a flexible, agile supply chain is now a necessity for retailers to survive. As more and more brick-and-mortar retailers embrace e-commerce they will need to bolster their supply chain to provide a successful multi-channel experience for the consumer.

The impact of e-retailing on logistics

Warehousing and fulfilment

e-retailers require distribution systems that often are more complex than traditional ones. Besides the need to manage an increasing number of suppliers and varying inventory, the management of multiple delivery options such as home delivery, in-store pick-up, lockbox or elsewhere also becomes more difficult.

e-fulfilment centres are being built to manage the unique needs of this growing retail segment. These centres tend to be highly automated with service offerings ranging from basic order management and storage to pick and pack, returns handling and value added services such as monogramming, gift wrapping and garment hanging services. Speed is very important – the quicker to fulfil and deliver an order, the greater the likelihood of a returning customer.

The size of these facilities also varies greatly. While Amazon operates warehouses that average 62,000 square metres, other companies use smaller facilities often located within urban areas close to where parcels are collected and also where customers can pick up their orders.

In the European and North American market many retailers are keeping warehousing and fulfilment in-house instead of out-sourcing to logistics providers. This is due to not only the complex distribution requirements and limited supply of facilities but also to the still undeveloped range of services currently available from 3PLs.

As online retailing matures and retailers expand into additional countries, warehousing and distribution requirements will change and will likely include the adoption of out-sourcing, particularly to those providers that adapt and introduce offerings for these changes.

Reverse logistics

The rate of online returns can average anywhere between 25 and 50 per cent. According to several retailers, customers are becoming more sophisticated in their online shopping – at one time they bought one item; now they buy two and return the one they do not like.

As such, many retailers are adding features such as panoramic viewing and virtual modelling to help minimize returns. However, these alone do not solve the amount of returns.

Other problems include regulations specific to online sales such as those relating to distance selling in the EU which dictate that retailers have to offer cash for return rather than just store credit.

In any case, handling returns is expensive and difficult for retailers to manage. Some retailers charge a restocking fee whilst others offer free returns. Most, if not all, logistics providers, including fulfilment specialists, offer returns handling as part of their solutions. For many of these providers, the solutions involve the gathering of returned items; determining if the items can be resold or disposed and then submitting the items into the proper channel of distribution. Because of varying individual country laws and regulations, much of this handling is done in the country in which the returns occur.

Courier, express and parcels sector (CEP)

The parcel segment has witnessed an impressive increase in volumes due to the rise in e-commerce. The industry's limited capacity for home delivery as well as the increased handling of returns amongst parcel carriers has allowed for the creation of new services as well as delivery and pick-up points.

For example, in late 2012, DHL introduced its DHL Easy Return. The service allows for consumers to return goods across Europe. DHL's service is a standardized process across Europe. Distance sellers are able to use a special software platform and web portal to provide returns labels for their customers or customers can choose to create and print these labels themselves from a web portal. The portal is available in English, French, German and Dutch languages. It also offers the option for consumers to send their return parcels via DHL's network of 80,000 drop-off points. Transit times range from 3 to 12 days and the company plans eventually to expand the service beyond Europe.

In B2C, convenience and prompt delivery is expected. The increasing demand for such delivery services has put a strain on parcel delivery companies and post offices alike, and this has led to the greater use of self-employed drivers.

Alliances are also being created to maximize and expand the services of partners. According to TNT Post and Hermes, shippers in Germany want a partner that can provide the entire logistics solution. Consequently, the two companies formed a delivery alliance in which Hermes will offer catalogue delivery via TNT Post and TNT Post will offer parcel delivery through Hermes – including access to the 14,000 Hermes parcel shops, charge-on-delivery shipment services, online identity verification and online real-time tracking.

As new delivery services increase, delivery points are also on the increase. Convenience and timing of deliveries are important to consumers when ordering online. To the parcel delivery company, additional delivery points may also assist them in maintaining fleet operations and thus keep delivery costs as low as possible.

Lockers

With its successful introduction of lockers to the United States, Amazon introduced its locker pick-up service to the UK market in 2011. Customers are able to choose to pick up goods from a locker location when placing their orders via Amazon UK's website. These lockers are typically located in various stores and there are also plans to expand the concept across the UK.

Parcel shops

GLS, DPD, DHL and many more parcel delivery companies have established parcel shops across Europe as a means for customers to drop off or pick up packages. Many of these shops are within other shops whilst others are stand-alone facilities.

Parcel shop networks in the UK include Yodel's CollectPlus network with 5,000 outlets; Hermes' myHermes network has more than 1,000 outlets.

In Germany, there are 14,000 Hermes parcel shops, 4,000 GLS parcel shops and DPD plans to grow its 2,000 network to 8,000 parcel shops.

UPS launched its network of parcel shops, UPS Access Points, in the UK in 2013, starting with about 500 outlets. In 2016, this number had grown to 2,800. According to UPS, one of the attractions of convenience stores providing parcel services is that B2C parcels are converted into B2B parcels by parcel shops, meaning a more efficient delivery model can be used. Launching a new parcel shop network meant driving UPS further into the B2C parcel market without having to significantly expand fleet operations.

Click and collect

Brick-and-mortar retailers, such as John Lewis, are now allowing customers the option to buy online and pick up at their stores. According to John Lewis, which has about 40 stores, this service includes its sister company, Waitrose, allowing the company to add an additional 300 outlets.

Asda, Tesco and Sainsbury's also offer this type of service. According to Sainsbury's director of direct channels, over a third of the supermarket's internet non-food sales already come through click and collect.

International commerce

Although the majority of B2C shipments are still domestic, international B2C is expected to gain importance as express providers build their cross-border networks. In the long term, larger e-commerce players will likely set up logistics operations in each of their key markets, which will convert international shipments into domestic ones. To cope with higher last mile costs in this segment they will need to develop innovative solutions particularly as e-commerce companies establish their own solutions.

The express segment continues to dominate in markets with a perceived poor quality of standard mail services such as in remote locations within Europe and in markets with high shares of volumes to or from non-European locations. Countries with more heavyweight business and with central positions in intra-European trade and traffic see more standard volumes.

As more e-commerce companies enter the market, the high levels of returned shipments, such as apparel, will need to be addressed along with the increase in parcels. CEP providers will need to either develop alternative solutions to cope with increasing costs or raise prices although the latter approach is unlikely given the fierce competition and the aim to transport returns free of charge in most European markets.

The four major integrators, DHL, FedEx, TNT and UPS, have a distinct advantage: well-established air and road networks. FedEx and UPS have both been keen to buy in Europe to strengthen their offering in this market.

For example, in 2012, FedEx completed the acquisition of the Polish courier company Opek. Through the acquisition, FedEx Express gained access to a nationwide domestic ground network with an estimated US $70 million in annual revenue and 12.5 million shipments handled annually. In the same year FedEx also acquired Tatex, a French privately held company. The company has a nationwide network with a central hub at Lieusaint, just south of Paris, and 35 shipping centres including six regional hubs. The acquisition gives FedEx Express access to a nationwide domestic ground network that carried 19 million shipments and produced approximately 150 million euros in revenue annually.

The role of the postal services

Many of Europe's post offices are struggling due to varying degrees of privatization and declining mail volume. Unlike traditional logistics providers, many of Europe's post offices continue to be governed based on procedures dictated by inter-postal bodies. At the international level, the Universal Postal Union defines the postal standards applicable to all countries. At the local level, bodies such as the E-Parcel Group set the delivery time standards and the penalties postal services owe their foreign counterparts should they fail to deliver a parcel within a specific time frame.

As such, many are reinventing themselves particularly as online retailing continues to grow and demand for parcel delivery solutions, e-fulfilment services and crossborder European solutions increases.

Along with the increasing selection of collection and drop-off points for parcels mentioned earlier in this chapter, post offices are also introducing additional solutions. For example, in Germany, customers can choose to collect parcels 24/7 from one of about 2,500 automated Deutsche Post Packstations and receive SMS/e-mail notifications. They can also send parcels using a touchscreen automated process. About 90 per cent of Germans can reach a Packstation in 10 minutes.

A number of other operators have developed similar automated postal pick-up solutions, including bpost, Cyprus Post, PostNord, Eesti Post and La Poste.

Austrian Post introduced 'Drop off Box' for 24/7 returns and 'Parcel Box' – parcels are placed in a secure box at select apartment buildings and a private access code is given with a notification card, which can be dropped into a personal mailbox.

In the UK, Royal Mail has trialled a 'Delivery to Neighbour' initiative where a neighbour can receive a parcel if the intended recipient is not at home.

CASE STUDY   Amazon drives the market in Europe

Headquartered in the United States, Amazon.com began operations in 1995, entering the European market in 1998. The UK is Amazon's largest European market. At present the company has eight fulfilment centres in the UK; one in Spain; four in France; one in Italy and seven in Germany.

Amazon's European fulfilment centres operate much like those in the United States. There are the people on the 'receive lines' and the 'pack lines'. They either unpack, check and scan every product upon arrival or they pack up customers' orders at the other end of the process. They place product wherever there is a free space. Employees use handheld computers to scan both the item they are stowing away and a barcode on the spot on the shelf where they put it.

When an order is received, the 'pickers' pick customers' orders from the aisles. Amazon's software calculates the most efficient walking route to collect all the items to fill a trolley and then simply directs from one shelf space to the next via instructions on the screen of the handheld satnav device.

As well as selling its own products, Amazon UK provides fulfilment services whereby customers can store their products in Amazon's fulfilment centres, and

Amazon staff will pick, pack and deliver them as well as provide customer service. Customers can also sell their products on other Amazon Marketplaces in Europe (Germany, France, Italy) and Amazon fulfils these orders from the customer's inventory stored in the UK.

Amazon has been experimenting with various delivery points and in 2011, the company installed lockers throughout London through a deal with Land Securities which owns several shopping centres in London.

Instead of delivering a parcel to a home or business address, the customer can select a locker location during checkout and pick up the parcel at a time that is convenient. Once the parcel is delivered to the Amazon Locker, the customer receives an e-mail notification with a unique pick-up code. When the customer arrives to collect the parcel, the customer will touch the Amazon Locker screen until there is an option to enter the unique pick-up code. Once entered, a message appears with the parcel's locker number and the locker door will automatically open.

All parcels delivered to Locker locations must be picked up within three business days. If the parcel is not picked up within this time frame, it will be returned to Amazon for a refund.

In 2012, Amazon introduced delivery to customers at nearly 5,000 convenience stores through collection network CollectPlus. More than 85 per cent of the UK population lives within one mile of a CollectPlus outlet.

e-retailing in Asia

The growth of e-commerce amongst Asia Pacific countries is rapid and the region is in the midst of becoming the largest as a percentage of global sales. Owing to the growth, infrastructure is strained and is proving to be a hindrance to adoption. Much of Asia's infrastructure was structured to meet export demand. However, because of the need to balance exports and imports, infrastructure projects are underway to establish road and rail networks, improve delivery service options and to expand warehousing and distribution centres.

Payments are another part of the supply chain that has proven challenging for the region. Traditionally, Asia is a cash-based society and looks upon credit with suspicion. As such, e-commerce companies have had to make allowances for cash-on-delivery which can slow the delivery process even further if frequent returns have to be made along with the prolonged financial payment cycle time.

The Asian e-commerce market is tempting for international e-commerce companies such as Amazon and eBay. Whilst both are amongst the largest of such providers in North America and Europe, it has not been the case for Asia. eBay pulled out of the Chinese market in 2006 owing to the fierce competition, but has operations in other Asian countries such as Korea and Japan. Amazon has had a difficult time in Asia as well. Although it is the second largest e-commerce company in Japan it has only about a 2 per cent market share within China's market. In India, it has had to partner with a local provider as required by India's government.

China's Alibaba and Japan's Rakuten dominate Asia's e-commerce and both of these companies are expanding into Europe and the Americas, and could rival Amazon and eBay for international sales.

CASE STUDY   China's leading e-retailer builds its own logistics

The Alibaba Group has identified logistics as the major hindrance for Chinese e-commerce companies. Jack Ma, the founder of Alibaba, noted: 'e-commerce sales are growing so quickly in China that logistics companies are in danger of being overwhelmed and unable to deliver merchandise ordered online to Chinese homes and businesses in a timely way.' As a result, it has partnered with investment company, Fosun Group, and banking group, China Yintai Holding Group to develop a logistics network.

Since 2011, Alibaba has worked on a strategy to develop a logistics network connecting all of China and provide delivery within 24 hours anywhere in China. Named the China Smart Logistics Network, Alibaba's strategy comprises four parts:

- Its consumer-focused subsidiary Taobao will develop its logistics initiative, which consists of the 'Taobao supply chain management platform' designed to help merchants handle inventory, a logistics partnership network and an industry code of standards guiding logistics service providers.

- Alibaba will establish an integrated logistics platform at group level that aims to bring together all players in the industry from warehousing to delivery.

- Alibaba will also invest in the establishment of a nationwide warehouse network across China.

- The group will offer warehousing facility support to small Chinese exporters.

Prior to this announcement, merchants were responsible for their own warehousing and fulfilment needs. However, during a one-day promotional event on Taobao mall, more than 21 million shoppers purchased more than US $146 million worth of goods. The unexpected volume caused the payment system to temporarily freeze and many merchants struggled to fulfil orders in the aftermath. Now, according to the founder of Alibaba: 'We are asking companies to keep their stock in our warehouses. We learned that their biggest concerns are goods storage and how to connect different parts of the logistics process.'

As such, Alibaba estimates the 10-year plan will cost more than US $15 billion with the Group investing more than US $3 billion itself to build a 'non-proprietorial' nationwide network of warehouses. In fact, the company plans to be a 'professional logistics property developer' with a centralized warehouse network dedicated to B2C services. Alibaba and its partners will establish the network in seven parts of the country – north-east, north, east, south, central, south-west and north-west.

Alibaba plans to expand its logistics network from 20 cities to 52 cities by the end of 2013. Initially, Beijing/Tianjin, the Yangtze River Delta and the Pearl River Delta areas were the first areas selected by Alibaba for warehouse construction because of their proximity to major population centres. It is expected that Shanghai, Tianjin and Guangzhou will have large warehousing facilities and an additional six to eight regional warehouse centres will be built.

e-retailing in North America

Of all North American countries, the United States clearly dominates the e-commerce market. Pure-clicks such as Amazon.com and eBay continue to expand their presence not only within their home country but within Canada, Mexico, and globally. In addition, brick-and-mortar companies such as Best Buy and Walmart are leaders in B2C e-commerce abroad as well as at home.

In the United States, e-commerce growth has outpaced total economic activity year-over-year, and that trend is expected to continue as businesses shift operating models to take advantage of the advantages of e-commerce and the growing population of internet consumers.

Although e-commerce sales are steady throughout the year, holiday shopping in the fourth quarter is the busiest season; the increase of e-commerce shopping in recent years has led to the adoption of the term 'Green Monday', the Monday after Thanksgiving, which is supposedly now the biggest online shopping day of the year, similar to the 'Black Friday' day after Thanksgiving shopping holiday for traditional retailers.

The undisputed leader of e-commerce in the United States is Amazon. Amazon, which began in 1994 as an online bookstore is now the model many e-commerce companies wish to imitate. Amazon's growth for the past several years has outpaced the sales growth of the US e-commerce market as a whole.

Many traditional brick-and-mortar US retailers are learning they need to embrace the e-commerce trend as brick-and-mortar retail sales continue to decline. Sales of Macy's, Best Buy, and others have declined as the e-commerce trend has taken off, and they have only recently begun to invest in their e-commerce sectors.

The location of online retail distribution centres/e-fulfilment centres is an important consideration. The placement of e-commerce facilities varies amongst companies, depending on their growth strategy. Retailer Macy's, for example, has opted for a regional approach and has at least four fulfilment centres devoted to e-commerce. These facilities are large and are in excess of 1 million square feet. Instead of a regional approach, however, Amazon.com has a different method, choosing instead to build facilities closer to its customer base and as a result facilities have proliferated.

When deciding upon a location for such a facility, key factors are considered such as sales taxes and state incentives, close proximity to major markets, a good labour supply to utilize in normal and peak seasons and close to transportation hubs.

State taxes have been a major issue for e-retailers for years. In particular, Amazon has been a focal point as it originally refused to locate facilities in states that enforced sales taxes on online purchases. However, as more states implemented these sales taxes, Amazon changed its strategy. Instead, the company has opted to work with states as its strategy shifts towards one of numerous facilities that are closer to metropolitan areas in which there are larger concentrations of customers. Many within the industry view this as an attempt to offer same-day delivery.

Locating facilities close to transportation hubs is another important consideration – particularly as many e-retailers operate in a two to five day delivery time frame. In order to achieve this delivery time, many facilities are locating to states such as Tennessee, Virginia, Ohio and Pennsylvania as these states are close to both UPS and FedEx primary hubs as well as to intermodal hubs. While many e-commerce orders are delivered via parcel providers such as UPS and FedEx, regional small parcel providers, US Postal Service, trucking companies, rail and intermodal services are used as well depending on service level and cost.

Amazon and other online retailers often require distribution centres of 500,000 square feet or larger and have different design requirements from those of traditional retail distribution centres. Quick turns and higher volumes of orders are typically the norm for online distribution centres.

Summary

The e-retailing revolution has had major implications for the logistics industry, and more specifically for the postal and express parcels sectors. As retailers develop new marketing channels to reach their customers a range of distribution opportunities have opened up. This chapter looked at how e-retailing has evolved in Europe, Asia and North America and spotlighted the supply chain strategy of one of the largest players, Amazon.

Key points to consider:

- A large proportion of e-retailing logistics is undertaken in-house. This is due to complex and fast-developing distribution requirements and the still undeveloped range of services currently supplied by LSPs.

- In developing countries, such as China, the lack of logistics provision has led the largest e-retailer, Alibaba, to develop its own logistics system and distribution centres.

- In the United States, Amazon has embarked on a strategy that will decentralize its distribution hubs. It is building numerous facilities closer to consumers, thereby compressing the time it takes to deliver goods and increasing customer service.

- Significant investment is being made in networks of lockers and drop-boxes which will enable buyers to receive goods more conveniently, thereby increasing the penetration of e-retailing.

Supply chain innovation and disruption   16

CHAPTER LEARNING OBJECTIVES

This chapter will provide the reader with:

- A characterization of the disruption process that has the potential to transform the global supply chain and logistics industry
- A description of the major macro, 'top-down' and endogenous 'bottom-up' trends that are creating an environment for innovation
- An assessment of the inefficiencies in the logistics industry that make the sector so ripe for disruption
- An examination of some of the major developments, such as the 'Internet of Things', 'autonomous vehicles' and '3D printing' as well as an assessment of their likely impact upon the logistics industry

The end of 'business as usual'

Much is presently being written about disruptive technologies and their impact upon societies and economies. One such book, *Bold*, by authors Peter Diamandis and Steven Kotler, looks at the various stages of what could be called the disruptive process. Although not all of the stages apply to the disruption of business models related to physical processes such as the movement of goods, their argument still holds good in parts and is a useful framework for analysis (Diamandis and Kotler, 2016).

The first stage of the disruptive process involves the 'digitization' of aspects of an industry sector. Although it is easier to imagine the effect that this would have, say, on a sector such as photography (the well-documented bankruptcy of Kodak, for example), digitization has also had a big impact on parts of the transport and logistics industry. The most obvious impact has been the migration of letters to e-mail reducing the number of documents being sent through postal operators and express parcels carriers.

Relevant as this may be, this is not the most important aspect of the digital revolution in terms of the logistics industry. More transformative has been the digitization of documents carrying the 'meta-data' accompanying goods throughout their storage or movement. Whilst once this would have involved a paper trail – a delivery note, Airway Bill or a proof of delivery, for instance – there is no reason why this data cannot be digitized and most frequently is.

This means that this data can be accessed more efficiently and used in ways that could never have been anticipated even a few years ago. This not only has implications for logistics operations but can provide far greater levels of supply chain visibility. Despite the ability of most companies to capture vast amounts of data, many are still unable to work out what to do with them all. Even if they have the capability to mine this 'Big Data' resource effectively, most will use it as a way of making their existing operational processes more efficient. However, more excitingly, for some smarter operators it is an opportunity to replace outmoded and inefficient business models.

This leads on to the second stage, that of 'disruption'. In the transport industry one of the major problems has been the inefficiency of the market. Estimates suggest that 50 per cent of vehicle trips are less than full, which means that less than optimal running is endemic (Eurostat, 2009). This not only has economic disadvantages but also consequences in terms of unnecessary emissions of greenhouse gases. The problem is that the transport industry is split into silos of unitized transport capacity, that is private fleets of vehicles. The allocation of these resources is only as good as the access of each individual company to demand (loads). Obviously, the capacity has to be of the right quality, have the right attributes (for example, temperature controlled/bulk, etc), be in the right place at the right time and, of course, available at the right price. However, these are largely secondary considerations. If the transport manager does not have access to the market information in the first case, these considerations are irrelevant. The inefficiency is entrenched as each company sees its ability to access loads as a key competitive advantage.

This is compounded by many shippers being unwilling to share contracted assets with other companies, competitors or not.

It is this environment of understandable vested interests, inefficiency and the poor utilization of data that suggests the transport industry is ripe for 'disruption'. The development of platforms that can match supply and demand by providing a closer-to-perfect market than presently exists could deliver huge value, which presently lies latent. It remains to be seen whether this will happen by incumbents being provided with additional loads, or by a more far-reaching move, such as disintermediating the industry to allow shippers to strike deals directly with owner-drivers. It could indeed be through the consumerization of the industry, by allowing private individuals to earn additional revenues by dropping parcels on their way to work, perhaps using public transport. Whichever form it takes, it would seem that given the conditions that exist a paradigm shift is inevitable.

The third (and for transport companies most worrying) stage of the disruptive process is 'demonetization'. In the Kodak example, this is the stage at which consumers stopped buying its film products in favour of new digital cameras. Could something similar happen to transport companies? Could the big beasts of the industry – UPS, FedEx and DHL – go the same way as Kodak? It seems improbable as, unlike the camera industry which went through an additional stage of 'dematerialization', products still need to be moved to market. That is, of course, unless 3D printing changes the game completely.

However, there are still considerable risks for medium and large transport companies. If disruptive technology providers are able to allow shippers (the cargo owners) to access the vast pool of owner-drivers that exists in every country in the world, they would be able to benefit from vastly lower cost bases. Owner drivers do not have legacy IT systems or pensions to fund, brands to support, or massive head office overheads, etc. These, of course, are all being funded indirectly by customers through higher-than-needed rates. Some of the largest shippers (such as Unilever) have already started the process of disintermediating their logistics operations by dealing directly with 'local heroes', rather than through regional or global logistics service providers. New disruptive technologies would give them even better visibility of the market and the opportunity to leverage its potential.

The final of Diamandis and Kotler's 'Ds' is 'democratization'. It could be argued that the logistics industry is already highly democratized as there are few barriers to market entry and exit. All that is required is a relatively small sum of money with which to buy a truck and you are a player in the market.

Contrast this with establishing a factory to manufacture camera film, for example, which needed vast investment in production facilities and brand marketing. However, disruption could lower the barriers in the transport sector even further, increasing the size of the relevant supply-side market from a few thousand transport entities in each national market, to many millions of individuals. Using either the free capacity in their own vehicles or indeed public transport, it is very foreseeable that parts of the industry (especially letters and parcels) could be transformed.

So is this the beginning of the end for the global mega-logistics companies, their business model eroded by a tsunami of micro-enterprises and individuals? Not necessarily. Although it is highly probable that many companies will fall victim to complacency, due to either being unwilling or unable to adapt to the new market environment, others will seek to harness the new technologies and change the market to their own advantage.

At the same time, not every new start up will be successful. Many, if not most, will fall by the wayside. Consequently, the largest players in the logistics industry should not feel threatened by every new 'disruptor', especially those who believe their own hyperbole. The smartest players in the industry are often, although not always, the largest companies who have been able to invest in new technologies. They are staffed by high quality and creative IT professionals. However, at the same time, the size and inertia that many large companies exhibit mean that they are at risk from these new start ups, regardless of how many internal innovation or research and development departments are created.

Supply chain and logistics: ripe for disruption

The logistics and supply chain industry is at the nexus of a multitude of demand-side trends and disruptive technology innovations, which will create a transformation in the way products are shipped, stored and delivered. This will have far reaching consequences for the industry and will mean that in a short period of time, many sectors will become unrecognizable.

The term 'innovation' can be used to describe a wide range of new practices. Some will have an impact on a part of the logistics process. For example, improving efficiency within a warehouse. Others have the potential to be far more systemic. For example, the impact which mobile apps (such as Uber)

Figure 16.1 A nexus of top-down and bottom-up trends

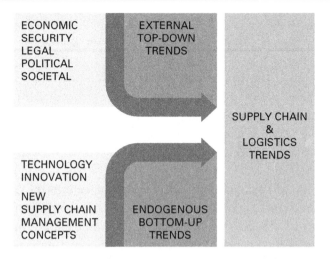

could have on the downstream movement of parcels, through the use of private cars or indeed public transport.

Figure 16.1 explains in more detail how these two sets of trends are coalescing to create a paradigm shift.

Economic, security, legal, political and societal trends are forcing top-down change upon the industry. For example, the growth of a wealthy middle class in many parts of the world is creating the need for more intensive, value adding logistics activities. Deregulation of sectors, such as retailing in India, will also lead to new opportunities that existing commoditized road freight operators are unable to exploit.

Alongside these shifts, the smartphone phenomenon has effectively democratized technology. Now everyone can have computing power in their own pocket. This, in turn, has encouraged technical innovation to flourish. No longer do very large computing companies monopolize the development of software; rather everyone has the opportunity to conceive and develop new technology solutions, as well as distribute them to a mass market. This has led to disruptive, agile and continually evolving applications. One example of this is Uber, which has transformed the taxi industry by ignoring the highly regulated, rigid market structure. It has provided a solution for customers based on the simple principle of matching unutilized capacity with passenger needs.

It is not only software that has created opportunities. Smartphones also have scanning functionality, cameras, satellite positioning features and much more, all of which can be deployed in some shape or form to facilitate or make the logistics process more efficient.

Running in parallel with the distribution of computing power and hardware throughout the population has been the generation of massive amounts of data. This has been brought about by the so-called 'Internet of Things'. By 2020 Gartner, the technology consultancy, believes that there will be 20 billion objects or 'things' with some form of embedded computing device (often very simple) connected to the internet or 'Cloud'. The amount of data ('Big Data') that is generated can inform decision-making opportunities, which can bring significant benefits: economic, safety, societal or environmental.

Perhaps the best example in the transportation sector is the potential for use in cars and trucks. Not only can sensors provide information about the whereabouts of a vehicle, for instance, to a central database, but they can also interact with other vehicles around them. They can, of course, provide much more information than this, including the condition of components, making maintenance programmes more effective, as well as the standard of driving.

One major trend that has been created by technical innovation, revolutionizing retailers' distribution channels and consumer behaviour, has been the e-retailing phenomenon. This has created enormous stress on the logistics industry, predominantly because innovation in logistics practice did not keep up with the transformation of demand-side needs.

Since e-retailing became a reality around the turn of the century, both the e-retailers and their parcels carriers treated the sector as if it were an evolution of mail order/catalogue shopping. This industry had developed in the 1960s and 70s and was popular at a time when delivery to homes was not seen as a significant problem, as there was usually someone there to receive the goods.

By the advent of e-retailing, a large proportion of women were at work and delivering to homes was problematic. Ignoring this, the market continued to regard home delivery and B2C as one and the same, despite the uneconomic nature of the model, which involves attempting delivery two to three times before returning a parcel to the sender. The use of this model is still placing huge stress on carriers, as well as creating frustration for the intended recipients.

However, finally innovative ways of getting goods to the consumer are being implemented. 'Click and collect' services, as well as smart locker boxes placed at stations, supermarkets, garages and so on, are now growing fast in popularity. Delivery is relatively cheap and quick for carriers, and consumers are able to pick up goods at their convenience. Options for delivery are now becoming more common, with consumers able to select the time and location of deliveries.

Cross supply chain innovations – the 'Internet of Things'

The 'Internet of Things' is a vague phrase that basically encompasses sensors, technology and networking to allow buildings, infrastructures, devices and additional 'things' to share information.

According to research company IDC, by 2020, this 'Internet of Things' and the technology surrounding it is expected to be a US $8.9 trillion market, growing at 7.9 per cent per year. IDC further suggests that the installed base of things connected will be 212 billion by the end of 2020, including 30.1 billion connected autonomous things.

> 'The Internet has changed the way we consume information and talk with each other, but now it can do more. By connecting intelligent machines to each other and ultimately to people, and by combining software and big data analytics, we can push the boundaries of physical and material sciences to change the way the world works.'
>
> Jeff Immelt, CEO of GE

Indeed, companies such as LG are creating 'smart homes' with IP-enabled televisions and home appliances, and related services. Samsung's internet-connected refrigerator tweets and streams music from Pandora, and Google's Nest thermostat allows consumers to monitor and set a thermostat online. Not surprisingly though, wearables (smartwatches and fitness trackers) are amongst the top categories expected to take off in the 'Internet of Things'.

GE has also embraced the 'Internet of Things' into its strategy and has announced a host of new 'Industrial Internet' technologies. For example, a GE locomotive is fitted with multiple sensors that transmit large amounts of data about performance. By heeding warning signals from these sensors, analysts can recognize an impending problem, schedule a train for service, and get a part ready to install – thus averting a breakdown on the tracks.

Fleet and asset tracking is another logistics aspect amongst the 'Internet of Things' concept. In 2013, Schneider National installed new tracking technology across its fleet of van trailers and intermodal containers. The technology from Qualcomm is designed to provide continuous, real-time information regarding the location and load status of each trailer and container. The technology uses solar and cellular power. According to Schneider, the tracking technology will also help the company pinpoint the exact location of empty containers and trailers, making the planning and dispatch process more efficient, whilst reducing drivers' wasted time and empty miles.

The proliferation of internet-connected devices that interact without human intervention is creating new possibilities in data gathering, predictive analytics and IT automation. As with many nascent technologies, there are still limitations: every company prefers to use its proprietary technology, which often is not compatible with other platforms. Not only do companies need to work together so their products can interact with each other, but there are also issues related to privacy that stand in the way.

Innovations in last mile delivery

Last mile delivery costs have been identified as the most expensive part of transportation operations. They are estimated to make up between a quarter to one-third of carriers' overall transportation costs. Consequently, carriers continually seek to optimize this stage of transporting shipments, especially in the B2C sector.

One of the biggest challenges facing B2C last mile delivery is that there is no guarantee that the recipients will be at home to receive their goods 100 per cent of the time, which is by far the most preferred option. The logistics and online retail industry has introduced a range of solutions to reduce the incidence of non-delivery and subsequently minimize the extra cost of additional delivery attempts.

For example, logistics carriers are now able to notify recipients of the intended delivery day and sometimes give a certain time window. If it is not possible for the person to be at home, they can give their permission for the goods to be delivered to a predetermined location on their premises, to a neighbour, or to another convenient location such as a shop or automated parcel terminal. They also have the option to reschedule delivery to an alternative location or date.

The ability to offer customers choice relies not only in developing technology solutions for sharing data with them (for example, delivery schedules), developing a range of locations where they can collect and return their goods, but also in the development of delivery service options.

Alternative delivery systems

The 'sharing economy' has become a disruptive force challenging government regulations and disrupting industries such as transportation, delivery, hotels and more. The logistics and supply chain sector will need to evolve to meet these challenges.

A number of start-up delivery companies have emerged such as Deliv, Postmates, Wun-Wun and TaskRabbit, which all address the same day/local delivery sector. However, most attention is focused on the plans of taxi app, Uber.

CASE STUDY   Uber's threat to the parcels sector

Founded in 2009, Uber offers transportation and taxi services in the United States and more than 50 countries around the world. Uber has developed from its roots as an app-based taxi network that uses technology to direct and connect vast taxi capacity with would-be travellers more efficiently. The app, which allows customers to see the location of nearby taxis and offers a choice of driver based on proximity, price and a review system, has proved to be hugely popular.

Its success in the transport sector has caught the attention of express parcel companies, which are beginning to see significant potential for an app such as Uber. The prospective adoption of such innovative technology has far reaching implications for the express sector and could render once-viable business models obsolete.

Uber has already begun to apply its technology to the express sector, running a trial of Uber Cargo in Hong Kong. The service works in much the same fashion as the Uber taxi app: customers select a vehicle from the app and direct it to pick up some cargo. The customer then loads the goods and tracks their journey in real time through to their arrival and delivery. Prices for the trial are based on the distance and time of the trip, with no extra charge applied for weight and volume.

Similar services to this have already been created in Asia Pacific by companies such as Lalamove and GoGoVan, both of which are operating in multiple cities in China and South East Asia. With the introduction of Uber's brand, and the critical mass it has the potential to bring, the express sector in Asia Pacific could be about to witness a revolutionary change and lead markets in Europe and the Americas to follow suit.

After all, the express sector is ripe for this sort of innovation. Across mature markets it is becoming increasingly plain that the sector cannot continue in its current form with huge inefficiencies brought about by failed deliveries and the costs of B2C deliveries not accounted for. Uber-style technology has the potential to dramatically increase efficiency with higher load factors, shorter trips between pick-ups and fewer missed deliveries. Its application will therefore move to the forefront of delivery companies' agendas as they aim to cut down costs.

However, some delivery companies may look upon the application of Uber's technology with caution; especially those whose business models are currently predicated upon the use of subcontractors and attempts to squeeze as much value out of them as possible. Uber technology has the potential to empower smaller subcontractors with the technology they need to secure business independently of the large delivery firms.

Augmented reality

Augmented reality (AR) has become widely adopted in a range of different environments since the application was first launched. Also known as 'mixed reality' (MR), the technology provides the user with 'layers' of real-time computer-generated data using either headsets, glasses, lens or in a car/airplane on the windscreen. This provides the viewer with a range of useful information that consequently can be used to improve their decision-making capabilities.

Augmented reality is being used in the retail sector to provide consumers with additional data on products that they view in-store, by surgeons in the medical sector undertaking operations, as well as for general interest. For example, through their camera, smartphones can be used to view a high street and provide data through 'tags' on the screen that may prove useful to the user; for example, showing them the location of a bank or pharmacy.

However, the logistics industry has also been quick to look at the benefits of using AR in the warehouse in order to increase efficiency of order picking. It has been estimated that picking accounts for 55–65 per cent of the warehousing costs, which in turn are approximately 20 per cent of overall logistics costs (Gibson, 2015). Logistics managers are always keen to develop more efficient working practices that can reduce these costs, as well as reducing pick errors. Usually picking schedules are driven by lists of orders that have been printed off in paper form, although other techniques such as pick by light have been developed. Another downside of this approach is that training of warehouse operatives is often costly.

AR in the warehouse, or 'Pick-by-Vision' as its application in this environment is known, has several advantages:

- The headsets or glasses being used allow for hands-free picking from warehouse racking.

- The optimal route to the correct picking face can be calculated and displayed for the operative to follow.

- The recognition software can then tell whether the user is in the right location and picking the correct product and quantity, increasing accuracy.

- The Warehouse Management System (WMS) is updated automatically.

- Much less training is required, allowing labour to be used more flexibly.

- In theory, this allows the warehouse operation to become more efficient, with fewer errors and greater picking volumes being achieved in a shorter period of time.

AR headsets and glasses also have positive safety implications. Positioning software is able to identify the location of forklift trucks in the warehouse and can inform an operative when to stop and when to proceed.

DHL has been at the forefront of using AR in the warehouse environment. It carried out a pilot project in 2014 in conjunction with customer Ricoh and wearable computing solutions expert Ubimax. Warehouse operatives were issued with head-mounted displays, such as Google Glasses and VuzixM100, at Ricoh's Bergen op Zoom facility in the Netherlands.

According to the companies involved, the test, which involved 10 pickers, 20,000 items and 9,000 orders, resulted in efficiency savings of 25 per cent, including zero errors.

Drones

In December 2012, Amazon shocked the market through a proposal to deliver packages by drone or 'unmanned aerial vehicle' (UAV). In a short press release, the internet retailer outlined its 'Prime Air' concept, the objective of which is to 'get packages into customers' hands in 30 minutes or less using UAVs'. The press release included a short video of the process of a package being picked and packed from the warehouse, loaded onto the drone and delivered to a house. The company said that 'from a technology point of view, we'll be ready to enter commercial operations as soon as the necessary regulations are in place'.

What Amazon appears to be attempting to invent are new processes for the rapid delivery of items and, in the spirit of innovation that Silicon Valley appropriates to itself, it has sought to use the newest of technologies to solve the problem.

Nonetheless, the solution does appear somewhat extravagant. The cost of 'drone' aircraft may be quite low; however, the sort of technology needed to navigate crowded urban skies may not be so cheap. Nor does the solution of a dedicated vehicle for each delivery appear particularly attractive. Certainly any delivery network with a moderately dense depot presence could be able to establish a responsive service, but it would seem likely that the sort of large distribution centres that Amazon operates would require a substantial fleet of drones travelling long distances to service customers directly.

The UAE has also revealed plans to use very similar four-rotor drones. It claims that very shortly these could be conducting unmanned deliveries of official documents, such as passports and driving licences. The problem of security will, apparently, be solved by the application of fingerprint and retina identification technology, which would allow only the intended recipient to receive the goods.

Questions of reliability, flight control and safety remain unanswered, whilst beyond these issues the spectre of civil air regulations looms large. There are key questions regarding drones that need answers before the future can be predicted.

The first is legislation regarding when and where they can be used. It is clear that the authorities around the world are waking up to this and there have been some sensible propositions, along with a practical solution from one of the vendors. The essence of the point is that drones cannot be allowed to interfere in airspace that is already regulated.

The second issue is practicality. This covers both the capabilities of drones (which are improving dramatically in terms of weight, size, range and power), along with the embedded software. Also, if you live in a high-rise flat or work in an office tower, a drone delivery will not work.

But there are some cases in which their use does make sense. These include the distribution of pharma products in Third World countries during seasons where conventional land transportation is impossible and the delivery of critical items in emergency repair situations, where time is of the essence.

As for Amazon Air Prime and other similar solutions, there may well be experimentation for low- to medium-cost items in areas where population density is low and transport costs are relatively high: for example, in rural Canada or Australia. But otherwise, the model is unclear at this stage.

Autonomous vehicles

There can be no more disruptive technology to the global road freight industry than 'autonomous driving' or to give it its more usual term 'driverless vehicles'. Although in many people's minds this type of technology is little more than science fiction, the fact that technology giants, such as Google, have invested heavily in developing the concept shows that it is perhaps closer to realization than people think.

Whereas the headlines have mostly focused on cars, one of the world's largest manufacturers of trucks, Daimler, recently revealed its own plans in this area. These included demonstrating a prototype that drove autonomously on an autobahn in Germany, successfully navigating a junction in real-life driving conditions. This is part of its Future Truck 2025 strategy. Trucks will be equipped with Daimler's Highway Pilot assistance system, which will allow them to navigate successfully at speeds of up to 85 kilometres per hour.

However, at this stage removing drivers from trucks is still a very long way off. It will face huge challenges, not only from labour organizations, but also safety and regulatory bodies, and even the wider population. A cursory look at the railway industry throws up some of the barriers faced. Although the technology has existed for many years for driverless trains or rapid transits, very few are in service. In theory, the highly controlled environment of a railway should lend itself ideally to the technologies. In fact, given the congestion which exists on many parts of a rail network and the expense of building new infrastructure, it would seem obvious that autonomous driving should have been adopted several years ago. At the very least, plans should be in place to implement such technologies. However, this is not the case, and this perhaps hints at the problems such initiatives in the road freight sector will face.

It is for this reason that vehicle manufacturers such as Mercedes-Benz (Daimler) are being very careful with the language they use, unwilling as they are to upset vested interests. For the foreseeable future the technology that they are developing will be to assist the driver rather than take over the driving. This would be comparable to airline pilots who use an autopilot once they have taken off and only return controls to manual when they are about to land. This is despite the fact that at many airports some newer airliners are quite capable of landing themselves.

What are the driving forces behind driverless trucks?

Congestion

One of the foremost reasons for the investment in this technology is the increase in transport efficiency, which has the potential to be achieved. With congestion forecast to rise substantially in the near future, there is a need to break the link between economic growth and vehicle movements. German authorities predict that truck transport volume will increase by 39 per cent by 2030, unless steps are taken. Construction of new roads is unpopular from an environmental perspective and many countries in Europe just do not have the money available to make the sort of investment required. Major trunk road networks in Western Europe have barely grown in the past decade. It therefore becomes essential to utilize existing road capacity more efficiently. New technologies can aid in this goal.

Costs

In many countries in Europe, it is estimated that around 45 per cent of total cost for road freight operators is related to the driver. Eventually, removing the driver (although no one is suggesting this is likely for many years) would obviously then have an enormous impact on road freight costs, profits and margins.

Another issue is the looming driver shortage crisis. Many people are increasingly unwilling to commit to a career as a driver, given the hours away from home, the relative low pay and the conditions. This will eventually translate into higher costs for road operators and their customers. By taking away most of the stress from driving by leaving most of the important decisions to a computer, the working conditions will become more attractive. There may also be the opportunity for the role to become more value adding as the driver will have the time and connectivity to undertake an enhanced role, perhaps in transport management activities.

Safety

The demand for absolute reliability is not so much a technical requirement; this can be achieved by embedding some degree of redundancy in the vehicles if they go 'offline' for a few seconds (although to put this in context

99.95 per cent reliability may be just about acceptable). However, public perceptions will demand that absolute reliability must be proven. Therefore, by definition, any operations involving autonomous vehicles 'in the wild' so to speak, will need to be as part of a much larger system. How long before this is a practical reality?

The technology

There have already been major developments in terms of assisting the driver. Daimler's Proximity Control Assist adapts the speed of the truck, depending on traffic situations, through an integral cruise control and braking function. Three-dimensional maps exist for a Predictive Powertrain Control system, and telematics products ranging from vehicle management and transport management, to apps for the driver and operator, have already been rolled out.

Future advances in technology will be in Vehicle-to-Vehicle (V2V) and Vehicle-to-Infrastructure (V2I) initiatives, which will build on the technologies already in place, adding in more cameras and sensors. Vehicle manufacturers at present believe that the driver will still be completely essential to the driving process in 2025. The technology is there to aid them, rather than take over their job.

V2V and V2I connective technologies are not strictly essential to autonomous driving, although if used in conjunction, will create more efficiencies. Vice versa, V2V and V2I technologies do not require autonomous vehicles.

Big Data and autonomous vehicles

It is increasingly possible to 'harvest' a huge amount of data from vehicles, both cars and trucks, which if analysed in a proper and timely way will result in efficiencies, mostly related to the avoidance of congestion. This data can be generated either by traffic authorities (such as municipalities or highway agencies), by private companies that provide information to users on speed of traffic, or more recently mobile applications that allow individuals to log incidents as they observe them. The latter can theoretically mobilize thousands of drivers who act as monitors of traffic situations in areas that no other organization could reach.

With vehicles having the capability to interact, not only with other vehicles around them, but also with highway infrastructure, a huge amount more data will be generated.

Embedded sensors in everything from transport infrastructure, through to smart devices on board the vehicles themselves, will be generating huge volumes of data. This data has to be assimilated and processed, with the resulting conclusions fed back into the system. This places huge demands on the communications topology required to carry the data. It has to be reliable and virtually 'fail safe'.

Legislative barriers to autonomous driving

Although other jurisdictions have not been slow to catch on, it is the United States that is leading the way in the development of autonomous vehicles. Three US states, Nevada, California and Florida, have enacted legislation that allows these types of vehicles to be tested on their roads. In Europe, Spain, Italy, Finland and Greece have also passed some form of legislation.

There are three main challenges, in addition to technology development, which will need to be overcome if driverless vehicles are to be widely accepted:

- safety (see above);
- data security (see above);
- insurance liability.

The last point may be the most difficult. If, for example, a driverless vehicle was involved in a collision with a pedestrian, who would be to blame? At present, the case depends on whether the driver is in the right or wrong and in most cases a judgment would be derived by assessing the driver's decision making or behaviour. However, if a collision was caused by a software or sensor failure, a case could be made to hold the car manufacturer responsible, unless, for example, it could prove that the owner had failed to maintain the systems to the requisite standard.

Prospects for autonomous vehicles

Autonomous road vehicles are under development by almost all major manufacturers. Their ability to operate as part of a coherent logistics operation will depend on a number of factors. Leaving aside the inherent technology on board the vehicle itself, consideration must be given to the operational environment in which it will function. This consists of a plethora of technical, legal and societal rules.

There is little doubt that the technology that will allow autonomous vehicles will be in place in five years, although owing to some of the reasons outlined above, it is more likely to be 10 years before it becomes a reality.

It will be much longer before legislators, vehicle manufacturers and road freight operators feel comfortable with removing the driver completely.

In summary, vehicle manufacturers believe that the efficiencies the technology will deliver will come in various forms:

- Reduced fuel consumption – the computer will drive the vehicle more fuel efficiently.

- Reduced emissions – for the same reason.

- 100 per cent connectivity and location services, which allow for 'perfect' route planning.

- Diagnostic services, which ensure correct maintenance and fewer breakdowns.

- Emergency braking will ensure fewer accidents; gaps between vehicles will be adhered to.

- Routes can be replanned around known areas of congestion.

- Accidents caused by human error (through tiredness, for example) will be considerably reduced.

- Communications can be shared with customers to provide visibility of delivery times, changing in line with the traffic situation.

Many vehicle manufacturers have developed their driverless vehicles to function within the constraints of prevailing transport infrastructures. In short, this means the driverless technology 'augments' drivers rather than replacing them. It is fair to assume that this will be the first step in an evolutionary path towards complete autonomous operation. During this period we will probably see vehicles operate as just one component in a huge data-generating transport system. As organizations learn to use and analyse the tsunami of data streams, they will be able to reap the potential efficiencies from both a cost and operational point of view.

The challenge for many transport operators will be how they modify their existing information systems to manage a sensor-rich environment. This will require not so much replacing or enhancing existing platforms, but more likely, a fundamental redesign of their approach to their business.

Advances in new technologies will have a direct impact upon the transport and warehousing industry. The sector, of course, is very labour intensive, both in terms of drivers and warehouse staff. In 20 years, however, this situation may well have changed dramatically. Google is already testing technology that will result in driverless cars and it seems reasonable that, once regulatory and labour organization barriers are overcome, we will see a growing proportion of driverless trucks on the roads. This would have obvious benefits in terms of costs, but would also consign tachographs and hours of service to history, thus improving supply chain efficiencies.

In Japan such tests are already underway, led by the New Energy and Technology Development Organization (NEDO). It has successfully trialled convoys of driverless trucks, using sensors to identify their position on the road and potential obstacles. The trucks are able to brake with a reaction time of just 20 milliseconds and hence can take advantage of the slipstream of the vehicle in front, travelling in intervals of just 4 metres. NEDO believes this will reduce fuel costs by 15 per cent but, of course, by removing the driver costs there will be far greater savings.

Caterpillar already uses six fully automated and programmed mining trucks at a facility in Australia. They can run 24 hours a day, which would normally require a team of four drivers. They are monitored from a remote control centre although they have the ability to make decisions on whether to stop, go round or over obstacles themselves.

Although there is a long way to go before we see driverless trucks on shared roads, ironically it may be safety that becomes the main argument for their adoption. Governments are keen to reduce the numbers of people killed or injured in bus and truck accidents, and a large number of these incidents are caused by preventable driver-error. For example, a driverless vehicle will not be distracted by an incoming mobile phone call and there would never be a blind spot for cyclists.

Autonomous transport in warehouses

Once the truck arrives at the distribution centre it would seem entirely possible for the unloading and put-away process to be entirely automated. Already in the United States, Amazon is using robots in some of its distribution centres. In 2012 it bought robotics company Kiva Systems for US $775 million. Its robots bring product shelves to a human picker, rather than the human picker walking the aisles to identify products. According to the company, this increases productivity by three or four times.

Essentially, Kiva is an operational concept that works by maximizing efficiency in the warehouse. This may sound self-evident, but its success has been based on the efficiencies it has been able to create, rather than using technology to replicate human work patterns within traditional operating environments. As with all good business ideas, the technology is not an end in itself, but a facilitator of innovation.

Therefore, in a Kiva warehouse, stocked items are intermingled. As the company says: 'Inventory is free from physical location constraints. Locations and positions are virtual, and move and adapt to the products. The result is that any item can be delivered to any operator, at any time.'

The operation works by Kiva's robots bringing goods to the human pickers standing at a workstation. When electronic orders are received, Kiva robots are automatically dispatched and navigate the warehouse by using barcodes attached to the floor. The robot then positions itself under the mobile shelves (which Kiva calls pods), lifts them and returns to the workstation. The human picker then uses a laser pointer, pick lights and barcode scanner to select the correct items.

The benefits are:

- Fast picking. A new pick face location is delivered to the picker once every six seconds. In addition, there is no walking required. Kiva claims that its pickers have twice the output of those working in conventional warehouses.

- Pick accuracy improved. Less human fatigue and a quieter picking environment aids human worker accuracy.

- The system, which works with multiple robots, has no single point of failure (unlike, for instance, a conveyor). In theory this can bring about zero-downtime.

- Flexible systems. As the robots and 'pods' are mobile, they can be scaled up or down depending on volumes.

- Installation of a new system takes significantly less time than an automated alternative, which relies on traditional technology. Kiva says that it could install an operation in two weeks in a new-build environment.

- Full cartons can be moved by robot to dock, onto conveyor and into the back of a truck with no human intervention.

- In addition to the ergonomic efficiencies that are delivered, there are obvious health and safety benefits from making the warehouse a 'human-free' zone.

One of the major problems with the concept is the space that is required. It may work well in countries where rents are low and land is not a problem, but in Europe this is often not the case. Many facilities work with high bays, which allows utilization of vertical space. In the Kiva solution, each pod is relatively low in order for it to be carried by the robot and then picked by the human. This means that distribution facilities have a large footprint. The success or otherwise of the business therefore lies in the trade-off between the benefits listed above and the cost of the real estate that the solution requires.

3D printing

'3D printing', or 'additive manufacturing' as it is also known, has the potential to become the biggest single disruptive phenomenon to impact industry since assembly lines were introduced in early-20th-century America.

New technologies that are currently being developed could revolutionize production techniques, resulting in a significant proportion of manufacturing becoming automated and removing reliance on large and costly workforces. This, in turn, could lead to a reversal of the trend of globalization that has characterized industry and consumption over the last few decades, itself predicated on the trade-off between transportation and labour costs.

Globalization has benefited shipping lines, airlines and freight forwarders enormously as vast quantities of consumer goods are moved internationally to Western markets from the Far East. Consequently, any challenge to globalization must be viewed as a threat to the global transportation industry. However, as with all disruptive technologies, it also offers opportunities. This section takes a look at the new technology, assesses the chances of its widespread adoption and examines its implications for the logistics industry.

What is 3D printing?

3D printing was originally developed as an automated method of producing prototypes. Although there are several competing technologies, most work on the basis of building up layers of material (sometimes plastic, ceramics or even metal powders) using a computer aided design. Hence, it is referred to as an 'additive' process; each layer is 'printed' until a three-dimensional product is created.

The logic for using 3D printing for prototypes is compelling. Traditional 'reductive' manufacturing techniques (where materials are removed) can take longer and are much more expensive. Mechanical parts, shoes, fashion items and accessories and other consumer goods, can all be printed for review by the designer or engineers, and revisions printed equally as easily. Whereas mass production is viable due to economies of scale, it is uneconomical for 'one-offs' and prototypes. 3D printing will remove this differential, where every item produced is an original (or perfect copy) and tooling for one is as cheap as tooling for many.

The final 3D printed product also has other benefits. Products can be lighter, but just as strong. There is also less wastage. In comparison, traditional reductive manufacturing is highly inefficient in the use of materials.

The way in which each product is individually manufactured means that it is ideal for 'mass customization' techniques. Consumers will, in theory, be able to have a much greater say in the final format of the product that they are buying, and have it manufactured to their precise specifications.

Can 3D printing revolutionize global industry?

There is obviously an enormous leap between a manufacturing process that can presently produce one-offs and one that can replace large-scale manufacturing. However, in theory, there is no reason why advances in technology could not increase the speed of production and reduce unit costs.

If this were to happen there would be many consequences, bringing about relatively minor (and then potentially major) changes to the global manufacturing industry.

For instance, 3D printing is already very good at producing products (even with moving parts) that previously would have required the assembly of multiple components. By eliminating the assembly phase there will be huge savings for the manufacturer in terms of labour costs, but also potentially in the removal of storage, handling and distribution costs involved in bringing together the relevant components.

However, systemic change will occur only if the automation of production rebalances global supply chain costs. The falling proportion of total costs made up by labour in the West would take away the rationale for producing goods in remote, low-cost markets (as relative transportation costs rise).

Instead, these manufacturing facilities could be sited close to the customer in Europe or North America where there would be fewer quality control issues and more responsiveness to market needs. Lower batch quantities would consolidate these benefits.

3D printing, combined with efficient manufacturing, will revolutionize the principles established in the first Industrial Revolution. Not only will local manufacturing re-establish itself close to end markets, but it will allow the flexibility to reconfigure in response to changing consumer demands.

The nature of manufacturing will be very different from traditional models in which it takes established production plants months (or even years) to retool.

The philosophy of manufacturing in which products are made precisely to customer demand could have big implications in certain sectors. For instance, in the healthcare vertical small 'one-off' production runs of drugs/compounds will reduce inventory holding costs. But this capability will also enable the rapid transport of entire production plants to areas where large amounts of drugs may be needed in times of emergency (for instance, pandemics or natural disasters).

Looking even further into the future, some household products could actually be manufactured in the consumer's home, once the cost of 3D printing technology has become affordable. This would have even greater implications for the logistics industry – this time on a domestic rather than international basis. This is not as far off as may be thought. 3D printers for consumers can already be purchased for just a few hundred dollars.

What are the implications for the logistics industry?

The implications of this new manufacturing technology for the logistics industry could be massive:

- Potentially a proportion of goods that were previously produced in China or other Asia markets could be 'near-sourced' to North America and Europe. This would reduce shipping and air cargo volumes.

- The 'mass customization' of products would mean that inventory levels fall, as goods are made to order. This would have the effect of reducing warehousing requirements.

- There would be fewer opportunities for logistics suppliers to be involved in companies' upstream supply chains, as manufacturing processes are increasingly re-bundled within a single facility. Tiers of component suppliers are done away with, as is the need for supplier villages, line side supply, etc.

- Downstream logistics would also be affected. Build-to-order production strategies could fundamentally impact the manufacturer-wholesaler-retailer relationship. In the future the shopping experience could also be vastly different. In some sectors, retailers will either cease to exist or become 'shop windows' for manufacturers, keeping no stock of their own. Orders are fulfilled directly by the manufacturer, and delivered to the home of the consumer.

- A major new sector of the logistics industry would emerge dealing with the storage and movement of the raw materials that 'feed' the 3D printers. As 3D printers become more affordable to the general public, the home delivery market of these materials would increase.

- The Service Parts Logistics sector would be one of the first to be affected. At present, billions are spent on holding stock to supply products as diverse as cars to x-ray machines. In some cases a huge amount of redundancy is built into supply chains to enable parts to be dispatched in a very short timescale to get machines up and running again as fast as possible. It does not take much imagination to understand the benefits for a service parts engineer of being able to download a part design from an online library, 3D print it and then fit it within a very short time window. This would make global and national parts warehouses as well as forward stock locations unnecessary to fulfilling customer needs.

The logistics company of the future

The changing supply chain dynamics will lead to the evolution of a new type of logistics company resembling a '4PL', or service management company, as much as anything else. Their businesses will comprise a mix of software development, delivery services, partner relationship management, contract management and brainpower.

The new logistics company will design solutions comprising demand planning, manufacturing, delivery, market monitoring, service parts management, and return and recycling services. In essence, they will become product lifecycle management service providers. This is a big opportunity for the major industry players that have the resources to establish these new organizations.

The service parts logistics industry could be either transformed or devastated by 3D manufacturing. With small 3D printing machines available, operations in remote locations – or even in an engineer's van – will only need electronic libraries of designs available to them on a local computer. They can then call up the design of the spare part required and immediately print it. Obsolete parts could simply be scanned in 3D, fixed in the computer's memory and the new part printed. The implications for inventory are clear.

Prospects for 3D printing

If the new technology is to completely transform global industry, 3D printing must be able to mass-produce goods in the same volumes as traditional manufacturing techniques. At present the jury is still out on whether this is feasible. Some in the sector (such as global manufacturing group GE) foresee a time when a whole engine, for example, could be printed. Others believe that at least in the medium term, hybrid solutions will develop, which combine new technologies with more traditional techniques.

However, what 3D printing is certainly not is science fiction. Its ability to create strong but light parts has been identified by the aerospace sector; components for the automotive sector are already being printed and the technology is being adopted by the mobile telecoms sector. It has been estimated that in 2015 more than 25 per cent of the 3D-printing market involved making production-ready items (Economist, 2013).

At the moment the following areas are in line for transformation:

Now:

- production prototypes;
- small manufacturing runs of high value/high complexity products;
- dental/aural healthcare forms/aids.

Soon:

- almost all service parts;
- complex high volume/high value forms;
- products related to fashion/trends that have a high volume/short lifespan profile.

Later:

- mass produced fast-moving consumer goods.

It is difficult to see that industry will undergo complete transformation for many years – probably decades – to come. What could happen, though, is that some sectors are penetrated by the technology at a much earlier stage, such as the manufacture of spare parts. In this case, the most enlightened logistics companies could even become early adopters of the technologies – investing in the 3D printers and providing facilities for engineers – rather than kicking against the progress. This would also provide a way of leveraging their capital and their own technological capabilities.

It is clear that if the larger logistics companies delay or ignore the implications of this trend, they are vulnerable to new kinds of organizations or associations that will match or leap ahead of their capabilities for very little outlay.

Summary

The supply chain and logistics industry is ripe for disruption from innovative companies looking at transforming systemic inefficiencies, such as poor asset utilization. The democratization of technology will open up the market to many more players, competing effectively with much larger express and logistics companies. This chapter reviewed many of the innovations that are starting to impact on the industry, such as the 'Internet of Things', 'augmented reality', 'drones', 'autonomous vehicles' and '3D printing'. It reviewed the likely impact of these new technologies and their potential for success.

Key points to consider:

- Technology has become cheap and the proliferation of smartphones has led to its democratization. This has provided individuals with a level of computing power that only a few years ago would have been the preserve of major multinational corporations.

- This, combined with digitization of shipment meta-data, has allowed new markets and business models to develop, which are challenging the transport and logistics industry's status quo.

- The ubiquitous nature of low-cost sensors means that a mass of data is being generated by the so-called 'Internet of Things'. The most successful companies will be those that can harness this data to create supply chain visibility – although many risk being overwhelmed.

- Uber has been the prime company to exploit the proliferation of smartphones within the personal mobility sector. Its entrance into the road freight industry has the potential for significant disruption.

- 'Augmented reality' in the warehouse environment could bring about significant savings due to enhanced efficiencies. This will become very important due to continued labour shortages in developed markets.

- 'Drones' and 'autonomous vehicles' are technologies that will inevitably impact on the logistics industry. The latter (including driverless vehicles) may well take many years to come to fruition, but will have by far the biggest effect, with the potential for a revolution in transport efficiencies.

- '3D printing' will also eventually transform supply chains. In the next few years, expect to see the service parts logistics sector most affected.

Ethical and sustainable supply chain strategies

17

CHAPTER LEARNING OBJECTIVES

This chapter will provide the reader with:

- A review of best practice employed in the supply chain sector, combining approaches that optimize profits whilst minimizing environmental and societal impact
- An examination of the impact of the logistics industry on the environment, looking at modes such as road, air, sea and rail
- An analysis of governmental response to environmental impact of logistics and the policies that have been introduced to mitigate climate change
- A review of the ethical dimensions of supply chains, looking at how some management concepts have resulted in practices detrimental to workers and the environment, particularly in the fashion and consumer electronics sectors

Profits, planet and people – the 'triple' advantage

Supply chain management concepts were originally developed with one goal in mind: to optimize business value by ensuring that product reached the end user in the most effective way possible. The adoption of supply chain practices has undeniably resulted in massive economic benefits, both in the emerging as well as the developed world. It has provided more consumer choice, economies that are more resilient to recessionary pressures, as well as improved living standards for many millions of people in poverty-stricken regions.

However, the gains have not been completely without cost. Just-in-Time supply chains are heavy and inefficient users of transport services owing to the trade-off between the high cost of inventory ownership and the low (financial) cost of transport. On occasion, this can result in what could be described as suboptimal operational decisions such as the more frequent use of smaller vehicles.

Many have argued that this trade-off is, in fact, artificial as it does not take into account transport's external costs such as the effect of carbon emissions on the environment. Political pressure and lobbying has made many manufacturers, retailers and logistics companies more aware of the impact of their businesses on the environment, and carbon reduction measures are now an integral part of most companies' strategic development plans.

However, there is a third factor that companies need to take into account if they are to create truly sustainable supply chains – that of the societal impact of their businesses. Perhaps one of the defining features of the next decade will be the pressure that retailers and manufacturers come under to justify sourcing decisions from a corporate and social responsibility (CSR) perspective.

There have been growing calls for companies to demonstrate that they implement ethical policies when it comes to the conditions in which their suppliers' employees work. No longer is it morally acceptable for manufacturers to out-source production or for retailers to purchase goods from suppliers without having full visibility of these issues.

That the CSR dimension is critical to the supply chain has been evidenced by the huge reputational damage caused by catastrophes such as the Rana Plaza factory collapse in Bangladesh in 2013. More than 1,100 people died in the disaster, implicating a number of international retailers whose goods were being produced in unsafe conditions.

This tripartite approach to supply chain management is critical to ensure long-term sustainability, although striking a balance between each of these core 'pillars' – economic viability, environmental accountability and social responsibility – will be challenging. Destroying value in the supply chain by burdensome government regulation is not welcome and nor is it the answer.

A smarter solution lies in convincing senior management that increasing visibility of supply chains in order to audit the corporate behaviour of their suppliers can provide them with the capability to make smarter sourcing decisions, especially in the case of a supply chain disruption. An opaque supply chain may not only hide unethical behaviour but also creates high levels of vulnerability and fragility from unknown risks.

This is not to say that governments and non-governmental organizations (NGOs) do not have a role to play in facilitating the development of these pillars. Companies can be nudged towards best practice and in an ideal world a partnership approach can successfully bring about positive results to all constituents.

In China, for example, consumer electronics manufacturer Apple is now working alongside the Fair Labor Association, a network of socially responsible companies, to ensure that the working practices of its main supplier Foxconn conform to a globally acceptable standard.

A combined corporate and governmental approach has also worked elsewhere in the developing world. High-tech manufacturers and governments have worked together in East Africa to create a reverse logistics solution, thereby reducing the amount of product being dumped and minimizing harm to the environment and human health.

What is clear is that economic, environmental and societal issues are bound tightly together, interwoven in deeply dependent relationships. In order to ensure a long-term, sustainable future for global supply chains, companies must build collaborative, multi-stakeholder approaches to creating value that do not impact on the environment or have a negative impact on people's wellbeing.

In many cases the problem goes to the very heart of corporate supply chain strategy. There is a failure of 'joined-up thinking' as regards the three goals of profitability, environmental and social awareness. What many companies fail to realize is that profit and socio-environmental outcomes are complementary not contradictory.

In a project recently undertaken by consultancy Accenture for the World Economic Forum, it was found that by initiating projects where social, environmental and economic benefits overlap, costs can be reduced by 9–16 per cent; revenue can actually be increased by 5–20 per cent; brand value increases by 15–30 per cent; labour standards rise and GHG emissions fall by 13–22 per cent (WEF, 2015).

The smartest companies see that there is much to be gained from adopting sustainable operational practices. For instance, companies that undertake driver training achieve a range of benefits. Vehicles are driven more efficiently, therefore cutting costs and increasing profits. However, a more economical driving style also reduces greenhouse gas emissions, is safer for drivers and pedestrians or cyclists and, consequently, reduces the risk to a company's brand as well as insurance/litigation costs.

However, the best-in-class companies go a step further and adopt a 'holistic' approach. For a logistics service provider this provides the opportunity to enter the same peer group as many of its customers. It places it on the tender list of companies to whom sustainability is not a 'take it or leave it' buzzword. Companies such as Unilever live and breathe sustainability and they are only willing to work with suppliers who take the same approach.

Figure 17.1 Towards best practice in sustainable strategies

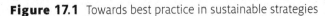

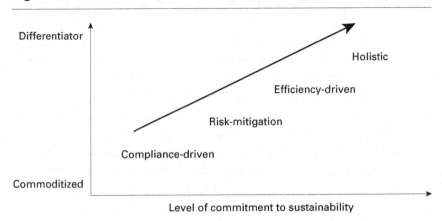

Environmental issues in supply chain and logistics

For many years, modern supply chain management concepts have been criticized owing to their supposed detrimental impact on the environment. In particular, 'Just-in-Time' (JIT) deliveries that take place on a more frequent basis than 'Just-in-Case' flows of goods have come under attack.

It is well known in supply chain theory that the extra cost created by the greater number of delivery journeys and the use of smaller, less-efficient vehicles is more than offset by the reduced costs in inventory holding. However, the green lobby believes that this trade-off only works as the full costs of transport are not fully passed on to the consumer as well as external costs to the environment, which are caused by the higher levels of pollution, noise, etc.

The flexibility and reliability required by JIT has also gravitated against the use of rail, which in terms of energy use and pollution is far more efficient than road. IKEA, one of Europe's largest shippers, estimates that transporting goods by rail reduces carbon dioxide emissions by 70 per cent compared with transporting the same amount of goods by road. In addition, particle emissions are less than half and the level of hydrocarbon emissions is less than 20 per cent of that for road transport.

Although IKEA has gone as far as actually running its own trains, it still relies heavily on road-based distribution. Where it does so, it measures many of its logistics service providers on the maximization of truckloads rather than on minimizing inventory. However, IKEA's distribution system is very much the exception to the industry and its ability to regard rail as a credible alternative to road is helped by its relatively unique distribution needs and management ethos.

Green Supply Chain Management (GSCM) as a concept has been growing in popularity over the past decade. It recognizes that companies have a responsibility for the environmental practices of their suppliers. Just because a company out-sources its production or logistics does not mean to say that it can out-source moral responsibility at the same time.

Logistics impact on the environment

The transport industry contributes to global warming as a result of greenhouse gas emissions such as carbon dioxide and nitrous oxides released during the combustion of fossil fuels. These gases provide additional layers in the Earth's atmosphere, gradually allowing less and less radiation through, and subsequently heating up the Earth. This is what many believe has led to a noticeable change in climate patterns.

Carbon dioxide (CO_2) is the most important greenhouse gas owing to the high levels released around the globe and the length of time for which it resides in the atmosphere.

Nitrogen oxides (NOx) produce ozone but reduce the concentration of methane within the atmosphere. Ozone increases dominate the effects on methane and lead to more gases in the atmosphere. Nitrogen oxide mainly contributes to over-fertilization of the subsoil and groundwater (eutrophication). In addition, NOx emissions are partly responsible for ground-level ozone and thus for summer smog.

Water vapour's effect on global warming is contested; when released from aircraft engines it forms 'contrails' which are thought to warm the Earth's surface and contribute to the formation of cirrus clouds, which may have warming effects. However, this impact is scientifically uncertain and many scientists think the opposite. 'Contrails' can actually block the sun's rays, and when aircraft movements are reduced or cease (such as in the immediate aftermath of the 9/11 terrorist activity) ground temperature is believed to rise. Both sets of views are very speculative.

Hydrocarbons are classified as methane and non-methane hydrocarbons. Methane is a greenhouse gas, but is only of very minor importance in the transport sector. Non-methane hydrocarbons and nitrogen oxides together contribute to the formation of ground-level ozone, and are thus a cause of summer smog.

Total dust/soot particulates are a severe health hazard. Soot particulates, which are produced by diesel combustion, are now regarded as a cancer risk. They represent the major component of the total dust emissions from diesel vehicles. In the case of electrically powered vehicles, on the other hand, dust emissions are produced entirely during power generation and distribution. While most dust emissions are dissipated into the atmosphere at great height (for example, power plant stacks), the distance travelled by airborne diesel soot particulates from their source of emission to the human being who inhales them is much shorter.

Sulphur dioxide is the main cause of forest dieback and the acidification of subsoil and groundwater. Sulphur dioxide can also lead to respiratory diseases.

Summary of environmental impacts

Carbon dioxide emissions
Greenhouse gas – climate change

Nitrogen oxide emissions
Eutrophication, summer smog, eco-toxicity, human toxicity

Non-methane hydrocarbons
Human toxicity, summer smog

Dust emissions
Human toxicity, summer smog

Particulate soot emissions
Human toxicity, summer smog

Sulphur dioxide emissions
Acidification, eco-toxicity, human toxicity

Transport factors impacting the environment

There are many factors that determine the level of environmental impact of freight transport, the key one being the choice of transport mode: truck, rail, inland waterways, ship or aircraft.

Even within the individual transport systems, there are considerable differences due to the vehicle technology, the capacity of the transport as well as other factors. For example, in the case of a truck, the key influencing factors will be the vehicle size (and thus the maximum permissible load), the capacity utilization level and the technical standards for the reduction of exhaust emissions (Euro standards).

Traction

With rail transport, the type of traction that is utilized determines environmental impact levels, so with electric traction, environmental impacts are produced entirely at the power station whereas the largest percentage of emissions are produced with diesel traction during the actual transport of the goods, as is the case with trucks. In addition, the trailing load of a freight train is yet another key factor influencing environmental impact levels (per transported unit of quantity).

Transport network

Each mode of transport is restricted to one specific transport network. However, the road network tends to be denser than a rail network or a network of inland waterways. As a result, shipments travelling by rail or water are in some cases forced to take a roundabout route, which increases the transport distances covered and thus the environmental impacts.

Vehicle capacity and utilization

Each mode of transport has a maximum loading capacity defined by the weight or the volume of the shipment. Whether the limiting factor is weight or volume depends on the type of cargo being shipped. In the case of dense goods such as coal or steel, a good level of vehicle capacity utilization is achieved on the basis of weight. So it is not unusual for the environmental impact per transported net tonne for these types of goods to be lower than for lighter weight goods, such as household goods or clothes. In the case of the latter, although vehicles might be full in terms of volume, the full utilization capacity in terms of weight may not be achieved.

Pre-supply chain energy use

Energy consumption and emissions in freight transport not only occur during the actual shipment, but also at a much earlier stage in the processes leading up to the supply of transport services. In the case of electrically powered rail transport vehicles, for example, the emissions are actually produced entirely in the pre-supply chain. To identify environmental impacts of a shipment and to make any comparison between different transport modes this energy pre-supply chain would need to be taken into account.

In some countries, Switzerland for example, the majority of the country's entire power production is based on hydroelectric power so electrically powered rail transport services produce no emissions. In other countries by contrast, a large percentage of the electric power is generated with coal or other fossil fuels.

Topography

In some countries, topography is also a factor in the environmental impact of transport. In road transport, significant differences in energy consumption and emissions can occur depending on the topography of the country. For example, the steeper the gradients encountered on the roads, the greater the fuel consumption will be.

Government policy and transport emissions

Governments around the world take a keen interest in transport owing to the level of emissions for which this sector is responsible. In the EU the transport sector is only second to the energy sector, emitting 24.3 per cent of greenhouse gas emissions compared with energy's 29.2 per cent.

As can be seen from Figure 17.2 road transport is the dominant subsector, accounting for 72 per cent of emissions, dwarfing those emanating from sea and air.

The EU has put a range of policies in place to reduce emissions from the sector. The European Commission lists these as the following:

- Aviation has been included in the EU Emissions Trading System (ETS).
- A strategy is in place to reduce emissions from cars and vans, including emissions targets for new vehicles.
- A strategy for reducing heavy duty vehicle fuel consumption and CO_2 emissions.

Figure 17.2 GHG emissions by mode and sector

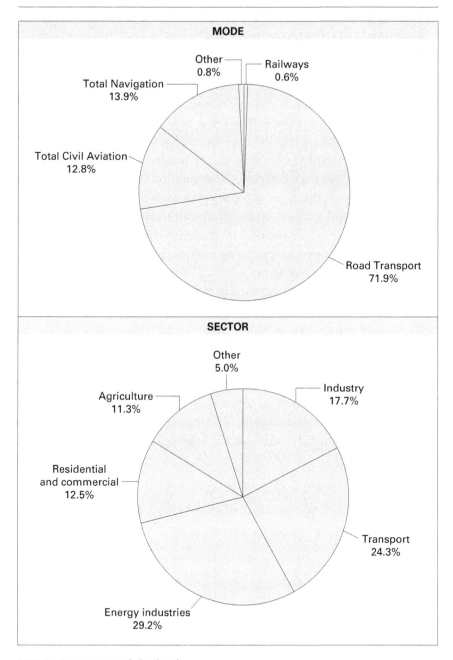

SOURCE: European Commission (2012)

- A target is in place to reduce the greenhouse gas intensity of fuels.
- Rolling resistance limits and tyre labelling requirements have been introduced and tyre pressure monitors made mandatory on new vehicles.
- Public authorities are required to take account of lifetime energy use and CO_2 emissions when procuring vehicles.

At a strategic level, the European Commission has published its ideas for the future of transport, entitled 'Roadmap to a single European transport area – Towards a competitive and resource efficient transport system'. The report's core principles are to '... break the transport system's dependence on oil without sacrificing its efficiency and compromising mobility'. This has led the EU to suggest that '... new transport patterns must emerge, according to which larger volumes of freight and greater numbers of travellers are carried jointly to their destination by the most efficient (combination of) modes. Individual transport is preferably used for the final miles of the journey and performed with clean vehicles.' (EC, 2011.) In other words the EU thinks both freight and passenger traffic should largely be based on rail and sea transport, with road only used for local journeys.

This would require an explosion in the level of multi-modal traffic. As the report says, for trips of more than 300 kilometres '... multi-modality has to become economically attractive for shippers. The EU needs specially developed freight corridors optimised in terms of energy use.'

As well as earlier initiatives foreseen in a 2001 White Paper, such as boosting rail and maritime connections for long-distance freight transport, the EC believes that additional instruments will be needed to achieve these objectives. They include:

- a freight logistics action plan;
- intelligent transport systems to make mobility 'greener' and more efficient;
- an action plan to boost inland waterways;
- an ambitious programme for green power in trucks.

The transport policy outlined in the review builds upon the 2001 White Paper. It includes actions to create a competitive European railway network through liberalization, technological innovation and interoperability of equipment and investment in infrastructure.

One key change of tone in the latest policy document is that the Commission has recognized road freight is essential to the working of any modern economy. Therefore, the Commission has moderated its opposition to trucks on environmental grounds. Nevertheless, it states that it intends to create 'Green Corridors' that are 'co-modal'. The Commission also restated its wish to create 'Motorways of the Sea', which it hopes will play an important role in restructuring long-distance freight transport in Europe and improving its sustainability.

The EU favours rail and wants to create a European freight network that will provide a better quality of service in terms of journey times, reliability and capacity. However, the EU does not control significant transport budgets, which remain firmly in the hands of the national governments. In a key state such as France the national rail freight organization (SNCF Fret) is in crisis and losing market share rapidly, whilst in the UK passenger volumes are increasing so fast that rail freight will have difficulty challenging for future capacities. Complex multi-country dynamics will make a pan-European approach difficult to implement.

Road freight

Europe

Whilst road transport emissions in Europe fell by 3.3 per cent in 2012 (EC, 2012), they are still 20.5 per cent higher than in 1990. The European Commission asserts that transport is the only major sector in the EU where greenhouse gas emissions are still rising. However, despite the headline figures, trucks and buses are responsible for only about a quarter of CO_2 emissions from road transport in the EU and for some 6 per cent of total EU emissions. Most come from cars and light vans, responsible for 15 per cent of overall emissions. The four main environmentally damaging chemicals to be released from diesel engines are carbon monoxide, nitrogen oxides (NOx), hydrocarbons and particulates.

There has been ongoing legislation related to van and lorry engine specifications, which has impacted on emission levels. According to the EC, new cars and vans registered in Europe in 2014 were on average 2.5 per cent more efficient than in 2013, according to data published by the European Environment Agency.

Average emissions of a new van sold in 2014 emitted on average 169.1 grams of carbon dioxide per kilometre, already below an EC 2017 target of 175 grams. Manufacturers still have to reduce emissions further to meet the target of 147 grams of CO_2 per kilometre by 2020 for vans.

Efforts to reduce pollutants from the engines of diesel vehicles have been orchestrated by the European Commission through a number of regulations, the most recent being Euro 5 and 6 standards.

The latest standard, Euro 6, came into force in 2014 and prevents the sale of new vehicles that do not conform to its provisions. Regulations are particularly aimed at reducing the levels of nitrogen oxides (NOx) and particulates.

Vehicle manufacturers started to introduce new engines that conformed to Euro 6 from 2012 and claim that performance is similar to earlier engine types. However, they are more expensive, which has added an extra burden to road freight operators.

To provide an idea of how vehicle emissions have improved over the years, a so-called Euro 0 engine of 1991 origin had the same level of emissions as 34 Euro 4 equivalents. However, although the 'Euro' initiatives have improved air quality – a health priority – the same cannot be said for carbon emissions.

The European Commission aims to reduce CO_2 emissions to around 60 per cent of its 1990 level by 2050, and in 2014 it published a White Paper looking at how this could be achieved. About 25 per cent of road transport emissions result from what the EC terms Heavy Duty Vehicles (HDVs) and these levels have increased in line with economic activity. CO_2 emissions grew by about 36 per cent between 1990 and 2010, surprising perhaps given the progress that has been made in air quality.

The EC believes that CO_2 emissions will be about 35 per cent greater than 1990 levels in both 2030 and 2050 helped by improved fuel efficiency of HDVs. However, this is far in excess of its published goal. The EC believes further improvements can be made through:

- technical improvements to engines and transmissions;
- improved aerodynamics;
- tyres;
- lighter construction materials.

On its own, improved aerodynamics on long-haul tractor-trailer vehicles can reduce annual fuel consumption by 6,000 to 7,000 litres, which leads to the elimination of 20 metric tonnes of CO_2. Aerodynamics can be improved by minimizing tractor-trailer gaps, adding side skirts and keeping tarpaulins tight. Improving driver techniques such as reducing idling time, smoother braking and acceleration and using optimal gearing can save 5 per cent of fuel.

In addition, it believes that road freight operators have a role to play in reducing emissions through:

- improved fleet management;
- better driver training;
- better vehicle maintenance;
- improved capacity management through technology solutions.

In the long term, the Commission is working on developing intermodal networks as an alternative, or at least a complement, to existing road networks. It is also promoting the use of cleaner fuels to reduce greenhouse gas emissions, such as natural gas and biomethane. It has also suggested increasing tax on the CO_2 element of fuels.

Specifically, the Commission would like to see adopted by member states the following provisions:

- HGV truck driver tests to include eco-driving requirements;
- road-user charging, which promotes the practice of polluter and user-pays principle;
- a carbon footprinting initiative to provide more information on the CO_2 impact of freight transport;
- increased levels of cabotage to make the road freight industry more efficient.

United States

Europe is not the only region to be concerned with the impact of road freight on the environment. A whole raft of legislation exists in the United States, which regulates the emission of greenhouse gases and other pollutants, especially those that have an impact on health. The industry is regulated by the Environmental Protection Agency (EPA) whose job it is to enforce federal law as well as provide latest research on environmental risks. In the Unites States, trucks have already reduced fuel consumption by 50 per cent since the 1970s.

In 2004, the EPA launched SmartWay, a public-private programme that is designed to help the transportation industry become more efficient and reduce emissions. It involves large and small trucking companies, rail carriers, logistics companies, commercial manufacturers, retailers, and other federal and state agencies.

Specifically, SmartWay transport programmes claim to lower emissions of carbon dioxide (CO_2), nitrogen oxides (NOx), and particulate matter (PM). Since 2004, SmartWay Partners report:

- saving 144.3 million barrels of fuel;
- US $20.6 billion in fuel costs saved;
- eliminating 61.7 million metric tonnes of CO_2;
- eliminating 1,070,000 tonnes of NOx;
- eliminating 43,000 tonnes of PM.

However, new regulations are being proposed by the Obama administration to limit CO_2 emissions even further and if they come into effect this will inevitably have a major impact on the US trucking sector. The new regulations complement existing initiatives taken to reduce CO_2 emissions in passenger vehicles and electricity generation. Larger trucks would be obliged to improve their fuel efficiency by up to 40 per cent. The benchmark would see the largest vehicles increase their miles per gallon from 5 or 6 in 2015 to 9 miles per gallon in 2017.

Potentially, the energy saved could be substantial. Although heavy commercial vehicles represent a few per cent of the vehicles on the road, they consume approximately 20 per cent of the vehicular fuels used in the United States every year. This is both because of their size and intensity of their use.

However, commercial vehicles are already more efficient than private passenger cars with more appropriate power-to-weight ratios and gearing. This is hardly surprising as the fuel is a major cost driver in any road freight business. Therefore, improving fuel efficiency will not be easy.

Such is the size of the target for fuel consumption it would imply that the main focus of the new regulations appears to be on improving engine technology. This is unlikely to be cheap, with suggestions that the price of the largest trucks could increase by tens of thousands of dollars. It could also imply that other fuels could be used, such as natural gas, although in the long term there are other options including forms of hydrogen-diesel mix or even electric power. These latter solutions, however, are some way off.

Assuming that these new initiatives are implemented, it might tentatively be suggested that the future of trucking in the United States is one of lower fuel costs but greater capital expenditure. Such a shift may influence the structure of the market in the long term with larger, better-capitalized providers becoming more competitive over their smaller, financially weaker rivals.

CASE STUDY   Telematics in road freight

At an execution level, vehicle and driver telematics already play an important role in reducing inefficiencies and hence improving sustainability. Telematics are able to gather data daily on mechanical performance of vehicles and behavioural patterns of drivers. The data gathered include: vehicle speed; direction; braking; performance of engine and mechanical components. At the end of each day, data can be uploaded to data centres and analysed.

The analysis can be used to improve driver behaviour, reducing wear on vehicle and fuel consumption (thereby reducing CO_2 emissions). Maintenance of vehicles is improved resulting in less downtime, fewer breakdowns and more fuel-efficient running. For example, incidents of harsh cornering, braking and speeding could be identified and retraining of drivers undertaken.

Operational impact

According to a survey by technology company Digicore:

- 77 per cent of companies that fitted telematics claimed they had reduced their costs;

- 64 per cent saw an increase in productivity;

- 52 per cent felt there had been an improvement in security;

- 51 per cent said they had enhanced fleet and employee performance.

This resulted in reductions of 11–15 per cent in fuel costs.

- Social benefits: better trained workforce; legal compliance over driver hours.

- Environmental benefit: reduction in greenhouse gases.

- Reputation/brand: fewer accidents/better public perception of standard of driving.

However, there are challenges in introducing telematics to an operation as in some cases it could be seen as invasive of employees' privacy. Buy-in is required from unions, senior managers and drivers. The business case would include everything from safer working conditions, less stress behind the wheel and less laborious paperwork to reduced tax liabilities, protection against false customer claims and a more equitable distribution of work.

Air cargo

Modern aircraft have high fuel efficiencies and manufacturers have made the most significant advances in fuel efficiency of any transport sector in order to drive down costs. Direct emissions from aviation account for about 3 per cent of the EU's total greenhouse gas emissions, which is equivalent to 13 per cent of GHG emissions of the transportation sector (EC, 2012). The large majority of these emissions come from international flights. However, of course, it is difficult to attribute which emissions relate to cargo and which to passengers, as in most cases cargo is carried on scheduled passenger flights. This means that with or without cargo, each flight would have generated a certain amount of emissions.

By 2020, global international aviation emissions are projected to be around 70 per cent higher than they were in 2005 even if fuel efficiency improves by 2 per cent per year. The International Civil Aviation Organization (ICAO) forecasts that by 2050 they could grow by a further 300–700 per cent.

For optimum fuel efficiency, aircraft need to be light, have low drag and fuel needs to have high energy content per unit volume/weight. Some alternative fuels that are being considered include:

- synthetic liquid fuels – being manufactured in South Africa by SASOL;
- biojet fuel – a soya derivative;
- ethanol fuel – only useful for short haul flights;
- hydrogen – fuel cells are being integrated on the ground, gradually being developed for aircraft.

Since 2012 emissions from all flights from, to and within the European Economic Area (EEA) have been subject to the EU Emissions Trading System (EU ETS), which it describes as the 'cornerstone' of its climate change policy. Airlines receive tradeable allowances covering a certain level of CO_2 emissions from their flights per year. The EU ETS works on the 'cap and trade' principle where a 'cap', or limit, is set on the total amount of greenhouse gases that can be emitted by an organization. This limit is gradually reduced over time. An airline can buy 'emission allowances' or 'off-sets', which are generated by emission-saving projects around the world, which allows it to go above the emissions cap. Exceeding its cap otherwise would attract large fines.

The theory behind what could be considered as a well-meaning but bureaucratic and complex mechanism is that it gives value to each tonne of emissions and encourages airlines to take steps to become more energy efficient. The EU also believes that it creates a major driver of investment in clean technologies and low-carbon solutions, particularly in developing countries, which generate the 'emission allowances'.

The ETS scheme was highly controversial and many non-EU airlines and governments threatened not to comply. This led to a watering down of the provisions, exempting international long-haul flights. China said the ETS rules would have cost their airlines US $123 million in the scheme's first year. At present the system is still in its early days and it is difficult to identify how successful it is for the intra-European flights to which it still applies.

Rail and intermodal

Railways have the capacity to move large volumes of goods in one single journey, with significantly lower carbon emissions, and thus fuel costs, in comparison to movement by road (see Chapter 11). Consequently, it has been part of many governments' environmental strategy to encourage a road to rail migration of volumes.

The European rail and intermodal sector has been re-energized over the past decade by a series of region-wide market reforms, which have allowed access to private operators from a range of different backgrounds. A market that was previously dominated by state-owned incumbents has become increasingly competitive with shippers now offered services from shipping lines, freight forwarders, intermodal operators as well as the national rail giants.

As part of a long-standing plan to revitalize the rail industry in the European Community, from January 2007 all European Union (EU) rail freight lines were opened up to competition. Up until then only international freight services, which represented approximately half of the total market for the rail transport of goods in Europe, were liberalized.

The European Commission is hoping as a result of this change that rail freight will now attract new investors and customers by offering services that are more adapted to the needs of the market. The main hope is that the railways will steadily increase their market shares.

However, many rail freight customers still believe that there is a long way to go before the railways offer an acceptable service. National rail operations in Europe are perceived to be more expensive, less flexible and unreliable with a distinct lack of customer focus, which only the private sector will be able to provide.

As far back as 2004 the association of Europe's railway supply industry, UNIFE, called on the European Commission and member states of the European Union to increase their investment in rail 'as an essential part of a competitive and sustainable transport system for Europe' with the emphasis on sustainability and reflecting the green issues that were becoming more prevalent.

One view, mainly held by the incumbent rail operators, is that attempts at liberalization have brought no new volumes and have split existing business between more operators, harming rail's ability to compete with road. As a result they believe that they are losing their dominant positions and the process of liberalization has led to the destruction of the existing system of cooperation between all the European railway networks and companies. Such a view is undoubtedly based on self-interest, although that is not to say that the existing European rail structure that has been adopted is working particularly well.

In the United States, the rail and intermodal sector has many advantages over its European counterpart. A true single market exists across the country, which allows the industry to take advantage of its competitive advantage over road – efficient and economic movement of containers or bulk goods over long distances. In the United States an intermodal train emits only 6.8 pounds of carbon emissions for every 100 ton miles, compared with a truck that emits 19.8 pounds. The Association of American Railroads asserts that 1 ton of goods can be moved 479 miles on a single gallon of fuel. Freight rail fuel efficiency improved by more than 100 per cent from 1980 to 2014 measured in terms of ton-miles per gallon.

Shipping

The World Shipping Council claims that sea freight is the world's most carbon-efficient mode of transport, requiring 10 grams of CO_2 to carry 1 tonne of cargo 1 kilometre. This compares with 21 grams for rail and 59 grams for road. Shipping accounts for approximately just 2.1 per cent of the world's CO_2 emissions and liner shipping accounts for around a quarter of the total.

For example, a tonne of freight shipped from the Port of Melbourne in Australia to the Port of Long Beach in California, a distance of 12,770 kilometres (7,935 miles), generates fewer CO_2 emissions than the same cargo moved in the United States by truck from Dallas to Long Beach, a distance of 2,307 kilometres (1,442 miles). Another way of looking at the comparison between modes is that an entire container voyage from China to Europe is equivalent in CO_2 emissions to about 200 kilometres of long-haul trucking in Europe. This means that, for most slow-moving freight, there is no real green benefit to moving production to Europe.

However, in the past, the shipping industry has gained a very bad reputation for polluting both the air and sea. Until regulations came into force in the 2000s, highly noxious heavy bunker fuels were used to power ships, resulting in high levels of emissions including sulphur oxides (SOx), oxides of nitrogen (NOx), particulate matter (PM) and carbon dioxide (CO_2).

The pollution is worst on heavily congested sea lanes or in ports and in order to reduce threats both to the environment and to human health, the International Maritime Organization (IMO) established a number of legally binding international treaties. Some governments have wanted to impose tighter restrictions on shipping lines, establishing, for example, annual fuel consumption limits or operational energy efficiency standards. However, this has been actively opposed by many parties in the industry who believe that the wide range of commercial and operational conditions in which ships are required to operate would make such an arrangement impossible to administer.

Emission levels have been helped by the trend to much larger shipping vessels. Shipping Consultants, Drewry, asserted that average ship sizes have increased by 40 per cent in the five years up to 2013, resulting in a 35 per cent drop in round-voyage emissions on a per slot basis. As well as greater economies of scale, ships are also using less fuel in real terms. This is through a combination of 'slow steaming' and more efficient engines and ship design. Since 2007 Maersk says it has achieved a 25 per cent reduction in CO_2 emissions per container.

CO_2 emissions are not the only focus of shipping lines and governments. Sulphur emissions have seen particular policy emphasis. Europe and the United States have implemented regulations that limit emission levels and Hong Kong introduced port rebates for cleaner shipping lines. This has been backed up by a threat to ban the use of high-sulphur fuels due to pollution problems in the port.

Vessel design has seen progress in the recent past. Talks at the International Maritime Organization (IMO) brought about an Energy Efficiency Design Index (EEDI). In 2011, energy efficiency standards applicable to newly built ships became legally enforceable.

Air pollution is just one issue facing the industry. Another is vessel discharges, such as ballast and bilge water, 'grey' and 'black' water (sewage). This can also include accidental spills of oil and fuel. There are international regulations that should in theory control these types of emissions and the World Shipping Council has created sets of guidelines for responsible practices.

A further environmental problem is the use of antifouling compounds on ships' hulls. These are important to prevent the build-up of barnacles and slime, thus indirectly reducing CO_2 emissions by minimizing resistance to movement through the water. However, they can contain 'biocides' that are harmful to the marine environment. One such biocide, tributyltin, was banned in 2008 owing to its impact on non-target species and its persistence.

Warehousing

As green logistics becomes a top public policy issue around the world, governments have begun enacting environmental standards for logistics property development. Warehousing users are being required to address many of the same issues as property developers. Initiatives include:

- using solar panels and wind turbines;
- reducing waste in construction;
- using environmentally friendly, recyclable materials;
- reducing CO_2 emissions;
- reducing water usage and use of rainwater ('grey water');
- reducing pollutants;
- increasing biodiversity and enhancing local habitats;
- increasing energy and resource efficiency;
- storm water collection and use of permeable paving;
- energy-efficient lighting;
- 'green' roofs.

In order to incentivize developers to work towards best environmental practice, governments have established initiatives that can measure and accredit the sustainability of warehousing projects. One such initiative is Leadership in Energy and Environmental Design (LEED), which has been developed in the United States and Canada.

LEED is a third-party verification organization that awards points for each property development based on levels of environmental compliance. Federal, state and local government can then make a decision to award tax credits, tax breaks, reduced fees, grants or loans based on the number of points that have been achieved.

CASE STUDY   IDI Gazeley and Porsche

Porsche Cars North America, Inc (PCNA), based in Atlanta, Georgia, is the US distributor of Porsche sports cars and sport utility vehicles. When company officials decided to build a new distribution and training facility to serve dealers and customers in the north-eastern United States, they made environmental friendliness and energy efficiency high priorities.

Working with developer IDI Gazeley, the combined team looked for ways to maximize the facility's energy efficiency and minimize environmental impact. They analysed 11 different models for lighting and insulation, the biggest determinants of energy efficiency; used only low-emission paints and adhesives; installed high-performance low-e glass in windows and insulation in office walls; and chose a roof made of highly reflective white thermoplastic polyolefin (TPO) membranes. The facility's customized motion detector T5 lighting system made it 60 per cent more energy efficient than a standard building. Combined with the natural lighting of clerestory windows, these lighting components reduce consumption whilst maintaining quality.

Waterless urinals, hand-washing faucets, and showerheads with aerators were used to reduce potable water demand compared with normal baseline standards. The HVAC system is equipped with high-efficiency filters and carbon dioxide monitors. The building is cleaned using a low environmental impact housekeeping programme.

Outside, IDI Gazeley's landscape engineers planted more than 70 trees, 400 shrubs and perennials, and native and adaptive plants to eliminate the need for a permanent irrigation system. They left more than 40 per cent of the site as vegetated open space to minimize disturbing the existing ecosystem and designed curb breaks to allow runoff from impervious areas to flow through grassed areas for cleansing, velocity reduction and temperature reduction before reaching the underground storm water system. A series of storm water best practices created a retention system that returns about 15 million gallons of water into the ground every year. Even the construction and demolition debris was treated responsibly, with 79 per cent of materials diverted from the landfill and recycled.

Return on investment – 'green and gold'

When environmental initiatives result in cost savings they are sometimes referred to as 'green and gold'. Below are three examples of where a focus on environmental impact can bring about benefits within a warehouse.

Return on 'green' warehouse lighting initiatives

Example 1

- 20,000 square metre clothing warehouse (three storeys of mezzanine racking) built in 2002 operating 12 hours per day, five days per week.
- Audit identified that implementation of lighting controls, lighting replacement and reduction of lighting levels could result in a 30,000 euros saving with a payback period of three years.

Example 2

- Ambient warehouse (1,000 square metres) operated 11 hours per day, Monday to Friday. Lighting cost savings identified of 37 per cent with a payback period of 2.4 years.

Example 3

- Audit of 25,000 square metre warehouse, operating 24/7, found that 10 energy-saving opportunities could save 51 per cent of costs with a one-year payback period.

Another way of looking at these initiatives is that for many businesses a 20 per cent cut in energy costs represents the same bottom line benefit as a 5 per cent increase in sales. But considerable challenges have also been identified. These can include:

- lack of senior management commitment and staff engagement;
- the need to communicate policy clearly to staff at all levels;
- no defined responsibility for energy use or performance monitoring;
- lack of technical knowledge resulting, potentially, in like-for-like replacement;
- lack of expertise to build the business case;
- a financial structure that works against improvement;
- maintenance or capital investment budget.

Retail logistics

One of the biggest challenges that the global logistics industry faces over the next few years is from environmental legislation as governments and consumers show an increasing interest in the level of 'food miles', that is the distance between where a product originates and its eventual market. Actually, although they are called 'food miles' the title applies to any consumer goods that are produced and then sold in different regions of the world.

Any legislation is likely to detrimentally affect the movement of goods from developing countries in continents such as Africa and the Far East to markets in Europe and America and would inevitably impact on the associated logistics sectors such as air cargo and sea freight. However, the simplistic concept of food miles tells only part of the story. Increasingly, environmental campaigners are looking at the 'carbon footprint' of all products, taking a more holistic view of their energy use.

Although more complicated in the way that it is calculated, the many various factors that are taken into account should provide a more equitable view of the global freight industry's role in carbon emissions.

For instance, many perishable goods that are grown in cooler countries need high levels of fertilizer or require greater energy levels to maintain warm temperatures in glasshouses. In terms of carbon footprint this is taken into account making goods grown in warmer countries more competitive in terms of energy efficiency. This is despite the fact that they may need to be airfreighted to their final destination.

One piece of research has shown that growing roses in Kenya emits just 17 per cent of the carbon dioxide compared with those grown in the Netherlands (Williams, 2007).

The situation gets even more complicated when seasonality is taken into account. Perishable goods such as apples require storage in temperature-controlled warehouses if they are to be supplied to markets out of season. Therefore the longer they are stored, the less 'competitive' they are against products that are supplied direct from remote markets.

In many cases, products grown in developed markets also have a substantial amount of domestic food miles, due to the centralization of retailers' distribution systems. This may be more efficient in logistics terms, but not as far as the carbon emissions produced by the extra transportation are concerned.

So, will the carbon footprint concept have a real and lasting impact on the global logistics industry? Although it is often difficult to say how these trends will develop, it seems that manufacturers and retailers, who must be the driving force behind these kinds of initiatives, are taking the idea very seriously. If they are required by law to account for their carbon emissions, then their logistics providers will have a key role to play in the measurement process.

Moreover, they will also be required to reduce their own carbon footprint and demonstrate how they are going to do it. The implications could be even more far-reaching. There may be significant changes to distribution systems in terms of warehouse location, and even modal choice. Depending on the level of government intervention, carbon footprints could, in theory, lead to a revolution in logistics strategies and operations.

Changes in the way retailers source and distribute their products may signal a change in the environmental habits of logistics providers. For example, Tesco has announced a new 'Carbon Cost' labelling scheme on all of its products that will include the energy used by logistics providers to source, make, store and ship each item. Logistics providers need to reduce their ecological impact to remain competitive.

Ethical supply chains

It is important to remember that globalization has been fundamental to lifting many millions of people out of poverty and has been a major factor in the industrialization of developing countries. Despite this, however, multinational manufacturers, retailers and logistics companies have come under sustained criticism from many quarters for undertaking practices that would seem unethical or environmentally harmful in their home markets.

The challenge that the world faces in terms of reconciling economic development whilst mitigating societal and environmental impacts has been brought about by systemic change in supply chain management over the past two decades. Traditional manufacturing back in the 1970s was characterized by largely vertically integrated, in-house production. Companies such as those in the automotive industry would design and make all the parts as well as assemble them. This has now changed to a model where manufacturing processes have been 'un-bundled and out-sourced' to suppliers who contract to what have become known as original equipment manufacturers or OEMs. Their focus is now on the design and marketing of products rather than their manufacturer.

This out-sourcing of production has had many benefits in terms of value creation for these OEMs. However, it has also meant that controls and management of the manufacturing process have moved to external companies and become more opaque and limited. Typically, many of these suppliers are located in regions of low-cost workforces, remote from the manufacturer and this has also made oversight of issues such as quality control more challenging. Many of these low-cost, remote markets also have poor governance structures in place.

Finally, whereas authorities and media have good visibility of practices in the Western markets, production in remote markets provides for diminished opportunities to scrutinize environmental or labour practices.

There are four main areas of concern:

1 in upstream supply chains, in particular related to the extraction and processing of raw materials;

2 in the downstream manufacturing and assembly of components;

3 in the way in which the product is dealt with at the end of its life;

4 throughout this process is the transportation needed to move the product from its raw state through the supply chain to the consumer and in some cases back again.

Each of these elements has related impacts on the environment and upon society. The best supply chains will mitigate these impacts and even use them to create more value for their shareholders.

Upstream supply chain issues

Some of the worst environmental and societal problems exist in the mining or extraction of raw materials. The worst examples are prevalent in Africa, Asia and Latin America where there is little oversight of bad practices. In many regions the use of child labour is frequent and there are no health and safety regulations in place. Some of these mines (for example, in the Congo) are run for rebel organizations fighting the lawful government.

Environmentally, mines can have a major impact, of course. Not only is there destruction of habitat but chemicals used in mining are uncontrolled and often have a massive impact on rivers.

Finally, there is also the issue of how the influx of large numbers of migrant workers impact upon the indigenous community. This can be very destructive for communities as well as creating health problems.

These issues are of major consequence to the global manufacturers of electronic goods. The majority of smartphones contain metals that have been mined in Congo – and manufacturers – as well as consumers – have a responsibility in making sure that the mining is done ethically.

The fashion and textile industry also has challenges in its upstream supply chains. At this stage of the process water is fundamental especially in the washing and dying process. Unfortunately, this can also lead to large amounts of chemical pollutants being released untreated into river systems. The waste water may contain solvents, heavy metals acids and alkalines. This means that the pollutants can get into the air and soil, impacting upon the human food chain. The vast amounts of water required can also be diverted from agricultural or human use, which has implications of its own.

Downstream supply chain issues

It is believed that about three-quarters of consumer electronics is outsourced to third-party companies. This means that whilst many brands such as Samsung, Apple and Hewlett-Packard have the responsibility for the design, marketing, sales and logistics of their products, they are actually made by contracted companies such as Pegatron, Foxconn and Catcher. These contractors have come under intense scrutiny and criticism for both their labour and environmental practices (the latter especially related to the improper disposal of waste and polluted water).

The issue of labour practices goes to the very root of supply chain management concepts. The electronics sector is influenced heavily by Just-in-Time delivery practices as manufacturers strive to reduce inventory. On top of this, cyclical and seasonal demand means that flexible workforces are required to meet the peaks and troughs of demand. Hence low levels of pay are augmented by very high levels of overtime – sometimes as much as 60–100 hours a week to meet the peak requirements. Also, employees are likely to be on short-term contracts or temporary work arrangements. It is asserted by research organization, SOMO, that in Mexico 65 per cent of Lenovo's staff are employed on a temporary basis to meet this cyclicality (SOMO, 2012). As well as this in many developing countries the sector has developed a reputation for poor working conditions such as exposing workers to chemicals, dust, pollutants and many other health and safety breaches.

It is not just consumer electronics where the downstream supply chain problems lie. Some of the most egregious examples relate to the fashion industry, in particular the Rana Plaza incident mentioned previously. The complex manufactured goods for companies such as Tesco, Gap and many other well-known brands. Despite many of these companies saying that they had audit processes in place, these turned out to be just 'box ticking' exercises, which failed to show up the structurally unsound nature of the building.

End-of-life reverse logistics

When a product reaches the end of its life in the West it is sometimes refurbished and sent on to secondary markets such as in Africa. This can be a legitimate use of a product, which is in the best interests of the environment and helps societies develop. However, sometimes it is a pretext for dumping product illegally and cheaply.

Recycling and processing facilities in Asia, Africa and elsewhere are often unregulated, putting at risk the workers, local communities as well as the wider environment. Computers and electronic equipment can contain lead and mercury and the uncontrolled burning of cabling can result in the emission of dioxins which can travel long distances and find their way into the food chain.

The problem here is fundamentally one of lack of supply chain visibility. Most companies in the Western world do care about the provenance of their products – if nothing else they have to be concerned about the risk of reputational damage. However, modern supply chains are remarkably complex and many manufacturers and retailers have little knowledge of the practices of their suppliers, and even less, their suppliers' suppliers.

Summary

It is no longer acceptable for multinational corporations to turn a blind eye to unethical supply chain practices. In fact, those corporations who pursue strategies that have positive societal and environmental impacts will also be those who maximize the most value in their supply chains, enhancing profitability. This chapter examined this 'triple advantage' of profits, planet and people, identifying best practice. It reviewed latest data on the effect of logistics upon the environment, and discussed the response of industry and government sector-by-sector. The chapter also reviewed how modern, out-sourced and remote supply chains risk lack of visibility and governance, providing a threat to Western manufacturers and retailers in terms of brand equity.

Key points to consider:

- The most successful corporations will be those who commit to a holistic approach to supply chain sustainability, integrating environmental, societal and value adding strategies.

- Modern supply chain practices, such as Just-in-Time deliveries, have brought about inefficiencies in transport, resulting in greater greenhouse gas emissions (GHG).

- Governments have acted to reduce carbon emissions and other pollutants by implementing regulations for engine efficiency, creating Emissions Trading Systems and attempting to break the relation between economic growth and emissions.

- Road transport makes up nearly three-quarters of transport GHG emissions.

- New technologies, such as telematics and Transport Management Systems, will be a major source of efficiency in the industry.

- Manufacturers and retailers must gain more understanding of their upstream supply chains in order to ensure that environmental and societal practices are consistent with an ethical policy. The enhanced visibility that this provides will improve decision making and hence supply chain resilience.

REFERENCES AND FURTHER READING

Airports Council International (2016) *Airports Council International releases 2015 World Airport Traffic Report*, ACI. Available from http://www.aci.aero/news

Alphaliner (2016) *Top 100 Operated Fleets 2015*, Alphaliner, France. Available from www.alphaliner.com/top100 [Last accessed 26 April 2016]

Baldwin, R (2011) *Trade And Industrialisation After Globalisation's 2nd Unbundling: How Building And Joining A Supply Chain Are Different And Why It Matters*, National Bureau of Economic Research, Cambridge, Massachusetts

Boeing (2015) *World Air Cargo Forecast 2014–15*, Boeing, Seattle

Boston Consulting Group (BCG) (2010) *Winning in Emerging-Market Cities*, BCG, Boston

Comité du Routier Nationale (2015) Average Cost Structure per truck 2013. Available from www.cnr.fr/Indices-Statistiques/Longue-distance-40T/Referentiel-prix-de-revient

Cooper, J, Browne, M and Peters, M (1994) *European Logistics*, Blackwell, Oxford

Diamandis, P and Kotler, S (2016) *Bold: How to Go Big, Create Wealth and Impact the World*, Simon and Schuster, New York

Donnan, S (2015) Trade talks lead to 'death of Doha and birth of new WTO', *Financial Times*, 20 December

Drewry (2015) *Container Shipping Faces More Overcapacity and Financial Pain*, Drewry. 10/15 Available from www.drewry.co.uk/news.php?id=408 [Last accessed 26 January 2016]

EC (2011) Roadmap to a single European transport area: Towards a competitive and resource efficient transport system, European Commission, Brussels

EC (2012) Reducing emissions from transport, European Commission, Brussels. Available from http://ec.europa.eu/clima/policies/transport/index_en.htm [Last accessed 26 April 2016]

EC (2016) Road Freight Price Index. Available from www.gscintell.com/graphs/

Economist (2013) '3D printing scales up', *The Economist*, Technology Quarterly: Q3 2013, 7 September 2013

Ernst & Young (E&Y) (2011) *Innovating for the next three billion: The rise of the global middle class*, Ernst & Young, USA

European Logistics Association/AT Kearney (2009) Supply chain excellence amidst the global economic crisis 6th European logistics study 2008/2009, ELA, Brussels

Eurostat (2009) Road Freight Transport Vademecum, European Commission, Brussels

Eurostat (2012) Transportation and storage statistics, European Commission. 10/15 Available from http://ec.europa.eu/eurostat/statistics-explained/index.php/Road_freight_transport_statistics_-_cabotage

Eurostat (2014) Road freight transport statistics – cabotage, [Blog] European Commission. 12/15 Available from http://ec.europa.eu/eurostat/statistics-explained/index.php/Road_freight_transport_statistics_-_cabotage [Last accessed 29 April 2016]

Gibson, H (2015) Augmenting Reality: Technology Offers Real Promise for Logistics [Blog] DHL 2/15. Available from http://goglobal.dhl-usa.com/blog/shipping/augmenting-reality-technology-offers-real-promise-for-logistics [Last accessed 29 April 2016]

Global Trade Alert (2013) 14th Global Trade Alert Report, Centre for Economic Policy Research (CEPR), London

Goel, A, Moussavi, N and Srivatsan, V (2008) Time to rethink offshoring?, The McKinsey Quarterly, USA

Harding, R (2014) Has trade growth become disconnected from GDP growth? [Blog] Price Waterhouse. 9/14, Available from www.pwc.blogs.com [Last accessed 26 April 2016]

IATA (2015) World Air Transport Statistics (WATS) 59th Edition, IATA, Geneva

Manyika, J, Dobbs, R and Woetzel, J (2014) Global flows in a digital age: How trade, finance, people, and data connect the world economy, McKinsey Global Institute, San Francisco

Maurer, A (2011) Trade in value added: what is the country of origin in an interconnected world? [Blog] World Trade Organization. Available from: www.wto.org/english/res_e/statis_e/miwi_e/background_paper_e.htm [Last accessed 26 April 2016]

National Intelligence Council (NIC) (2012) Global Trends 2030: Alternative Worlds, NIC, Washington

Roberts, D (2015) The Chinese Can't Kick Their Savings Habit, Bloomberg Businessweek, 1 May

Savills (2012) European Warehousing Markets, Savills. Available from http://pdf.euro.savills.co.uk/european/european-office-and-warehouse-markets/european-warehousing-markets-autumn-2011.pdf [Last accessed 26 April 2016]

SOMO (2012) Temporary agency work in the electronics sector: Discriminatory practices against agency workers, Stichting Onderzoek Multinationale Ondernemingen, Amsterdam

Transport Intelligence (2012a) Global Contract Logistics 2012, Ti, UK

Transport Intelligence (2012b) Global High Tech Logistics 2012, Ti, UK

Transport Intelligence (2014) Global Automotive Logistics 2014, Ti, UK

Transport Intelligence (2015) European Logistics Mergers & Acquisitions 2014, Ti, UK

Transport Intelligence (2016) *Global Contract Logistics 2016*, Ti, UK

Transport Intelligence/Eurostat (2016) *European Road Freight Report 2016*, Ti, UK

UNCTAD (2014) Review of Maritime Transport 2014, UNCTAD, Geneva

UPS (2014) Supply chain management is the key to top-line growth in the 21st century for pharmaceutical and medical device manufacturers, UPS, Atlanta

WEF (2013) *Building Resilience in Supply Chains*, World Economic Forum/ Accenture, Geneva

WEF (2015) *Beyond Supply Chains: Empowering Responsible Value Chains*, World Economic Forum/Accenture, Geneva

Williams, A (2007) *Comparative Study of Cut Roses for the British Market Produced in Kenya and the Netherlands*, Cranfield University, UK. Available from www.fcrn.org.uk/sites/default/files/Cut_roses_for_the_British_market.pdf [Last accessed 26 April 2016]

World Trade Organization (2016a) *World Trade Growth: Value of world merchandise exports*, Available from www.wto.org/english/res_e/statis_e/short_ term_stats_e.htm [Last accessed 26 April 2016]

World Trade Organization (2016b) *China Exports 2009–2015*, Available from www.wto.org/english/res_e/statis_e/short_term_stats_e.htm [Last accessed 26 April 2016]

INDEX

Note: The index is filed in alphabetical, word-by-word order. Numbers and acronyms are filed as spelt out. Page locators in *italics* denote information contained within a Figure or Table.

CPSIA information can be obtained
at www.ICGtesting.com
Printed in the USA
BVOW06s2146011116
466664BV00015B/135/P

9 780749 478254